LEGENDARY BRITAIN

An illustrated journey
Bob Stewart and John Matthews

Illustrated by Miranda Gray

Photographs by Tim Cann

BLANDFORD

To Rosemary Sutcliff and Meriol Trevor
who first mapped the Legendary Lands for me
J.M.

To Rudyard Kipling – Master of Legend
And Lewis Spence – Master of Magic
B.S.

Blandford Press
An imprint of Cassell
Artillery House, Artillery Row
London SW1P 1RT

First published 1989

Distributed in the United States by
Sterling Publishing Co, Inc,
2 Park Avenue, New York, NY 10016

Distributed in Australia by
Capricorn Link (Australia) Pty Ltd
PO Box 665, Lane Cove, NSW 2066

British Library Cataloguing in Publication Data
Stewart, Bob
Legendary Britain: an illustrated journey.
1. Great Britain. Description & travel
I. Title   II. Matthews, John, *1948–*
914.1'04858

ISBN 0–7137–2027–1

Typeset by Litho Link Limited, Welshpool, Powys, Wales.
Printed in Portugal by Printer Portuguesa.

contents

ACKNOWLEDGEMENTS

vii

INTRODUCTION

viii

1 · WESTWARD TO LYONESSE

Arthurian Cornwall and the West Country; Tristan and Isolt in Cornwall

Drustan's Ghost (by John Matthews)

1

2 · CAERLEON: THE CITY OF THE LEGIONS

The Kingly Shadow (by John Matthews)

16

3 · MERLIN AND DINAS EMRYS

Merlin and His Location; Dinas Emrys; Merlin; How Dinas Emrys Gained Its Name

The Girl Who Met Merlin (by Bob Stewart)

28

4 · WAYLAND'S SMITHY AND THE WHITE HORSE

The White Horse and Dragon Hill

The Smith King, or Three Rogues Underground (by Bob Stewart)

47

5 · AQUAE SULIS: TEMPLE OF THE UNDERWORLD,
HOME OF THE FLYING MAN

Sacred Springs and Wells; The Goddess Sulis; King Bladud;
The Legend of the Pigs; The Flaming Head; The Flying Man and the River Avon

The Goddess Speaks (by Bob Stewart)

63

6 · THE ISLAND OF GLASS
Fortress of the Holy Grail; A Grave for Arthur?
The Struggle for Spring (by John Matthews)

79

7 · ROBIN HOOD AND THE GREEN MEN
Who Was Robin Hood?; Gentle Robyn: The Mythological Argument;
The Green Men of Sherwood; The Good Yeoman: Robin Hood in History;
The Landscape of Robin Hood
The Death of Robin Hood (by John Matthews)

93

8 · THOMAS THE RHYMER IN THE EILDON HILLS
The Eildon Hills; The Hawthorn Tree; The Underworld Initiation; Merlin's Grave;
The Ballad of Thomas the Rhymer
The Tongue That Cannot Lie (by Bob Stewart)

110

9 · IONA AND THE SACRED ISLES
Pagan Origins; Celtic Christian Roots and the Arrival of St Columba;
Columba Is Exiled; The First Monastery; Death of Columba and the Fate of Iona;
The Relig Oran, Burial Place of Kings; Iona Today;
Fiona Macleod and the Island of the Grail
The Island of Sorrow and Joy (by John Matthews)
The Hermit (by Bob Stewart)

125

10 · THE ORKNEYS: ISLANDS OF THE OTHERWORLD
The Isles of the Dead; Prehistoric Orkney and the Settlement of Skara Brae;
Wolves of the Sea
The Hidden Runes (by John Matthews)
The Mystery of the Women (by Bob Stewart)

149

AFTERWORD
171

BIBLIOGRAPHY
172

INDEX
176

acknowledgements

The authors, photographer, and artist all wish to thank Gothic Image Tours of Glastonbury, Somerset, organisers of *Magical Britain – A Journey Through the Myths of Time*. Much of the site research and photography for this book was done during one such tour in the autumn of 1987. Acknowledgement is also due to the various individuals and groups who joined us or, more importantly, transported us, on exploratory trips to ancient sites between 1970 and 1987. Bob Stewart wishes specifically to acknowledge his debt to John Wooton who first introduced him to the ancient sites of Cornwall, and to William G. Gray who first introduced him to the Otherworld aspects of ancient sites in the Cotswolds, Oxfordshire, and Wiltshire. Thanks are due also to the Museum Department of Bath City Council, who kindly gave permission to take new photographs of Romano-Celtic monuments for this book.

B. S. and J. M.
Bath and London, 1988

íntroductíon

The concept of this book is such that many sites are not included: there is no value judgement in this, merely the simple fact that space would not allow us to cover more locations and legends. Rather than content ourselves with a few paragraphs for each of a large selection of sites, we have tried to penetrate the legendary and cultural roots of Britain through a harmonious sequence of locations from the far south-west to the far north. This concept and its various sub-themes are described in more detail in our Introduction.

Some of the omissions, such as the famous stone temples of Avebury or Stonehenge, were relatively easy to make (though no such omission is ever without regret) as they have been so extensively covered by other writers over the years. Others, especially little-known but clearly significant locations and sites, were far more difficult to exclude. We hope to have the opportunity to deal with a further selection of both major and minor sites and legends in a second volume.

ORIGINS

 RITAIN IS A very ancient land, both geologically and culturally. Many of the remains of its early cultures may be traced back to the most distant prehistoric past — there are structures in Britain that predate the pyramids of ancient Egypt. Perhaps the most notable ancient culture, the root culture, is the megalithic civilisation that stretched from Orkney in the far north to the Channel Islands a thousand miles to the south, and had settlements and extensive structures to the west in Ireland.

These mysterious people were builders of considerable sophistication and technical skill. The outdated Victorian notion that they were savages wallowing in ignorance and darkness is clearly nonsense when we consider their works still standing today — and remember that these are only part of the whole picture, for many were destroyed during later centuries. Yet the concept of hard primitivism is still upheld to a greater or lesser extent by modern education and by some archaeologists. Stone circles and alignments, earthworks, and (more rarely) megalithic burial and household artefacts have been extensively examined by archaeologists, but the primal people left a more subtle and no less substantial heritage that underpinned many later cultures. Their sacred circles and enclosures were held in reverence for millenniums, with successive peoples using them as worship and burial sites. Some of these places and the associated legends handed down through enduring tradition are described in our later chapters.

The modern conception of both ancient and historical Britain has changed radically in the last fifty years. Indeed, as little as twelve years ago an academic reviewer could pronounce gravely that 'British heritage had little to do with the Celts' when commenting upon a book by one of the present authors. No one would make such a statement and publish it today . . . but the Celts are, after all is said and done, a relatively recent phase in the culture of Britain. Though we have little 'proof' in the scientific sense, it seems likely that the lost early cultures of the land contributed much to the foundations of Celtic beliefs, ritual, and social practices. The thread of that mysterious inheritance runs through the locations chosen for this book.

If we examine British legends and their locations – for a true legend is always located upon a specific place or places and is never a mere tale without a home – certain patterns and themes are generally repeated. Many detailed works on folklore and legend have been published correlating and analysing traditional material, and there is no intention here of repeating this type of work, no matter how valuable. We have, instead, selected locations and legends that seem to illustrate best the primal themes that are found in a quest for the essence of British lore and legend. It must be no coincidence that some of these locations are world famous and visited by thousands of people every year, yet we have not chosen sites and legends out of mere popularity, and many of the most significant locations in Britain are still, to this day, unvisited and difficult to reach. We have, instead, tried to strike a balance between these sites and areas that are relatively popular and easy to reach, and those that are so essential to the roots of Britain legend that they should be included, regardless of their obscurity or remote location.

The reader who wishes to visit the places selected will be pleased to hear that none of the sites chosen is beyond the reach of basic modern travel and determination, and that most of them are easily accessible by rail or road, with occasional well-established ferry-crossings. Indeed, some of the most astonishing British remains are not on remote islands but right in the heart of modern cities, or close to major routes. Despite an astonishing wealth of history and ancient locations, such as would amply fulfil a far greater territory, Britain and Ireland are a relatively tiny group of islands, heavily over-populated in many regions. This leads to the land acting as a kind of 'time machine', for the most ancient remains and legends are found in the heart of the most modern locations. London is a typical example of this, where we may find a temple of the Romano-Oriental god, Mithras, within a modern business, or a sacred hill and castle within a few metres of international politics and commerce. Indeed, the capital city demands a separate book of its own, so great is the wealth of history, myth, legend, and sacred sites within it. Bath, in the west of England, is a striking example of a city visibly extending through time, due to its compact nature, where a Romano-Celtic temple and ancient worship site is revealed underground in the heart of the Georgian and modern city. It seems strange, even to an author familiar with the place, that these words were written on a computer, a product of late twentieth-century technology, within an eighteenth-century house standing upon the foundations of a first-century Roman temple that in turn was built upon a Celtic and Druidic worship site that may in turn have been developed from an even earlier culture drawn to the copious hot springs of Bath. Much of this is discussed in Chapter 5.

The careful revelation of buried sites is, of course, due to the painstaking work of archaeologists, but the vast majority of legendary locations and ancient structures are visible upon the surface of the land, for they are stones, mounds, chambers, and in some cases extensive re-structurings of the very landscape. The British have tended to be very casual about their heritage, and in previous centuries have been indifferent or even hostile to it . . . but this is not through mere ignorance. When we consider the immense periods of time, and the richness of the remains from all stages of the past, it is perhaps a matter of over-familiarity – so there is little harm in stating, in this Introduction, some simple facts that seem glaringly obvious, even dull, to those who live daily with visible evidence of the distant, even prehistoric, past. Yet, paradoxically, there are many thousands in Britain who have never seen a standing-stone, visited a sacred site, or had the opportunity to delve into the wonder and terror of their own inheritance of legends and mysteries.

The legends and their specific locations are underpinned, as we said above, by certain enduring themes. The origins of these themes are not necessarily obscure problems of a distant or tribal mentality (as we are so often led to believe), but fundamentals of human consciousness: the collective wisdom and entertainment drawn from thousands of years of people living upon a land, and relating to specific locations within it. Put more simply, there is much within us all, even today, that resonates to the places, people, and practices found in the old legends. Furthermore there is, as in all human traditions worldwide, a universal quality to the great legends, and a power within the places associated with them. We do not need to be wildly mystical Celts or pagan Saxons to appreciate this mysterious universal appeal, for it resonates through all traditions worldwide, and derives from humans living upon the planet. But to make something concrete and defined out of our legendary and essential *magical* inheritance from the past, we need to relate to specific examples. British legends are such examples, linked to places, underpinned by powerful themes.

These themes are best represented as follows:

1. Underworld or Otherworld and prophetic traditions.
2. Fairy and ancestral traditions.
3. Grail and kingship traditions.

The three themes are closely related to one another, yet have a powerful individual identity and specific traditions of their own. It is essential to grasp both their unity and their individuality if we are to relate to the deepest levels of British legends and their close concern with the land itself. Once we have grasped this relationship, we find that it incorporates the entire range of British and European legend and tradition, though some items are well disguised and obscured either through rationalisation, literary meddling, or the bizarre influence of modern culture.

Fig. 1 shows, in the broadest sense, how the three major themes relate to one another. It is not designed as a rigid formula, merely as a general indicator of harmonic connections found within the huge body of British and Irish legend and tradition. When we consider specific legends, we find that each of the themes listed is personified by a powerful figure or archetype, though these figures can and do appear in many guises, and with many examples ranging through the centuries. Occasionally the archetype seems to connect to a historical person, as in the case of Thomas the Rhymer or Robert Kirk (Chapter 8). The three figures or archetypes are as follows:

1. Merlin (Underworld/Otherworld/prophecy)
2. The Fairy Queen (fairy/ancestral)
3. King Arthur (Grail/kingship)

Fig. 1
Thematic correspondences of people and places

Table of places

1. Aquae Sulis (Bath)/ Orkney/Dinas Emrys/Iona

2. Eildon Hills/Wayland's Smithy/Sherwood Forest

3. Tintagel/Caerleon/ Glastonbury

Table of people

1. Merlin/King Bladud/ saints/primal cultures

2. Robin Hood/Wayland Smith/Thomas the Rhymer/Robert Kirk

3. Ambrosius Aurelianus/ Arthur/Tristan/Vortigern

Note These are general rather than detailed correspondences and the relevant chapters show how frequently the functions of places and the roles of characters overlap and interact in British legend.

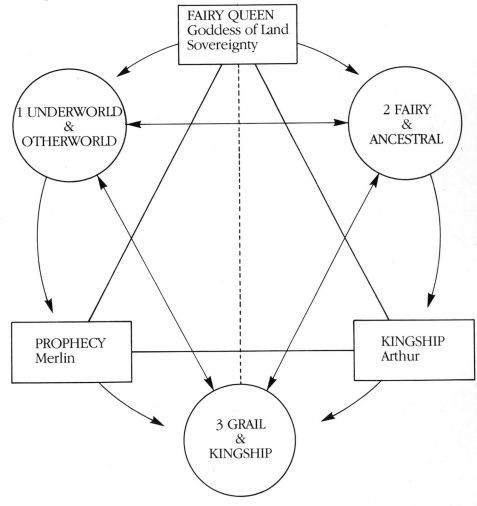

FAIRY QUEEN
Goddess of Land
Sovereignty

1 UNDERWORLD
&
OTHERWORLD

2 FAIRY
&
ANCESTRAL

PROPHECY
Merlin

KINGSHIP
Arthur

3 GRAIL
&
KINGSHIP

But in the diagram, we have returned the role of Fairy Queen to her original, more potent aspect, that of Goddess of the Land, represented in Irish tradition by the figure of Sovereignty. Thus we have a threefold relationship between goddess, king, and seer. In many legends this becomes maiden, hero, and magican, but the fundamental themes remain.

Legendary Britain is not, therefore, a gazetteer, nor a selective guide-book or collection of legends in the familiar sense, but an attempt to trace the three essential themes (kingship and the Grail, the Otherworld and prophecy, fairies and ancestors) through aspects of the legendary history of the land. This legendary history frequently overlaps with actual sites such as Caerleon on Usk, Sherwood Forest, or the Eildon Hills (see the diagram), and such sites are discussed in detail in later chapters. Other locations with more complex backgrounds, such as the Orkney Islands and the West Country, are dealt with in more general terms, though the locations of Glastonbury and Bath (Aquae Sulis) are given special attention.

In all cases it is the mythic, heroic, or magical associations that have been concentrated upon or developed, either through direct commentary, or through the added dimension of retelling certain tales connected to sites. The original stories that follow each chapter are based upon mythic or heroic patterns within genuine tradition, but have been dramatised or retold to give further insight into the deepest legendary foundations, the three themes outlined earlier, and shown in our diagram. The new tales are not restricted to a recreation of the past, however, as some are set in the present, or even in the future.

One of the three themes that emerged early on in the writing of the new tales, and indeed in the research, writing, and compilation of the entire book, was that of kingship. The sacred bond between the king and the land over which he has been granted rulership was central to early British culture; in ancient times it may have been sealed, literally, in blood through a ritual sacrifice. But we must never assume that this was a cruel or barbaric or vicious matter, for it was the foundation for many profound and ennobling religious and cultural matters, of which even Christianity partakes in some measure.

No maimed or crippled king could rule, in Celtic culture, and this gave rise to the world-famous stories of the Waste Land in Arthurian legend, for the devastation was caused by the incurable wound of the Fisher King. There is much in modern society that is resonant of that Waste Land, in both warfare and indiscriminate poisoning and plundering of natural resources for sheer greed. This theme is restated in part, using a Waste Land of the not-too-distant future, in the story of *The Smith King* (following Chapter Four), which also draws upon the legend of Wayland Smith, who is a fusion of both Saxon and Celtic or earlier deities and ancestral beings.

The original Quest, that of the Grail, was undertaken to heal the wounded king, a frequent feature of British legend, and to cause the wasted land to flourish once again. This major theme, that of the Grail and kingship, is found in the subjects of Ambrosius and *The Kingly Shadow* (Chapter 2), Robin Hood and *The Death of Robin Hood* (Chapter 7), on Tristan and *Drustan's Ghost* (Chapter 1). In these legends and retellings we see the effects of a design or pattern that overrides personal need, setting it aside for the impersonal or transpersonal good of the land and its people.

Curiously, this theme is greatly strengthened by its counterpart, that of the Underworld and prophecy. In such legends an individual undergoes magical transformation and experiences that give devastating insights into reality or truth. In late Arthurian legend and literature, it is the aged Merlin, having undergone such transformations in his early life, who assists the young Arthur through his wisdom and insight. In earlier traditions, however, we find that Merlin and Arthur have little contact, despite popular belief to the contrary. This entire theme is dealt with in our Chapters 3 and 8, and the stories, *The Girl Who Met Merlin* and *The Tongue That Cannot Lie*.

In the tales, *The Struggle for Spring* and *The Island of Sorrow and Joy,* based upon the locations and legends found in Chapters 6 and 9, events take place that touch upon the life or sacrifice of the Royal Blood. The primeval megalithic culture is touched upon in our Chapter 10 on Orkney, and in the time-jumping tale *The Goddess Speaks,* Chapter 5, based upon the legends and location of Aquae Sulis, now called Bath.

The third major theme, that of the Goddess of the Land or Fairy Queen, underpins the other two, for it is from the goddess that the king and the prophet or bard gain their power, blessing, and insight. We shall meet the Fairy Queen in our Chapter 8 and in *The Tongue That Cannot Lie,* though she also appears in many guises in the other chapters and stories. In the ancient text of *The Prophecies of Merlin* set out into Latin by Geoffrey of Monmouth around 1135, but certainly drawn from much earlier bardic verses in the native British language, we find the Goddess purifying the land by transforming its rivers, and holding the forests of the north and the fortresses of the south in either hand. She also summons the ancestors and, eventually, in her higher or more universal aspect of the Weaver Goddess, unravels the solar system at the end of time. Thus it should be no surprise to discover that the Fairy Queen of British tradition is no mere tinsel sprite, but a powerful and often terrifying force personified by a dark, beautiful woman who rules an Underworld realm and grants the powers of prophecy to those brave enough to travel with her.

LEGEND AND HISTORY

NE OF THE earliest historians of England was the Venerable Bede, writing in 731. In his book, *The History of the English Church and People,* he described Britain as follows:

Britain, formerly known as Albion . . . extends eight hundred miles Northward and is two hundred in breath, except where a number of promontories extend further, so that the total coastline extends three thousand six hundred miles. . . . Britain is rich in grain and timber; it has good pasturage for cattle and draught animals, and vines are cultivated in various localities. . . . The country has both salt springs and hot springs, and the waters flowing from them provide hot baths, in which people bathe. . . . The land has rich veins of many metals, including copper, iron, lead, and silver. . . . In old times the country had twenty eight noble cities, besides innumerable strongholds, which also were guarded by walls, towers and barred gates.

(trans. L. Sherley-Price)

Bede's *History* was based, of course, on earlier accounts and surveys, some being Roman. For an early text it was remarkably accurate, but it lacks an important dimension, that of legend. The legends of Britain lie like a substrata beneath the people, cities, ploughed fields, and motorways of the land. They live in the megalithic stone circles and the great abbeys and castles of the Middle Ages . . . even in the concrete of the modern cities.

Britain has had many names in the past: Albion, Prydein, Clas Merddyn (Merlin's Enclosure), the Island of the Mighty. Each in its own way represents a layer of legend. These legends ultimately make up the secret life of the land, which can never be truly forgotten until the land itself vanishes. The heroes of a land are always attached, either historically or magically – or both – to certain sites or areas. Arthur, Hereward, Robin Hood, Boudicca, Merlin, and a whole legion of saints (mainly forgotten) sleep beneath the land of Britain until such a time as they re-awaken in an hour of great need. These ancestral and legendary people are the deepest part of Briain, remembered through the ages as part of the national heritage and identity.

The poet, David Jones, writing of King Arthur in his poem, *The Sleeping Lord,* asks

> Are the slumbering valleys
> him in slumber?
> are the still undulations
> the still limbs of him sleeping?
> Is the configuration of the land
> the furrowed body of the lord?

This same theme was used by the great British poet and prophet, William Blake, when he identified Arthur with Albion, the Sleeping Giant of the Land. It is the hidden mysterious side of the land that we will examine in these pages, the myths and legends associated with certain key places within the unending story of Britain. Some of the stories will be retold, bringing fresh forms to the protean traditions and characters. Slowly, we shall delineate the shape of an inner landscape, a primal land, the secret Britain that was called Logres in Arthurian tales, but that bears many names both in and out of time.

Bob Stewart and John Matthews
London and Bath, 1989

1·westward to Lyonesse

ARTHURIAN CORNWALL
AND THE WEST COUNTRY

RTHURIAN ASSOCIATIONS WITH the West Country date back at least as far as the Middle Ages (some would say earlier) and extend to Devon, Somerset, and Cornwall in particular. Some sites, such as Tintagel Castle in Cornwall or Glastonbury in Somerset (see pp. 79–92)have almost become pilgrimage centres for Arthurian enthusiasts, though in the case of certain places any real connection with Arthur is doubtful.

For a number of years now a debate has raged over Arthur's supposed country of origin. Geoffrey of Monmouth, writing in the twelfth century but deriving his information from earlier sources, placed Arthur's birth-place at Tintagel, a dramatic and romantic site overlooking the Atlantic from high cliffs. He also placed Arthur's greatest battle, Badon, at Bath (see pp. 63–78), while his demise took place in Cornwall.

Aside from Geoffrey's testimony, other texts and oral traditions associate Arthur with Cadbury Camp in Somerset, widely held to be the original site of Camelot, Arthur's fabled capital; nearby Glastonbury as a possible repository for the Holy Grail; and somewhere in the region of the River Camel or Cam, Arthur and his son, Mordred, are believed to have fought their last battle of Camlan, in which the pride of the Round Table knights perished.

These, together with numerous other sites, have established Arthur firmly in popular belief as a West-Country hero – though, of course (as applies wherever one places him) the stage of his activities ranges far beyond any localised boundaries to cover most of Britain.

If, as we must, we examine the evidence for these West-Country locations, we become aware at once of certain facts. Geoffrey of Monmouth appoints Tintagel as Arthur's birth-place, and the dramatic remains of the Norman castle are still pointed out as the site of his nascency – with Merlin, as described so

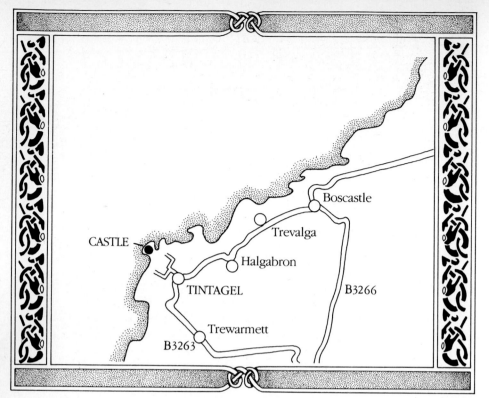

Tintagel.

vividly by Tennyson, carrying the child Arthur down the steep cliffs from the postern gate in the great walls. Unfortunately, there was no castle there in the sixth century, when Arthur flourished; instead, the remains of a Celtic monastery have been found on the island promontory below the castle and this is unlikely to have witnessed the birth of so renowned a hero.

As to the battle of Badon, this could indeed have taken place near Bath, perhaps at Solsbury Hill, which overlooks the present town, or indeed at any one of several other sites in the area: Liddington Castle near Swindon, or Badbury Rings in Dorset have both been plausibly suggested.

Other notable sites with Arthurian connections include Dozmary Pool, on Bodmin Moor, one of several supposed sites for the lake to which Bedivere reluctantly consigned the great sword, Excalibur. Certainly, on a visit to this site – especially in the early morning when mist still shrouds its banks – it is not hard to imagine the scene, with the wounded Arthur laid nearby and the faithful knight watching in wonder as, having flung away the sword, a hand and arm cleft the water and snatched the sword from human sight.

Similarly, Cadbury Camp, some miles distant across the Somerset Levels, is convincing as the site of Arthur's centre of operations in the south. Originally an Iron-Age fort, Cadbury was excavated in the 1960s and shown to have been re-fortified in the period usually ascribed to the Arthurian revival.

However, does all this add up to a West-Country Arthur? When all the evidence is weighed it seems to depend as much upon oral tradition as upon fact. An equally valid case can be made for a northern Arthur (see Chapter 9)

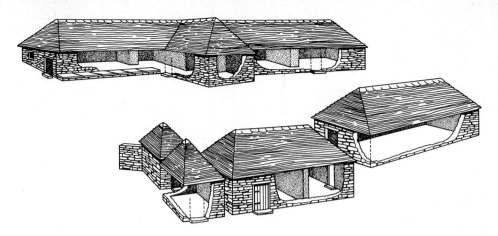

Conjectural reconstruction of the settlement at Tintagel.

Dozmary Pool, traditionally the site where Bedivere, on the wounded Arthur's instructions, cast the magical sword, Excalibur, back into the waters from which it had come.

and indeed the consensus of opinion, based on the latest archaeological and textual evidence, tends towards the north as a more likely place for the majority of Arthurian activity. However, it must be said again that no single place or area of countryside can claim to be 'the' Arthurian locale. The very nature of the sixth-century war-leader was his extreme mobility, which enabled him to appear at any one of a dozen places quickly – usually where his enemies least expected him. For this reason, as much as because of Arthur's deeper associations with the land, the numerous locations ascribed to him or to other characters associated with him remain equally valid.

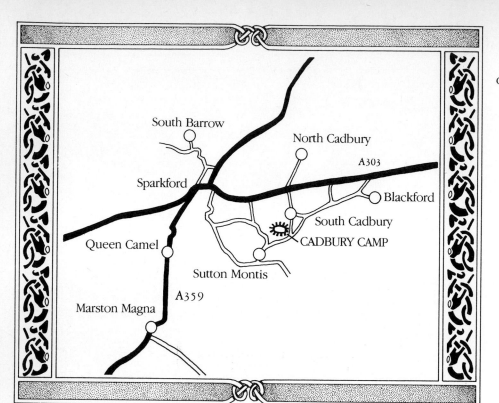

TRISTAN AND ISOLT IN CORNWALL

QUALLY STRONG ARE the claims made for several sites as a setting for the ill-starred love of Tristan and Isolt. Throughout Cornwall in particular, sites abound that chart the adventures of the lovers almost every step of the way.

Like the legends of Arthur, those that grew up around the figure of Tristan were largely Celtic in origin. Again like Arthur, they were taken up by the wandering tale-tellers of Europe, who in time gave rise to the troubadours and *trouvères* with their complex courtly epics of love and chivalry. Tristan and Isolt became favourite subjects, and a number of romances were written that told their story in increasing complexity. One of the earliest of which we have any knowledge is the *Tristan* of Thomas (*c.*1170). Here the story is still simple enough, but it was soon elaborated into a full-scale romantic epic, of which the best known and probably the finest was written by the German poet, Gottfried von Strassburg (*c.*1210). His work is rich in symbolism and contains some of the finest descriptive passages to be found anywhere in medieval literature. An English version of the story was written in the thirteenth century and attributed to the same Thomas of Erceldoune (Thomas the Rhymer) referred to in Chapter 8.

Prose versions of the story followed throughout the thirteenth and fourteenth centuries, by which time the lovers had become part of the vast

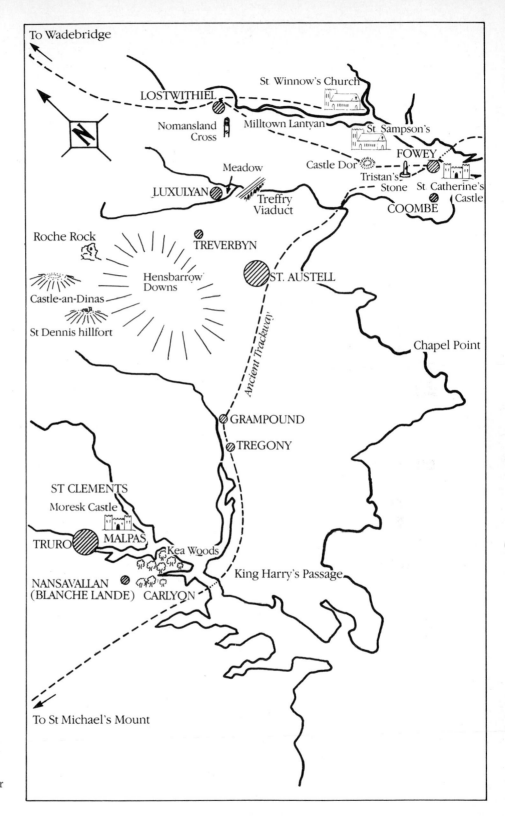

Tristan in Cornwall (after
E. M. Ditmas).

panoply of the Arthurian mythos. Tristan became a great knight of the Round Table, second only to Lancelot in bravery and strength, and versions appeared as far away as Norway and Iceland. The story became, to all intents, a text book example of the ethos of *amour courtois* (courtly love), which presupposed that love between married people was not possible (a reflection of the arranged dynastic marriages among the courtly class) and raised the theme of adultery to an almost mystical status.

The whole matter of nineteenth-century romanticism grew from this and there are, not surprisingly, numerous poetic versions (generally bad) from this period. Wagner's opera *Tristan und Isolde* (1865) is perhaps the single best modern work to come out of the original medieval tale. It is justly famed for its elevation of love to spiritual heights of intensity, and the famous love – death leitmotiv that runs through the opera has been written about extensively, and has helped keep the story of Tristan and Isolt alive into the present day.

Lyonesse, Tristan's homeland, has long been associated with the Scilly Isles, which may possibly be all that remains of this ancient land, and which is believed to have sunk beneath the waves at a time probably too distant to identify properly – despite the record of no less a source than the *Anglo-Saxon Chronicle* that describes it as overwhelmed by a high tide on 11 November 1099.

This lack of specific information as to the cause or date of the disaster had led to theories that Lyonesse was once part of Atlantis, or that it was inundated, like Ys in Brittany, as the result of some great unspecified wickedness on the part of its ruler, or else that like other 'lost lands' of Britain it sank beneath the waves over a lengthy period of time.

This last belief, perhaps the most readily acceptable, has found support in recent years by such investigators as F. J. North and Nigel Pennick, who have devoted time and effort to restoring Lyonesse and its fellows to the maps of legendary Britain.

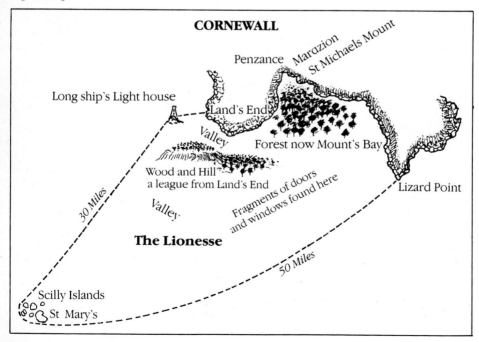

Agnes Strickland's map of Lyonesse from Beckles Wilson's *The story of lost England* (1902).

A continuing fascination with lost lands has helped to preserve stories relating to parts of the original coastline of Britain long since vanished beneath the sea. Thus a map, included in the 1902 book *The Story of Lost England,* shows a forest surrounding St Michael's Mount, and stretching between Land's End and Lizard Point. Also marked are placed where 'fragments of doors and windows' have been found, well out in the stretch of sea between Cornwall and the Scillies. Rumours of drowned bells that signal warnings of disaster or death are frequently told, and it seems somehow appropriate that Tristan, whose original name was changed by the romancers to echo the French word *'tristesse'* – sadness – should thus lose his homeland, as well as his life and love.

Inland, as far as Castle Dor or even Maiden Castle in Dorest, are the lands supposedly once ruled by Tristan's uncle (or father) King Mark; while St Sampson's Isle, where Tristan fought the Irish giant Morholt, has been traced both to Samson Island in the Scillies, and to an islet in the Fowey Estuary, near the church of St Sampson at Lantyan – which may itself house the site of Mark's palace.

The episode of Tristan's leap has been variously sited. In this the hero escaped his captors by asking to pray in a chapel overlooking the sea, then squeezing through a narrow window and leaping down the sheer cliff-face to the sea. Tradition places this death-defying feat at Chapel Point near Mevagissey though it has been pointed out by more than one commentator that this is rather far from the scene of other events in the story, which are

Maiden Castle, one of several re-fortified Iron-Age hillforts that may have been the headquarters of King Mark during the Arthurian period.

grouped within a fairly small area. The fact that Beroul, one of the earliest compilers of the saga, who seems to have known the countryside of Cornwall rather better than most of his contemporaries, refers to the fact that 'the Cornish still call this stone Tristan's Leap', does suggest that he is basing his description on an actual place with a well-established tradition.

The Forest of Morrois, where Tristan and Isolt hid from Mark's soldiers, may have been the present-day Forest of Moresk, which appears in the *Domesday Book* as Moreis, and was once part of a far more heavily wooded area. This is not too far from the extraordinary Roche Rock, which lies about 8 km (5 miles) north of St Austell, and is a possible setting for the hermitage of Ogrin where Tristan and Isolt sought refuge after they finally escaped for a time from Mark's vengeful pursuit. Today there are the remains of a fifteenth-century chapel, reached by a series of ladders from the flat plain below, but tradition makes it the habitation of a hermit from much earlier times. Though far inland, it makes a splendid alternative to the famous leap, though this is purely speculative.

The most impressive and interesting pieces of evidence connecting Tristan with the West Country is the so-called Tristan Stone. Nowadays it stands at a cross-roads 2.5 km (1½ miles) from Fowey and some 3 km (2 miles) from Castle Dor – perhaps Mark's home – though once it stood nearer to the site of the great earthwork. It is nearly 2m (7 ft) long and once probably lay on its side, though it has been re-erected to point like a finger at the sky. On one side is a partially obliterated inscription that has been interpreted to read

Roche Rock, possible origin of the story of Tristan's miraculous escape from the soldiers of King Mark. He is said to have leapt from a high window and fled across country.

DRUSTANUS HIC JACET
CUNOMORI FILIUS

—

DRUSTAN HERE LIES
OF CUNOMORUS THE SON

Portrait of Tristan
(Chertsey Abbey).

We approach here several mysteries at once. 'Drustan' (Drust or Drostan) places Tristan as possibly a Pictish or even Irish hero. His name (and parts of his story) crop up in sources as various as an early Irish *Hymn to St Muirgint* and an eighth-century legal document now in the Abbey of St Gall.

Elsewhere, we find reference to a 'Drust, son of Talorc' who may have given his name, if nothing more, to the later hero, and who appears to have flourished only slightly later than the Arthurian period with which Tristan became associated.

As for 'Marcus Cunomorus', he is to be found under several guises: as March ap Meirchiawn in the Welsh *Triads,* as Kynvarch in the ninth-century *Life of St Paul Aurelianus*, and in the tenth-century Irish *Book of Lecan* as Marcan. Kynvarch is clearly a variant of the Cunomorus of the Tristan Stone inscription. Though while Cunomorus refers to a 'dog', Kynvarch means 'horse', possibly referring to a one-time horse deity or at least to a king who worshipped such a one, and almost certainly giving rise to the curious folk-tradition that March or Mark had horses' ears – itself a sly reference to the 'horns' worn by all cuckolded husbands.

Professor Sigmund Eisner has reconstructed the story in a challengingly original manner, setting it firmly in the Strathclyde area of Britain where March ap Meirchiawn probably ruled in the sixth century. Drust or Drostan, a Pictish warrior related to him, takes service with his 'uncle' and falls in love with the beautiful Essyllt (the Welsh version of Isolt) with the inevitable outcome.

Whether we accept this version or not, it does not preclude accepting the Tristan Stone as genuine. Mark could just as easily have been a Cornish lord, and Tristan could have indeed come from Lothian, or Loönis as it was called by the romancers, a name close enough to Lyonesse to confuse the two. His mother could have been of Pictish origin and have married Mark or March or Marcus as a dynastic union. Equally, Tristan could have take service with a Cornish 'uncle' at a later date, as the stories themselves seem to suggest.

Tristan teaches Isolt to harp (Chertsey Abbey).

Whatever the truth, the legends are inseparable from their adopted home, and add a rich strata to the legend-haunted lands of the west, while the story of the lovers has assumed an almost archetypal status in which *amour* (love) has become elevated to a spiritual dimension seldom recognised today. Unlike the story of Lancelot and Guinevere, whom Tristan and Isolt superficially resemble, there is something wild and powerful (at least in the earlier versions) about their story that has caused it to transcend time and space. The best modern re-telling to date is *The White Raven* by Diana Paxson (Hodder and Stoughton, Sevenoaks, 1988) that restores something of the original Celtic vitality to the tale. Our own version, which follows, seeks a further dimension.

Drustan's Ghost

The central idea underlying this story is one touched on elsewhere in this book – the marriage of the land and the king. This mystical relationship worked on two levels: the king mediated his rulership via his relationship with the Goddess of the Land, Lady Sovereignty herself, but he also derived his kingship via the sovereignty-bestowing maiden whom he married, for in earlier times queens were drawn from the holy bloodline and suitable husbands were found to be their consorts.

The story of Tristan and Isolt and Mark has always seemed to mask a deeper reality than that of the human tragic-love triangle. In the story, we revert to the earlier characters of Drustan and Marcus. Instead of sending Drustan to Ireland, Marcus sends him to the Otherworld to fetch his bride, for it is within these realms that Isolt really resides. It is only by such a union that Marcus can restore the Waste Land. But the dynastic mingling of the ancient blood of the Sidhe (the Faery Folk) with the Royal House of Cornwall was not to be: this burden falls to Arthur and Guinevere – another such faery bride, for only so can her role be truly understood. However, as in this story, fate strikes by the introduction of a younger, more able man in the shape of Lancelot, who, as Tristan does, interposes between the king and the land. Thus an ancient pattern is endlessly rewoven, and the Waste Land returns until that most elusive of Otherworldly redemptions – the Grail – is finally found and another sacrifice of royal blood is demanded (see pp. 137–143).

I said I would follow her forever, and so I have; but now she is gone where I may not follow (unless she comes for me) and all I can do is sing of our joy and our sorrow, of the love that burned us and left the land riven and unhealed.

All this because of a cup, drunk without thought in a midsummer gale on the ocean, with the salt spray blowing in our faces and the gulls flying high above the swaying mast-head. So much to tell and so little time in which to tell it, before the sun rises again and I am bound once more to the stone.

It was winter when my father, Marcus Flavius Cunomorus, self-styled king of Dumnonia, first showed signs of the illness that was to change the lives of us all. He had been out hunting, as was his usual practice, but this time he came home a changed man. Before he was familiar: bluff, hearty, a big man in every sense; after he was meaner, pinched, somehow fearful as well as angry, as though at an adversary neither he nor any of us could see.

He sent for me, that same afternoon, and when I arrived in his private chamber I found Andret there also. There was no love lost between my brother and me, but we both knew when our father's wishes were not to be refused.

He looked at us both in turn with eyes that had grown feral and red-rimmed in the space of a few hours. Then he smiled, which in its way was as terrible. He took something from a pouch at his belt and laid it on the table before us. It looked like a long, pale-gold hair, finer than the finest harp-string I ever possessed.

'There,' said my father, smiling that happy, empty smile, 'there is her token. You must do the rest.'

Andret who was always the bolder of us when the need arose, took the chance. 'What is it you wish us to do, father?' he asked.

Our father's smile vanished. 'What! he cried, 'can it be that you are too stupid to understand? What must I do to explain it to you?' He paced slowly around the table, towering over us, though we were neither of us beardless boys. 'I see that I must spell out even the most obvious things,' he said at last, but the way he said it brought a chill to my heart. 'Very well, then. This hair is from the head of the woman I shall marry. You must find her and bring her to me. Is that clear enough for my two brave young sons?'

That was obviously as clear as anything our father had to say to us was ever going to be, so we looked at each other and when Andret shrugged I picked up the golden hair, intending to cut it in twain, one half for Andret, one for me. At once a strange feeling overcame me. Everything looked suddenly altered, as though it was not quite solid any more. Both my father and my brother were changed as well, at least my father was more or less as he had become in those last few hours, while Andret — Andret became suddenly 'dangerous', leaner, harder, more rat-like. All the small, unhappy tricks he had played on me were suddenly brought to mind. In that moment I hated Andret with an all-consuming hatred; I found that, without thinking, my hand had sought the hilt of my dagger.

Then, as quickly as it had come, the mood passed, to be replaced by an even stronger feeling — a desire to discover the owner of the hair. It was so deep and strong a feeling that I was halfway to the door before Andret knocked me down. We began struggling with a silent ferocity quite foreign to our usual battles, and might indeed have done each other serious hurt had not our father fallen upon us roaring and dragging us bodily apart. He tore the golden hair from my hand, cut it in two with a swift slash of his knife, and gave one piece to each of us.

'Now, go!' he said, with scarcely contained anger. 'Get out of my sight, and don't come back until you've found her!'

Andret and I backed off, glaring at each other — but strangely, the moment that he had a piece of the hair, my desire to attack him vanished, as apparently did his to get at me. We left the chamber together, hastened to our rooms and gathered a few necessary possessions, took our horses and left the court.

We went separate ways, myself going west, Andret north. I never saw my brother again, nor do I know what happened to him. Perhaps he wandered into a land where her influence did not stretch and there found rest. Perhaps he fell victim of outlaws or other evil powers. I think, perhaps, he was lucky.

For myself, I pressed on through lands that were at first familiar but soon became less so and were finally strange. I had no clear idea where I was going, but there is little doubt that I was in some way guided by my possession of the golden hair.

After a while I entered the forest, a region of that vast, dark wood of which the bard Taliesin has sung and which is called in the tongue of the French, Broceliande. It was a place not much visited in those times, and its vast enclaves were little explored. It was not a place I would have chosen to go, but I had no choice — so completely was I bound by the power of the hair.

And so I came, after a period of travelling that has no borders in my mind, to the place where I was always intended to go.

At sunset I came to an edge of the wood and looked out upon the sea. It stretched flat and empty to the horizon, where I could just discern the shape of hills. And beached and waiting on the verge of the land was a small coracle of the kind much favoured along the shores of Dumnonia. I knew well how to sail it and since this was the way I must go, I stepped aboard and taking the small, single paddle, pushed off from the shore of Britain and set sail for the other shore, where no land that I had ever heard tell of existed.

And though it had seemed far off when I first glimpsed it from the edge of the forest, now it seemed that distance was deceptive, for it took me less than a day of paddling to reach that other shore. And it seemed to me that the coracle knew its own way and needed little effort on my part to steer it. This did not surprise me, and at last I did little, but lay back in the shallow craft and took out my part of the golden hair and looked at it.

If it had seemed fair and bright before, now it seemed positively to glow, and by this I knew that I was nearing my destination. Sure enough, when next I raised my eyes from the contemplation of my token, I found that the shore was near. Great, frowning cliffs rose from the sea close at hand and there I saw a channel leading into a bay, and my fine craft was easy to steer between the rocks until it lay at rest on a margin of white sand.

I stepped ashore and for the first time since I had laid hand upon the hair I felt at peace. There and then I sat down upon a rock and took out my harp, which had suffered surprisingly little from its journey, and was quickly tuned. I began to play, softly at first, an ancient tune I had learned from a travelling bard only the winter before. So lost did I become in the music that I neither heard nor saw her approach. Only when I had played enough did I look up and see her. And from that moment my fate was sealed.

The hair that had come from her head in no wise matched the splendour of its companions. Like white gold it fell, to her hips and beyond, and it framed a face more beautiful to me than the dawn. I loved her at once, with a deep and unshakeable love, and in a thousand years it has not dimmed.

The Ghost of Tristan.

CRVSTAVS HIC IACIT
CVNOWORI FILIVS

Her voice, when she spoke to me, was as sweet as the sweetest songbird's and matched everything about her that was itself matchless.

'Welcome, Drustan, that was sweetly played.'

To hear praise from her lips was to dwell in Tir na nOg itself, and I knew myself utterly lost from that moment. When she stretched forth her hand I placed mine willingly within it and went with her into the silence of that place.

And so I dwelt there, on the island of Caer Siddi, which has also been called Spiral Castle, with the woman I came to know as Isolt — though I know now that she has many other names. And time passed not at all it seemed, though the sun rose and set and rose again. By its light we walked on the sweet grass of the island or climbed the hills until we could look out at the restless sea; or else we lay at rest beneath the shade of the apple trees that grew in the sheltered groves amid the valleys of that place. And at night I sang to her and played such music as I had never known was in me and I loved her as much as a man sometimes loves a woman, with all the fierceness of consuming flames.

In those flames I was myself, somehow, consumed. And when I had no more will or wish to be anything other than I was, or to know any other life, Isolt came to me and told me that we must depart. When I sought to protest, though weakly, she laid a finger on my lips and said, smiling, 'It must be so, my love. It must be so.'

Then, though I had seen no other living soul save animal or bird in that land since first I set foot upon it, suddenly there were people who came forward with rich clothing for us both and who washed us in scented water and garbed us as a king and queen. Then they led us to the shore where a great ship awaited and we went aboard.

Two things I remember of that voyage, which somehow took longer than my own short passage from shore to shore. One was the game we played on the first day, a strange game played with jewelled pieces on a golden board, and the second is the cup with which we pledged each other as we sat together on the deck of the ship, with its great sail billowing above us and the salt spray on our faces and gulls flying high above the swaying mast-head.

A simple cup it was, though of gold, as was everything that came of Spiral Castle. But the drink. Ah! That was not simple. In it lay the fate of the land, though I knew it not, and in it also lay the bitter draught that was to bind me here until the ending of all things.

Isolt, when she offered it to me, said only, 'Let us pledge ourselves each to other, and swear that we will abide by what must be.'

I drank, and with that draught came both joy and endless sorrow. Joy because it sealed our love across all time; sorrow because it brought also knowledge. Then I knew what had changed my father. I seemed to see, far off and distant in my mind as though I watched it happen, his meeting with Isolt that distant day of hunting, and of the pledge made between them for the good of the land, for she was not made for any one man, or for any mortal lover. Her destiny was greater. So, too, was my father's, for despite his Roman pretensions, his blood was far older and carried the strength of the land. By their mating would come a new flowering, the dried-up wells would flow again in despite of the harm done long ages since by Amangons and his men.

For the rest, the story is well known, how 'Tristan' (they changed my name to mean 'the sad one') brought 'Iseult' to King Mark, and how he used her ill so that she began to love the son who had brought her to Dumnonia rather than the father she was meant to wed. And how those two became lovers and fled to the forest and dwelt there in lawless bliss. So, too, is it told that the land grew sick and the wells remained dry and the fields fallow, and how there was war between King Mark and the Emperor Arthur, and great evil besides. And it is said that 'Tristan' fell sick at last, and died, and that she who loved him perished from sorrow and was laid by his side, and that two thorn trees grew from their grave and put forth red and white flowers and that they twined together . . .

Such is the story, but it happened otherwise. The truth is that our love was too strong for the tide of fate that bore us, and that the mating of my father's blood with the blood of the goddess came not to be, and that the land grew sick. But what is not told is how that evil was undone and what truly became of 'Tristan' and 'Iseult'.

We fled, it is true, from the madness of my father to the safety of the wood. But there time does not cease to move as it had for us on the island, and once departed from there no mortal may return again. And with this knowledge came a bitter sorrow that I could not transcend. It threatened even our love that, though it grew no cooler, yet became like a sword laid between us.

And at length, Isolt spoke to me of the land and the sickness, from which we were saved within the enclave of the wood. And when she had spoken we were silent for a long while, until I found the words to say what had begun to fill my mind of late: that I could not bear to grow old while she remained unchanged; that I would as soon die than watch our love grow cold.

Thus it was that Isolt spoke of the way in which we might always be one, until time itself ceased and the lives of the wood were rolled up and laid away until the next day of Creation.

Easy enough, it seemed to me then, to sleep the long sleep and yet be free; to be bound forever to my love. I know now that the ways of the people of Caer Siddi are not for mortals, any more than our ways are for them. I drank the cup, the second draught that brings sleep and forgetting; but I did not forget, and my sleep is shallow. You who walk here, who see me and hear my words, understand this better than I ever shall.

Yet I believe that she will come. Time means nothing in Caer Siddi. It is but a moment since I drank, and from that moment I have waited. The land has flowered again, and sickened and flowered many times since then. But still I wait and soon, I believe, she will come, and we shall both be set free.

2·caerleon:
the city of the legions

According to Geoffrey of Monmouth, Caerleon was founded by Belinus, a fictitious Roman leader whose name disguises that of the British god, Bel or Belin. In those days it was known as Caer Usk, the City by the Usk, and Geoffrey calls it the mother city of South Wales.

It lies in a sheltered valley accessible from every side by land or water, but easily defensible for all that. During the Roman occupation it was known as Caer Lleon, the City of the Legions, though the Romans themselves called it Caerleon.

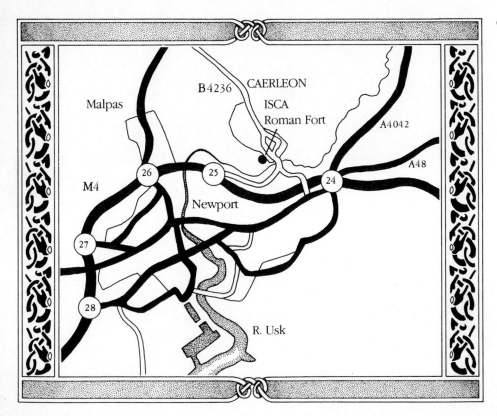

Isca Silurum after the river and the local tribe of the Silures. From *c*.AD 75 it was the headquarters of the 2nd Augustan Legion and served as a base for the governing of South Wales.

Initially set out after the manner of all Roman forts, covering some 50 acres (20 ha), with wooden buildings and a turf ditch and rampart surmounted by a palisade, it was rebuilt in stone some time after AD 130 by the soldiers who had worked on Hadrian's Wall. From this point onward it became one of the three permanent legionary posts in Britain (the others being at York and Chester) that together controlled the whole of the country.

Today, thanks to painstaking archaeological work, there is much to be seen of the original Roman buildings, in particular the remains of the fine bath-houses, which include an open-air pool, a changing-room once heated by a hypocaust, and a *frigidarium* or cold room, in which the bathers plunged after their swim. They are a tribute to Roman engineering skills and their love of comfort.

Giraldus Cambrensis (Gerald of Wales), a contemporary of Geoffrey of Monmouth, drew particular attention to the baths in his celebrated *Journey Through Wales* of 1188, according then to have been constructed with 'extra-ordinary skill', perhaps wishing that such luxury still existed in the draughty castles and monasteries of his own time.

Bronze horseman, wearing a cloak and Corinthian helmet, and bearing the shield of an auxiliary.

Nearby, the north-west corner of the fort, now known as Prysig Field, contains the foundation of three barrack blocks, one of which is original and the others of which are reconstructed. The original foundation is the only one of its kind ever discovered in Britain. The remains of 24 rooms in pairs of 12 can still be traced, with additional housing for the centurion close to hand (a room like the one described in the following story). Also close by are the remains of the latrines – including a stone channel through which water was flushed and which at one time would have been surmounted by a row of wooden seats.

Parts of the original defensive walls still stand, and just beyond lies the extraordinary amphitheatre, the finest example of its kind to be excavated in Britain. Some 24 m (80 ft) long, oval in shape, it was large enough to seat an entire legion (some 6,000 men) and was probably used for drills and exercises, as well as for games and religious ceremonies.

The walls still stand to a height of 2 m (6 ft) in places, some bearing the names of the Roman centurions who may have worked on them. There are eight gangways dividing the terraced seating areas that would once have had wooden benches to sit on. Two massive entranceways, complete except for their capstones, lead into the arena, and to each side of these are small, narrow chambers, where the gladiators (or sometimes prisoners) waited. In one of these is a niche that probably contained a shrine to Nemesis, the Roman goddess of fortune.

The Romano-British practice of inscribing leaden tablets with offerings made to the deity of the place has lead to some notable discoveries including several at Bath (see p. 66) and one at Caerleon itself, on which is written 'Lady Nemesis, I give you this cloak and boots. Let him who wore them not redeem them save by the life of his *sanguineus.*' (This last word probably refers to the owner's chestnut horse, on whose skills he presumably relied in battle or in the arena.)

Before it was excavated, the arena was covered by a grassy mound known

locally as Arthur's Table, and it is this connection that gives Caerleon its legendary dimension. For here, according to Geoffrey of Monmouth, and in consistent references throughout the *Mabinogion*, was Arthur's greatest court. Long before the better-known Camelot (possibly sited at Cadbury Camp in Somerset) Caerleon was the centre of activity for such famous Round-Table heros as Gawain, Kei, Bedwyr, Gereint, and Owein. Here also Arthur is described as holding his first great gathering of kings and nobles after his war against the Emperor Fliolle, and of receiving the royal diadem of Britain at Whitsuntide. For, says Geoffrey,

Situated in a passing pleasant position . . . and abounding in wealth above all other cities, it was the place most meet for so high a solemnity. For on the one side there flowed the noble river aforsaid [the Usk] whereby the Kings and Princes that should come from oversea might be borne thither in their ships, and on the other side, girdled about with meadows and woods, passing fair was the magnificence of the kingly palaces thereof with the gilded verges of the roofs that imitated Rome.

(Bk IX, Ch. 12, trans. S. Evans)

Geoffrey is, of course, here describing a medieval Arthur, who perhaps bears little resemblance to the sixth-century hero and warrior, though there is, as we shall see, reason to suppose that the siting of the Arthurian court at Caerleon is not without some foundation.

Geoffrey also mentions one of the chief glories of the city, two churches dedicated respectively to the martyrs, Julius and Aaron. Nothing is known of either of these two personages, though they are mentioned in Bede's *History*, and in various charters dating from a period just *after* Geoffrey was writing. They may be the same martyrs described as meeting their deaths during the reign of the Emperor Decius (249–51) but there are no records of any churches dedicated to them.

An even more significant detail (for our present purpose) in Geoffrey's account is his reference to

A school of two hundred philosophers [priests?] learned in Astronomy and in other arts, that did delight to observe the courses of the stars, and did by true inferences foretell the prodigies which at that time were about to befall unto King Arthur.

(Bk IX, Ch. 12, trans. S. Evans)

This has been justly compared to the description of Merlin's observatory in Geoffrey's *Vita Merlini*, as well as being a distant memory of Druidic colleges that at one time performed a similar, if not identical, function.

This is by no means the end of the Arthurian connection with Caerleon, however. As already noted, in the *Mabinogion*, Arthur's court is almost without exception described as being sited here. We may imagine the famous scene from *Culhwch and Olwen* where the young prince Culhwch arrives to request the aid of Arthur and his warriors in winning the hand of the beautiful Olwen. He is met and challenged by Arthur's porter, Glewlwyd Mighty-Grasp, and then finally admitted to find Arthur surrounded by a band of heroes of truly mythic proportions: Kei, who could hold his breath under water for nine days and nights; Sgilti, who could walk over the forest branches; and Clust, who could hear an ant moving 50 miles (80 km) distant. This is not unlike a similar guest-list of Arthur's coronation feast in the *Historia*, which also, of course, took place at Caerleon.

A much-vexed question in all matters of Arthurian scholarship is the location of the twelve famous battles against the Saxons described in the *Historia Brittonum* (*c.*900) attributed to the monk, Nennius. Much speculation has gone into the identification of the sites where these battles were fought. One that has seldom caused contention is that of the City of the Legions, otherwise Caerleon. It is possible that we have here a historical basis for the attribution of this particular city to Arthur's time.

While there was probably little or no human habitation before the Romans established their fortress, such a permanent settlement would have attracted civilians of all kinds, thus founding a township that grew until it expanded into the medieval city described, however extravagantly, by Giraldus:

Caerleon is of unquestioned antiquity. It was constructed with great care by the Romans, the walls being built of brick. You can still see many vestiges of its one-time splendour. There are immense palaces, which, with the gilded gables and their roofs, once rivalled the magnificence of ancient Rome. ... Here, too, archbishop Dyfrig handed over his supreme function to David of Menevia, for the metropolitan see was moved from Caerleon in accordance with the prophecy of Merlin Ambrosius: 'Menevia shall be dressed in the pall of the City of the Legions'.

(*The Journey Through Wales*, Book 1, Chapter 5)

It is known that many strongholds, both native and Roman, were re-activated during the Arthurian period; and it is more than likely that Caerleon, significantly placed for the defence of South Wales, would have proved important to the historical Arthur and his men.

Tennyson, centuries after in 1875, chose to begin his epic cycle of poems, *The Idylls of the King*, at Caerleon. Perhaps he knew of the local story that claimed Arthur was sleeping under a nearby hill, for certainly it is for its Arthurian associations that the city of Caerleon deserves an important place on the map of legendary Britain.

The Kingly Shadow

In the story that follows, an imaginary meeting takes place between two men, one of whom already rules over the kingdom of Britain and the other who will do so in a time yet to come.

Kings and kingship were always a sacred matter to the people of Britain. Descriptions still exist of ceremonies in which the king symbolically married the land, either in the shape of an Otherworldly woman who represented the Goddess of the Island or, as in Ireland, where the king mated with a white mare in whose blood he ritually bathed and whose flesh he afterwards consumed. (A description of this ceremony can be read in Giraldus' book, *A Journey Through Ireland* – he was deeply shocked and scandalised by what he considered a barbaric anachronism in twelfth-century Donegal.)

Ambrosius Aurelianus, who held together the war-torn kingdom of Britain in the interregnum between the demise of Vortigern (the Gwytheryn of this story) and the coming of Arthur, was perhaps of mixed Roman and British blood – though Gildas the Wise hints at Ambrosius' family being of imperial stock. If he was indeed of mixed native and Roman blood, this may have been of great advantage in enabling him to weld together both peoples into a force strong enough to repel the invading Saxons, Picts, and Scots until the young King Arthur arrived on the scene.

Of Ambrosius' life and death very little is known. This particular period was one of great turmoil, and there is little in the way of verbatim reportage: most chronicles covering the period 460–85 (roughly the time of Ambrosius' campaigning) date from several centuries after this time. Nennius calls Ambrosius, Emrys Wledig or the Overlord, and relates the story of Vortigern's Tower with him as the opponent of that treacherous king, thereby aligning Ambrosius the warlord with Merlin the mysterious prophet. Geoffrey of Monmouth drew fruitfully upon this confusion as well as upon the oral traditions relating to Merddyn or Merlin, as he called him.

Certainly there is a strong line of tradition connecting Ambrosius, Merlin, and Arthur that persists, and which the following story sustains.

There have always been kings in these lands. Sometimes seen and sometimes unseen. But always, it seems, there is the right man waiting to come forward at the right time. If one failed to do so a surrogate had to be found. Often he rules as well as any man and is none the worse for not being the true king. But still, only when the true and rightful heir steps upon the King Stone is all right with the land. That is the way it has always been and that is the way it will always be.

Now at the time I want to speak of, some knew, by signs and portents in the heavens, that a king more great than any seen so far was soon to come. The *Druidim* had seen it long since, and the college of priests, who studied the heavens daily from their great foundation in the City of the Legions, had begun to suspect that it might be so. And, in this time of which I speak, there was one called Merddin, whose history I will tell another time, who had been appointed by the dwellers in Avalon to seek out the new king and see to it that he found his throne and his true destiny. For he that was coming was to be the King Before and the King Hereafter, he that had ruled before and died, and now was about to be reborn. This time, it was said, he would not die, returning instead to Avalon when the moment came, there to await a further time when he would be needed to govern the land.

Now the man who ruled over most of Britain at this time was named Ambrosius Aurelianus in the Roman way, and he wore the toga with a wide, purple stripe and had his chin and cheeks shaved for him and wore his hair short. But for all that it was known that his mother was of the Silures, so that he had the royal blood of the Maiden in his veins, as well as the iron blood of Rome; so that he was at least half fit to rule, even though he was not the chosen king and had not married the land.

Those were troubled times, as you will recall, when the legions had been called away to fight in Gaul and beyond, and when the chieftain Gwytheryn, he of the thin lips, had invited the Saxon hounds into our land, at first to fight against the Picti and the Scotti; but soon enough they began to help themselves to lands and to plunder.

So when the people saw how Ambrosius began to organise resistance, and how he seemed to represent the best of Rome *and* Britain, they were not slow to follow him. For the first time in living memory, men of more than one tribe fought alongside each other under Ambrosius' banner – with the result that the Saxons were pushed back within the boundaries of the lands originally gifted to them by Gwytheryn, and kept there, for a time at least. But they were still not driven out of the land.

Ambrosius was no longer young. He had fought with the legions in Gaul, learning his skills from no less a man than the Riothamus Uthyr, before he fell, or vanished, fighting the Parisi. So there were a few who began to wonder about a successor; while others, who had heard about the coming of the true king, fell to wondering how and when he would announce himself.

And Ambrosius had thought of this often in the past year, lying awake on his narrow army cot, thinking of all the opportunist kinglets who had left the body of the land torn and bleeding, wondering who would follow him, and which of his own men he could put forward when the time came. None, it seemed, even began to measure up the enormity of the task – that of keeping together what had been, so often, broken.

Long years of army service, followed by more years of the task he had found awaiting him when he returned to Britain – the restoration of Roman order in a land at war with itself – all this had left no time for his own life. There would be no successor of his own blood.

In the end the coming of the king happened naturally, though the true story is strange enough.

Ambrosius had his headquarters in the old Roman fort at Isca Silurum, or the City of the Legions as it was still known. He lived simply enough, like any soldier, adopting none of the pomp and ceremony he might have affected. This brought reluctant approval even from the haters of all things Roman, who chose to remember Ambrosius' British blood at such times, and to acknowledge his abilities as a soldier.

So it was that as Ambrosius sat late one night reading over a fresh set of dispatches from the far north, the leather curtain across the door was pushed back and there came in a figure with eyes more deep and black than the night itself and a face made all of sharp lines and edges and little flesh, and whose voice when he spoke was as harsh as a raven's.

'Ambrosius Aurelianus, I must have speech with you.'

And, though he was taken somewhat off guard by the sudden and dramatic appearance of the stranger, Ambrosius answered coolly enough: 'Speak, then, since you are here; but be brief, for as you see, I am busy.'

The stranger's face seemed to take on a glow of its own as he answered. 'You have held the land well, Ambrosius, but the time has come for you to relinquish your place to another.'

'Who are you?' demanded Ambrosius, unable to suppress a shudder at the import of the words.

'I am called Merddyn Emrys. I am the Steward of this land.'

Now Ambrosius looked with open wonder at the newcomer. The name he uttered was one he knew well for it was already touched with the glow of legend. Few there were who did not know the story of how the traitor, Gwytheryn, fleeing from Ambrosius' own army, had attempted to build a refuge in the mountains of Eryri, and how each night the work of his builders was thrown down by an unseen agency. It was then that the child, Merddyn, had come, revealing that two dragons fought beneath the hill, which was sacred to the Goddess of the Land. Subsequently he had prophesied the imminent death of the tyrant, which had been proved correct when Gwytheryn perished in the flames after Ambrosius had caught up with him at last and burned his camp to the ground.

But of the child, Merddyn Emrys, nothing more had been seen since that time.

That had been little more than ten years since, and then Merddyn had been a child of perhaps ten summers; this Merddyn seemed a mature man; yet the more Ambrosius looked at him the less able he was to put any age upon him.

'Be seated, Merddyn Emrys,' he said. 'Your name is not unknown to me. But I would know what business you have here at this time.'

'I am but the messenger,' replied the mage, 'the one with whom you must speak is elsewhere.'

Ambrosius answered: 'Am I to know whom? Indeed, am I to know why I should speak with this person?'

'In time all will be made plain,' was the reply. 'For the moment I ask only that you trust me and believe that I mean you no harm.'

And Ambrosius, though he might well have done otherwise, nodded his head in assent, and when the mage led the way out into the night he followed, noting without surprise that they passed through the barracks and into the narrow streets of the town unchallenged.

The sun was a red stain on the horizon as they reached the great amphitheatre, pride of Roman Isca, built in the time of the Emperor Titus and rising thirty feet above the earth. Its walls were already beginning to crumble into disrepair and grass and weeds grew tall between broken flagstones and along the stone seats where once citizens and legionaries alike had gathered to watch the games.

So it was that by the light of the setting sun, Ambrosius Aurelianus, *Dux Britanniarum*, came to the centre of the great oval space at the middle of the arena and so stood, waiting for he knew not whom nor what, wondering perhaps why he had allowed himself to be brought there, unarmed, with the evening cold beginning to strike through his cloak and the clothing beneath, until he shivered.

Of the other, of whom the mage was but a messenger, there was at first no sign, while from the moment they had reached the amphitheatre Merddyn himself had vanished into the shadows.

Then as Ambrosius waited, there came the sound of light footfalls and his soldier's sight identified a dark shape hesitating amid the crumbling stones.

'Come forward!' Ambrosius demanded, more sharply than he had intended. 'Show yourself!'

The figure who emerged from the shadows was no fearsome and terrible warrior, no wild monster from the dark Otherworld, but a slight youth of no more than fourteen or fifteen summers, simply dressed and unarmed. When he spoke his voice was light and uncertain.

'My lord?' He spoke in a native dialect familiar to Ambrosius.

'Who are you? What is your name?'

'I have no right to any name until it is won by right.'

'Then how shall I call you?'

'My family used to call me Gwri.'

Ambrosius found himself smiling. 'Very well then, Gwri it shall be. What do you want of me?'

'Something more and something less than your blessing.'

'Oh, and what may that be?'

'I have a task to undertake. I must marry the land.'

Ambrosius and Arthur,

Ambrosius felt his scalp prickle as an involuntary shudder ran through his body. Though he already knew the answer, he said,'You must explain what you mean.'

In formal sing-song the youth answered: 'I have met the Old One by the stream and have danced her dance; I have drunken of the Red Drink of Lordship and have kept vigil at the lip of the Well. Still must I play the game of light and dark and seek the Cauldron in the four-sided island. But before I do these things I must ask the Word of him who is the Protector of the Island of the Mighty, that when the times comes I may take his place and stand where he stands.'

Ambrosius, every hair on his body standing up, asked: 'What word is this that I must give?'

'The Word of Passing, the Word that gives the right to the one who comes after. You must ask the Question.'

As he heard these words a strange feeling came upon Ambrosius – that he had heard these self-same words before, and that he knew the answer to them even before it was out of his mouth. He said. 'What are the duties of a king?'

'To love the land and to serve the land.'

'What more besides?'

'To be patient, to know self-government without haughtiness, to speak truth and keep promises; to honour the gods, respect poets, and to be boundless in charity towards all. To lift up good men and suppress ill-doers; to give freedom to the just, restriction for the guilty. To light a lamp in the minds and hearts of men whom he honours, and to appear as splendid as the sun in his own hall.'

The ancient formula sounded familiar to Ambrosius, as though he had always known it. The response came unbidden to his lips. 'And when the time comes to lay down your life for the land, what then?'

'Then I shall go willingly to the place where all men must go and drink of the Dark Drink of Forgetting.'

As he heard these words Ambrosius had a strange sensation that more than one voice was speaking – as though a chorus of voices spoke from within the depths of the earth, an endless chain of those who had served the land. And among them, somehow, he stood, Ambrosius Aurelianus, *Dux Britanniarum*, his native blood calling out from the depth of his being . . .

The moment passed, and as though a shadow had passed over the world, Ambrosius blinked and was once more aware that he stood in the old amphitheatre of Caerleon. Before him the boy who had been king before and would be king hereafter, stood quietly, and for the first time Ambrosius noticed that where their two shadows slanted away to one side in the light of the sunset, the boy's towered hugely. A kingly shadow, crowned, and with a sword. Ambrosius blinked and again it seemed that he had imagined what he saw. His eyes met those of the boy, a long and appraising look that spoke of all that he had felt and dreamt and all that was to be. 'Will you tell me your true name now?'

'Artorius I am called in the language of the Romans; Artos in our own tongue.'

'Artos. Artos, I believe you will indeed be king after me, perhaps sooner than I had realised. And I believe you may be the hero this land has needed and has so long awaited. A dark time is coming for us all; it will need great strength to meet it. It seems to me that you have both.'

'He has indeed, Ambrosius the Roman.' The voice of Merddyn spoke from the shadows, but Ambrosius never took his eyes from those of the young Artos. With as much ceremony as he knew how, he placed his hand on the boy's shoulder. 'You asked for the Word that would make the passing of one king and the coming of another happen as it should. Now I can give it. The Word is "service" — serve the land and the people who *are* the land, and they will serve you . . . Do what must be done, Child of the Future. Time will do the rest.'

And Ambrosius turned away and walked out of the amphitheatre without looking back. He told no one of what had occurred that night, until he lay dying of poison, introduced by a Saxon spy into the well from which he habitually drank. Then he told the tale to one who was close to him, a young officer named Bedwyr, whose native blood assured him that it would be understood and not forgotten.

It is said that that young officer became one of the foremost warriors in the war-band of the young king, when he finally drew forth the Glaive of Light from the Stone of Kingship and married the Land's Lady; but of that story others will have to speak, for I know no more of it.

3·merlin
and dinas emrys

Traditional or legendary memory is surprisingly accurate: old tales and notions regarding places, almost forgotten people, and mysterious events have often been proven by modern scientific archaeology. This does not imply that archaeology defines truths exactly as found in legend, but that both legend and archaeology can reveal surprisingly harmonious conclusions. Each shows us one side of the mirror of history: legend reflects the past to us in dreams, riddles, potent myths, tragedies, and adventures; archaeology examines the material itself from which the mirror is constructed. Providing we do not accept the legends literally or expand the archaeology poetically, they can work well together to give us insights into the culture of the past, and therefore into the relationship between ourselves and the land in which we live. This last subject is not a matter of quaint antiquarianism, but cuts right through into crucial problems of environmental preservation and survival. Thus we might say that such insights into the past contribute to the welfare of the future.

This situation, of a balanced supportive relationship between tradition and archaeology, is fairly recent. Early antiquarians had not developed the technical tools and intellectual disciplines used by modern researchers and field archaeologists, and they tended to rely excessively upon legend and early literature. This created an expansive and often wildly inaccurate picture into which the rapidly developing modern disciplines of archaeology cut deeply; for a generation or more tradition was regarded as a spurious or at least dangerous source by hard scientific archaeologists. But in recent years, between approximately 1960 and the present day, a re-assessment of tradition has taken place on many levels. At one extreme, ancient texts and anonymous folk-tales and legends have been examined and much of their inner or fundamental mythic content has been defined, interpreted, and most important of all, related to British tradition, history, and to specific localities or regions. At the opposite extreme, in archaeology, material discoveries from specific sites have been found to relate in many ways to legends, either in early literature or from folk tradition, of those same sites . . . and, of course, to the overall patterns of legend and myth that enfold specific localised examples. Although we are examining this development in a British legendary context, we should remember that it applies worldwide.

Many examples of the interweaving of legend and history, myth and archaeology, could be cited; some of the major ones form the foundation for this book. While a few are factual and prosaic, many more present riddles or paradoxes that may never be solved. We might think, superficially, that a correlation between hard scientific disciplines and legend helps to prove and define the truth of early history, but this is not entirely so. Do the legends, myths, and powerful images generate development of locations (such as the famous temple at Aquae Sulis), or are tales attached to ruins or natural features of the land, and so develop into complex legendary structures? Clearly, neither of these simplistic proposals can provide an adequate answer.

The patterns of *interaction* between a geographical site or location and its cultural history, and again between its development, history, and legendary or mythic content are impossible to separate and correlate truly. We may, for convenience, approach the factual aspects alone, or the legendary aspects alone, but the truth lives in the fusion of the two. We might take this concept a step further and suggest that the truth of any ancient location is found upon an inner level that gives rise to both its history and its legends, through the interaction of people and the land in which they live and develop. This applies both upon a regional, national, and specifically limited local level. The local cases are specific and often uniquely formulated examples of broader regional and national motifs: this applies equally to history as it does to myth.

MERLIN AND HIS LOCATION

NE OF THE major figures who embodies some of these fascinating paradoxes is Merlin, the prophet and wise man of British tradition. We find Merlin appearing in an extensive literature, ranging from early medieval manuscripts to highly fantastic modern novels; but we also find him located at specific sites in Britain, mainly in North Wales, lowland and midland Scotland, and (less certainly) Cornwall.

Some sites have acquired Merlin through pure contrivance and have no historical or legendary connection with him whatsoever. Glastonbury is the best (or worst) example of this process: it has no Merlin legends in genuine tradition, and there are no early literary references connecting Merlin specifically to the region. Yet modern enthusiasts and writers insist on attaching Merlin to Glastonbury, perhaps because of the delightful monastic 'discovery' of what was supposedly the grave of King Arthur and Guinevere in the twelfth century. Alas, this was also spurious, and the beginning of a long, muddled sequence of fake-lore in Glastonbury that persists increasingly today, and actually obscures the true Glastonbury legends that are fascinating examples of Celtic lore connected to an ancient site (see Chapter 6).

But we do have a very short reference in Geoffrey of Monmouth's *Vita Merlini* in which Merlin and the bard Taliesin take the wounded Arthur to the Fortunate Isles, and a further reference in *The History of the Kings of Britain* to Avalon, where Arthur's sword, Caliburn (Excalibur) was made. Such magical

islands are part of the mythic Otherworld of Celtic legend generally, and many examples of actual islands or Otherworld locations are found all over Britain. Now neither of the mythic places referred to (the Fortunate Isles or Avalon) is said specifically to be Glastonbury by any writer or source of tradition before the twelfth-century works of Giraldus Cambrensis, and of William of Malmesbury, who was invited by the monks to write his influential work, *The Antiquities of Glastonbury*, completed around 1139. Unfortunately, the passages describing the finding of Arthur's grave were inserted after William's death, as in his *Acts of the Kings* (1125, revised 1135–40) he follows the traditional Welsh statement that the grave of Arthur is unknown. The later passages are probably the work of Adam of Domerham, but an eye-witness account of the opening of the tomb was given by Giraldus Cambrensis in two of his works (*De Principis Instructione* and *Speculum Ecclesiae)*, where he also explains the Welsh-language origins of the name Avalon.

The classical historian Procopius relates *(De Bello Getico,* I, i) that in the west of Britain there were certain islands where the souls of the dead were carried, while the name Ynys Avallach was used for the island ruled by Avallach, king of the Otherworld. It may be from this last name that Avalon derives, through a metathesis with the root word for *apple,* as the Fortunate Isles were the source of eternal fruit, and the apple was sacred to the early Britons. This is the explanation used by Giraldus Cambrensis, who also wrote some perceptive remarks on the identify of Merlin (in his two major books on Wales, published as one volume in *The Journey Through Wales/The Description of Wales,* translated by Lewis Thorpe, Penguin, Harmondsworth, 1978).

It may well be that a fusion of this Glastonbury link to Avalon, which was part of the monastic claim that Arthur was buried in the abbey precincts, has led to the false placement of Merlin in Glastonbury in later literature, through the tale that Merlin and Taliesin carried the wounded king to the Fortunate Isles or Avalon. We should remember, though, that while an Arthurian claim was made by the monks of Glastonbury, and described as an addition to the *Antiquities* by William of Malmesbury and later writers, Merlin never formed part of it.

Thus we have an example of the type of fantastical use of legend that is the bane of the developing student of myth or tradition: for a true legend or mythic sequence or character is *always* connected to a locality, and may always be proven to connect to that locality by a number of different sources, time periods, and correspondences. We cannot find Merlin at Glastonbury in British legend . . . he was never there, but we do find him at a number of other places supported by legend, early literature, place names, and (surprisingly perhaps) by archaeology. It is in this last context, the fusion of legend, history and archaeology with the figure of Merlin, that we should consider the little-known but impressive site of Dinas Emrys in Snowdonia.

DINAS EMRYS

ITUATED IN CAERNARVONSHIRE in North Wales, Dinas Emrys is one of a number of hillforts re-occupied in the late Romano-Celtic period after the official abandonment of Britain by the Empire. It is probably from this period that the site gained its associations with certain semi-historical characters found in *The History of the Kings of Britain*, but as we shall see shortly, the figure of Merlin has ancient connections pre-dating this period.

Although the site is isolated, it is possible to reach it by road, with a short walk and hill climb, so it is by no means inaccessible. In an area rich with early Celtic or British tradition, and with the mountain ranges still echoing of Druids,

Dinas Emrys.

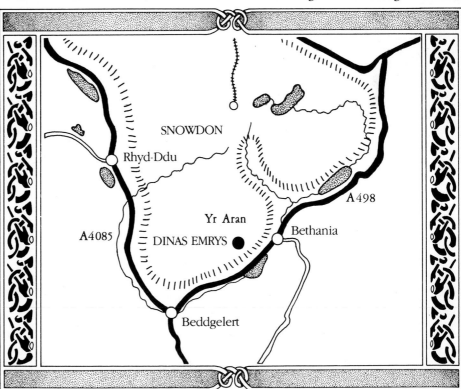

dragons and magic, Dinas Emrys surely repays the trouble of a visit. It is not a tourist site, however, and it may be necessary to obtain permission to cross private land to visit, depending upon the approach taken. This little-known yet important legendary hill-top site has a long connection with the primal legends of Britain, and with the figure of Merlin and the Two Dragons associated with Druidic or Celtic prophecy.

Dinas Emrys is basically an Iron-Age prehistoric fort or enclosure on the summit of a commanding hill. It has been excavated several times, due to its legendary associations, and provides an interesting example of archaeology corroborating legend – and indeed finding its subject-matter through legend in the first place. Building upon Dinas Emrys ranges from the Norman-Welsh period of the eleventh and twelfth centuries, backwards in time to its prehistoric fortified settlement, with several stages of use and re-occupation in between.

The name of the site simply means the hill or fort of Emrys, a name associated with both Ambrosius, the Romano-Celtic war-leader, and Merlin, who is sometimes said to be of the same family. But the associations are complex, and revolve in part around the legend of King Vortigern's Tower, and the deeper myth that this legend encapsulates. In the *History of the Kings of Britain*, we find that the traitor Vortigern has invited Saxon mercenaries into the land to bolster up his rule – he has usurped the rightful ruling house of Ambrosius Aurelianus, and of Uther Pendragon, who eventually became father of Arthur.

Dinas Emrys. The remains of settlements from prehistoric times to as late as the twelfth century are found upon this legendary hilltop associated with Merlin and King Vortigern.

But at this stage the legends of Arthur are not developed, and we are encountering much earlier strata in which the figure of Merlin plays a major role. The tale is a fusion of myth, legend and factual history, assembled by Geoffrey of Monmouth in the middle of the twelfth century from various written and oral traditional sources (trans. Giles, 1896):

At last he had recourse to magicians for their advice, and commanded them to tell him what course to take. They advised him to build a very strong tower for his own safety, since he had lost all his other fortified places. Accordingly he made a progress about the country, to find out a convenient situation, and came at last to Mount Erir, where he assembled workmen from several countries, and ordered them to build the tower. The builders, therefore, began to lay the foundation; but whatever they did one day the earth swallowed up the next, so as to leave no appearance of their work. Vortigern being informed of this again consulted with his magicians concerning the cause of it, who told him that he must find out a youth that never had a father, and kill him, and then sprinkle the stones and cement with his blood; for by those means, they said, he would have a firm foundation. Hereupon messengers were despatched away over all the provinces, to inquire out such a man. In their travels they came to a city, called afterwards Kaermerdin, where they saw some young men, playing before the gate, and went up to them; but being weary with their journey, they sat down in the ring, to see if they could meet with what they were in quest of. Towards evening, there happened on a sudden a quarrel between two of the young men, whose names were Merlin and Dabutius. In the dispute Dabutius said to Merlin: 'You fool, do you presume to quarrel

Approach to Dinas Emrys. The hill would have been an ideal watch and guard point, as is testified by re-occupation of the prehistoric hillfort in the sixth century, and the remains of a Norman tower, originally thought to be that of King Vortigern. Vortigern's building, if it is on Dinas Emrys as tradition suggests, is more likely to be the re-occupation of the hillfort.

View from Dinas Emrys. In the old Welsh legends of the *Mabinogion,* this hill is also called 'Hill of the Flaming King' — a title that may refer to the primal solar deity of the Celts, with whom both Merlin and King Bladud (at Bath) are associated.

with me? Is there any equality in our birth? I am descended of royal race, both by my father and mother's side. As for you, nobody knows what you are, for you never had a father.' At that word the messengers looked earnestly upon Merlin, and asked the by-standers who he was. They told him, it was not known who was his father; but that his mother was daughter to the king of Dimetia, and that she lived in St. Peter's church among the nuns of that city.

(Bk V, Chap. XVII)

Vortigern inquiries of Merlin's mother concerning her conception of him.
Upon this the messengers hastened to the governor of the city, and ordered him, in the king's name, to send Merlin and his mother to the king. As soon as the governor understood the occasion of their message, he readily obeyed the order, and sent them to Vortigern to complete his design. When they were introduced into the king's presence, he received the mother in a very respectful manner, on account of her noble birth; and began to inquire of her by what man she had conceived. 'My sovereign lord,' said she, 'by the life of your soul and mine, I know nobody that begot him of me. Only this I know, that as I was once with my companions in our chambers, there appeared to me a person in the shape of a most beautiful young man, who often embraced me eagerly in his arms, and kissed me; and when he had stayed a little time, he suddenly vanished out of my sight. But many times after this he would talk with me when I sat alone, without making any visible appearance. When he had a long time haunted me in this manner, he at last lay with me several times in the shape of a man, and left me with child. And I do affirm to you, my sovereign lord, that excepting that young man, I know no body that begot him of me.' The king full of admiration at this account, ordered Maugantius to be called, that he might satisfy him as to the possibility of what the woman had related. Maugantius, being introduced, and having the whole matter repeated to him, said to Vortigern: 'In the books of our philosophers, and in a great many histories, I have

found that several men have had the like original. For, as Apuleius informs us in his book concerning the Demon of Socrates, between the moon and the earth inhabit those spirits, which we will call incubuses. These are of the nature partly of men, and partly of angels, and whenever they please assume human shapes, and lie with women. Perhaps one of them appeared to this woman, and begot that young man of her.'

(Ibid. Chap. XVIII)

Merlin's speech to the king's magician, and advice about the building of the tower.
Merlin in the meantime was attentive to all that had passed, and then approached the king, and said to him, 'For what reason am I and my mother introduced into your presence?' – 'My magicians,' answered Vortigern, 'advised me to seek out a man that had no father, with whose blood my building is to be sprinkled, in order to make it stand.' – 'Order your magicians,' said Merlin, 'to come before me, and I will convict them of a lie.' The king was surprised at his words, and presently ordered the magicians to come, and sit down before Merlin, who spoke to them after this manner: 'Because you are ignorant what it is that hinders the foundation of the tower, you have recommended the shedding of my blood for cement to it, as if that would presently make it stand. But tell me now, what is there under the foundation? For something there is that will not suffer it to stand.' The magicians at this began to be afraid, and made him no answer. Then said Merlin, who was also called Ambrose, 'I entreat your majesty would command your workmen to dig into the ground, and you will find a pond which causes the foundation to sink.' This accordingly was done, and presently they found a pond deep under ground, which had made it give way. Merlin after this went again to the magicians, and said, 'Tell me ye false sycophants, what is there under the pond.' But they were silent. Then said he again to the king, 'Command the pond to be drained, and at the bottom you will see two hollow stones, and in them two dragons asleep.' The king made no scruple of believing him, since he had found true what he said of the pond, and therefore ordered it to be drained: which done, he found as Merlin had said; and now was possessed with the greatest admiration of him. Nor were the rest that were present less amazed at his wisdom, thinking it to be no less than divine inspiration.

(Ibid. Chap. XIX)

Accordingly, while Vortigern, King of the Britons was yet seated upon the bank of the pool that had been drained, forth issued the two dragons, whereof the one was white and the other red. And when the one had drawn anigh unto the other, they grappled together in baleful combat and breathed forth fire as they panted. But presently the white dragon did prevail, and drave the red dragon unto the verge of the lake. But he, grieving to be thus driven forth, fell fiercely again upon the white one, and forced him to draw back. And whilst that they were fighting on this wise, the King bade Ambrosius Merlin declare what this battle of the dragons did portend.

(trans. Evans, 1912, Chap.)

It is interesting to note that Geoffrey locates the tower upon Mons Eris or Snowdon, in the same broad geographical location as Dinas Emrys, which tradition has connected with Vortigern, Ambrosius, and Merlin, from at least as early as the ninth century. Indeed, when early archaeologists dug up the remains of the Norman-period tower upon Dinas Emrys at the turn of this century, they thought that they had uncovered the Tower of Vortigern, for the site fulfils several of the legendary attributes. Dinas Emrys has the ruins of a tower, sited, of course, upon much earlier settlements dating back for approximately a thousand years; it has a cistern and spring that seem to have

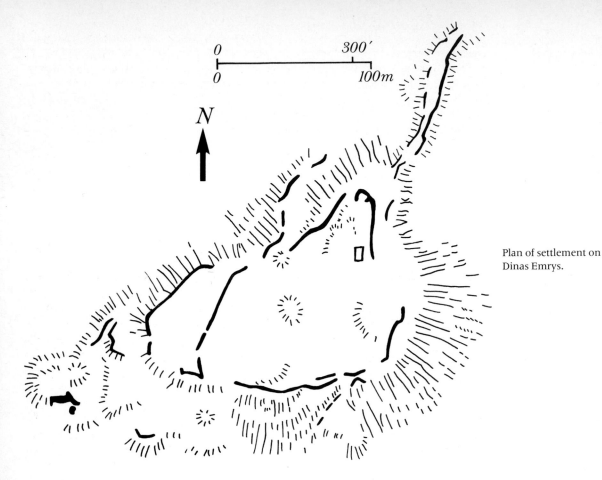

Plan of settlement on Dinas Emrys.

undermined certain structures, and it is in North Wales with the famous name of Emrys attached to it.

In the late Roman period, after the official 'withdrawal' (which was in effect a long-term organic collapse of Romanised society, in the south of Britain), a cistern was built in the settlement upon Dinas Emrys to increase the effective use of the water supply, and this was further developed around the time of the building of the historical tower in the Norman period. Thus we have a relatively modern and accessible historical structure that fulfils the requirements of a legend . . . so we would be forgiven for assuming that local people had attached the legend to the ruins sometime after the twelfth century.

But this cannot be the case, for Geoffrey of Monmouth, writing in the twelfth century, elaborated the history and legend already known and current in his day, drawing from the writings of Nennius and from oral bardic tradition. It was at this time, of course, that the Norman tower would have been built and occupied upon Dinas Emrys . . . so the legends and mythic history predate the historically defined buildings of the Norman-Welsh period; a tower contemporary to the chronicler would hardly be mistaken for that of Vortigern, least of all when it was likely to be in current use at the time of his writing – this same obvious conclusion would apply to localised Welsh legends and tales about Dinas Emrys. Thus the early antiquarians and archaeologists made the natural error of assuming that they had found Vortigern's Tower, but in fact they had found one level of a series of lengthy occupation and re-occupation, upon a site with legendary associations.

We must always bear in mind the defensive and observational potential of Dinas Emrys: situated upon a high spur of rock, with views along the neighbouring valleys, it would have been the perfect site for early settlement. The Celts re-occupied many such hill-forts after the collapse of Romanised society, and it was this increasingly nationalistic revival, both in political and sheer practical terms of survival, that led to the legends of Ambrosius and Arthur. Such legends were based, in part, upon historical characters and events, but what of Merlin? How does he fit with a physical, historical site, associated with mythical dragons and the themes of prophecy and kingship?

MERLIN

O UNDERSTAND MERLIN truly, and his relationship to specific sites, certain as Dinas Emrys, which is one of several locations in Wales and Scotland connected with him, we must dispose of the idea that he is solely an 'Arthurian' character. Even in a literary historical sense, it is clear that the Merlin texts, such as the *Prophecies* and *Life of Merlin*, and those parts of the *History* that deal with the young Merlin (quoted above) represent a separate and in many ways primal or magical tradition. Before Geoffrey of Monmouth wrote about Arthur, there was very little material upon this most famous of British kings. After Geoffrey had opened the gates, a veritable flood of material followed. Within less than a century of Geoffrey's original description of Arthur's birth and exploits, a vast range of material had appeared in various languages in Europe . . . not only were writers and poets developing upon the theme used by Geoffrey, but they were drawing upon established traditions preserved in poetry, legend and – to a lesser extent – in other texts.

The massive corpus of Arthurian material tends to absorb the earlier Merlin traditions, as if Merlin was merely an adjunct to Arthur. But Merlin derives from very detailed and enduring traditions that connect the land, prophecy, and, to a smaller degree, the cosmology and magical psychology of the bards and Druids. These traditions are essentially separate from the kingship legends that are found in the figure of Arthur, but both traditions are concerned with humanity's relationship to the land. While the kingship traditions (of which Arthur is part) deal with balance of power routed through a ruler and leader for the welfare of the people and the land, the prophetic traditions (of which Merlin, Thomas the Rhymer, and others are a part) deal with power routed through an individual for purposes of magical transformation, wisdom and enlightenment. The two traditions merge, of course, within the ancient Celtic structure in which seers, bards and Druids attended upon the king. This pattern is best known to us from Irish tradition, which often helps in our interpretation of later and often confused forms in British legendary literature.

Thus, when we have Merlin at Dinas Emrys, or at Vortigern's Tower, or even the later figure of Thomas the Rhymer (who was a historical person in the thirteenth century) at the Eildon Hills in lowland Scotland, we are dealing with a primal tradition of power. The evil Vortigern represents illusion, arrogance, folly and unlawful rule. The prophetic child, Merlin, represents purity, Otherworld vision, and acts as the opener, gatekeeper, or herald of lawful rule. In this last sense he begins with his childhood utterance before Vortigern what he will try to conclude as a mature man with the rule of Arthur — a task that ultimately failed through other agencies.

The entire matter rests upon ancient beliefs concerning power within the earth; that certain sites or locations were essentially sacred because energy or power flowed through or out of them. Nowadays this type of thought has been greatly confused and trivialised by modern theories concerning 'ley-lines' and similar fashionable escapism, but to our ancestors the matter of power within the earth was a practical concern. It appears in the most obvious sense in the location of settlements, farms and temples, utilising geographical, geological, and other natural occurrences to generate a harmonious and successful environment. But it originally went much deeper, for the land itself was regarded by the ancient Celts as a sacred entity, symbolised in Irish manuscripts and in other Celtic literature by the image of sovereignty: the Goddess of the Land. It is no coincidence that this goddess appears in the *Prophecies of Merlin*, first uttered beneath Vortigern's Tower.

The Red and White Dragons represented the Britons and Saxons warring with one another, but on a deeper level they derive from an ancient understanding of energies within the land. When these energies fused with the awareness of the young Merlin, he could see to the very end of time. For the

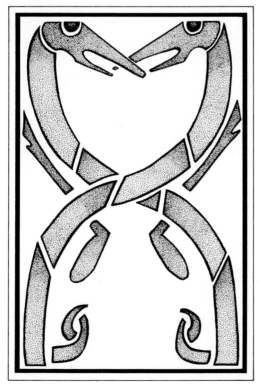

Two dragons.

38

Prophecies that he uttered were not merely concerned with the immediate problems of Britain – they reached far into the future and eventually described the ending of the solar system, an apocalyptic vision quite different from that found in orthodox medieval Christianity (see the author's *Prophetic Vision of Merlin,* Arkana, London, 1986).

We can trace this primal theme even further, for Merlin may be followed through several expressions. The first is the historical Merlin, who seems to have been one or more people (for Merlin is a title rather than a single individual name) living in the fourth to sixth centuries. (Much of this research is admirably dealt with in *The Quest for Merlin,* by Nikolai Tolstoy, Hamish Hamilton, London, 1985.) Beyond this historical level, we have the image of the Druid, prophet and seer, who was closely attuned to the natural powers of the land. This level fits in many ways with the remaining knowledge that we have of Druidism, where three orders (vates or seers, bards, and Druids or judges) were known to operate. But on a deeper level again, we may have some trace of Merlin as a divine figure, perhaps the power that inspired the vates or seers and bards, to make their utterances. Thus a human prophet, Merlin is the vessel for an ancient god-form, the Celtic or possibly pre-Celtic god of inspiration, prophecy, and the vital energies of the land.

The young child Merlin, as found in the extracts quoted above, seems almost identical with the Celtic Apollo, and the god-child Mabon. One of the most important collections of Welsh legends, the *Mabinogion,* is derived from the name and character of Mabon, though he hardly appears in the tales at all. Whenever we hear of Mabon in Celtic legend, we hear of a young and perfect spiritual child, and this is exactly the condition of Merlin when he prophesies before Vortigern. This youthful god was important to the Celts, and always appears in association with his mother, the Goddess, sometimes known as Modron. Inscriptions to Mabon or Maponus are found in Britain and Gaul, and may even be known across the Atlantic if we give credence to the work of Professor Barry Fell. (See *America B.C.* and other books by Professor Fell, in which structures and inscriptions found upon the Atlantic seaboard are described and interpreted to show that Celtic and other early settlers were active in America long before the customary 'discovery' by Columbus.)

HOW DINAS EMRYS GAINED ITS NAME

 E FIND THE theme of the Red and White Dragons occurring in the *Mabinogion* in the tale of Lludd and Llevelys, which draws to a certain extent upon themes from the *History of the Kings of Britain* and perhaps from the earlier chronicle history of Nennius, which is the first written source for the tale of Vortigern and the dragons. In Lludd and Llevelys the dragons are described as plaguing the land with a terrible screaming as they fight, and the motif of the tower is absent. Lludd is set the kingly task of capturing them, and turning their terrible energies to good advantage:

When you arrive home measure the length and breadth of the island [of Britain] and when you find the exact centre dig there a pit. Place in the pit a vat of the best mead, and a silken sheet over the vat, and stand guard upon it all yourself. You will see the dragons fighting in monstrous shapes, until they finally rise as dragons into the air. When they have wearied of the terrible combat they will sink onto the sheet in the form of two little pigs. They will drag the silken sheet to the bottom of the vat, drink the mead, and fall sound asleep. When that happens you must wrap the sheet around them and lock them in a stone chest, and then bury them in the earth in the strongest place that you know of in the island. As long as they are in that place no plague will come upon the land of Britain.

(Lludd and Llevelys, *The Mabinogion*, trans. Guest, Daniel Nutt, 1904.)

In this curious tale, again relating to kingship and the purification and guardianship of the land, we find a theme that seems to suggest how the dragons, released by Merlin in the presence of Vortigern, came to be entombed in the first place. When Lludd undertakes the kingly task of ridding the land of the fighting dragons, they become guardians:

Lludd wrapped the sheet around them and secured them within a stone chest in the strongest place that he could find in Eryri [*Snowdon, the Mons Eris described in the* History] and thereafter the place was called Dinas Emrys, though before it had been known as Dinas Ffaraon Dandde.

(Ibid.)

Here we have the dragons secured in Dinas Emrys, in a tale written out in the fifteenth century in Wales, but drawn from much earlier Celtic tradition, just as the important chronicles of Geoffrey were drawn from oral tradition and written sources in the twelfth century. Ffaraon Dandde, the tale tells us, was one of the Three Noble Youths who broke his heart with dismay, though we are not told why.

It seems unlikely that this branch of the legend would have been inspired by Norman-period ruins, any more than the theme recounted by Geoffrey could have been. Dinas Emrys is a sacred hill, a place that not only serves as a fortress centre in times of hardship, a defensive place for the warriors and their people at time of need (as in the re-occupation during the post-Roman period), but also a location for powers and legends associated with kingship, prophecy and dragon-power. The Norman-Welsh tower would have been part of the terrible pacification of Wales — built to prevent nationalists from using the ancient site for their own purposes as they had during the post-Roman period.

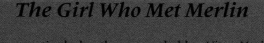

The Girl Who Met Merlin

In early sources, particularly the remarkable *Vita Merlini*, it is made unquestionably clear that Merlin derives his power from the influence of, or under the guidance of, a feminine archetype, goddess, or power. We find this restated clearly in the legend of Thomas the Rhymer (see p. 111) in which a mortal is given Otherworldly powers through his relationship with the Fairy Queen. Such motifs refer back to a pre-Christian culture, and are at the foundation of bardic inspiration; nor were they abandoned in the Christian era, for we find constant re-workings of the goddess-inspiration motif, such as courtly love, the cult of the Virgin, and in more recent times the poetic themes rediscovered from the ancient world by writers such as Robert Graves.

Yet literature has made Merlin into a besotted old fool, seduced by the alluring young Nimue and entranced. Somehow the motif has been stood on its head, and we may lay much of the blame for this on Victorian authors, particularly Alfred Lord Tennyson. But the inversion began long before the nineteenth century, and is inherent in the propagandist Christian suppression of women and, of course, of the principles of womanhood and sexual equality.

In *The Girl Who Met Merlin* I have brought the entire convoluted and multifold question into the present day, yet the encounter between a teenage girl and a mysterious man is beyond time. The story contains a few magical matters, which may require some explanation in advance for the reader unfamiliar with such things. Janet stands on one foot with one hand over one eye (apparently to shut out the glare of the setting sun); this is a posture found in Gaelic tradition, used for developing the second sight, and seeing into other worlds. In earlier Celtic culture it was adopted by bards or Druids who wished to utter satires, spells, or curses; it is echoed in the folk-tales of one-legged, one-armed, one-eyed Otherworld beings who haunt certain spots in Scotland and Ireland. In a more popular sense, it is found in Renaissance tarot, in the trump of the Hanged Man, which reflects the major Celtic magical and religious theme of the Threefold Death. The Threefold Death was experienced by Merlin in the earliest Scottish legends (see p. 39), and is found in a number of early Welsh and Irish texts relating to sacrificial kingship and magical arts. The entire subject is dealt with at length in my book, *The Merlin Tarot* (book and full-colour set of cards published by Aquarian Press, Wellingborough, 1988), in which such pictorial and emblematic traditions are restored for modern use from early texts and tales.

The root of this story is found in the theme of sacrifice, epitomised by the Threefold Death in British tradition. Merlin (if indeed it is he) says to Janet, 'There is love, and then there is love', for the most significant traditions regarding his disappearance suggest that he merged with the land voluntarily, foregoing human pleasures for a greater end. Janet, too, makes a sacrifice, right at the end of the story, but being a sensible modern girl it is only a sandwich and a bottle of Coca-Cola.

It had always seemed wrong, to Janet, that a girl was blamed. This blame permeated several otherwise delightful stories. It was particularly unfair, she thought, in the stories concerning Merlin. There he was, prophetic, wise, powerful; yet somehow she was supposed to accept that a girl not unlike herself had brought about his magical and mysterious downfall by freezing him into a hawthorn tree . . . of all unlikely things!

As a little girl she had loved to hear her uncle tell the old stories. They gave satisfaction to her mind and heart, while videos and computer games made her tense and jumpy, like all the other tense, jumpy people who punched buttons, twitched joysticks, beeped beepers, and were flashed, bleeped, peeked, poked and erased by plastic toys in their bedrooms, arcades, offices. In the old stories was a reality, a fulfilment that Janet could not easily explain, least of all to herself.

When she grew a little too old for hearing stories, she read them for herself. The reality of the tales was reconfirmed, except, she thought, for the accusation and blame upon women – or as she came to identify it, upon girls of about her own age. Growing a little older, reading a little more, she felt that the blame had crept into the original stories through the nasty minds of re-writers: surely the pure tale was free of such nonsense and agitation. Yet she still felt almost guilty, as if she was personally implicated, as if the blame in the stories was really directed at her. She did not like this.

So it was, upon a fine summer's day, that Janet set out for a long walk in the country, armed with food and drink and a vile, plastic coverall forced upon her by her mother, 'just in case'. The weather was hot, fine, golden. Bright flowers burst out of the hedgerows and a dust of pollen shook and erupted as she brushed past each caressing stem. The seething, humming insects bothered her not at all, nor did the heat and brightness. She drank up the sun and loved him, innocent (perhaps) of the urging procreation all about her.

She had planned her route that morning, before catching the bus out of the suburbs. It was a circular route that would bring her back home by a set of long lanes leading ultimately to the park beyond her garden wall. A friend had dropped out of the adventure at the very last moment, meeting Janet at the bus stop to say that she was really going to watch the new break-dance movie but had to tell her mother something to get permission. So Janet, like all the Janets in fairy tales, went out to walk alone.

By mid-afternoon she had eaten her sandwiches – all but for one, to be kept

Merlin upon Dinas Emrys.

in reserve for hunger pangs *en route.* She had drunk most of her drink, which was a bright-red, vivid, glowing gassy liquid high in lethal additives and chemical agents. It was delicious, of course. Following her map, folded carefully in her pocket with the paths showing outwards, Janet crossed fields, leapt into secret lanes as they prepared for autumn fruiting, and once came right through a farmyard full of smiling sows who wheezed and winked at her knowingly from their pen. Beyond the farm a footpath led through hazel woods, up to a long fold of land that was marked upon the map as an ancient prehistoric track. Here tiny hard bushes grew by the wayside, and dry, deep ruts emitted clouds of chalky dust from beneath her sandals.

This curious old track led further up towards the rising downs (silly that downs were always up). On the other side of the ridge she would begin to descend back towards the town where she lived, only two or three miles distant.

So it was that with the heat and the excitement of it all, she sat down to rest under a twisted old tree that marked the crest of the ridge. And there, of course, she fell asleep. It was late, late, when she awoke to the sound of a calling bird that bubbled and wept high in the evening sky. The road ruts were pooled in shadow, and the tree above her was a hawthorn tree.

As Janet sat up, worried that her parents might be worried (but not worried for herself), a man stepped out from behind the tree. She did not move suddenly, or squeal, or even blink; she sat still, looking at him in the sunset light. He seemed old to her, wrapped in a dull brown coat tied about the waist. His eyes were black as polished stones, and he stared right into her face without speaking. An absurd thought occurred to her that this might be . . . but she banished it from her mind, and stood up slowly. He flinched back for an instant, putting his hand upon the tree-trunk for support. This gave her confidence.

'Well, I must be going. My father is waiting for me.' It seemed a good line, neither friendly nor unfriendly, neither inviting nor condemnatory. It hinted, quite truthfully, that someone larger than herself was waiting, even if he was not as close as she had (without lying in any way) implied.

'Why are you here?' asked the dark-eyed man, in a voice of rust and old unopened doors. 'What do you want here?' As he spoke he seemed to age, his face collapsing inwards, his mouth drawing down. It was surely a trick of the light, from the dissolving sun far to the west.

'I'm on a short walk, just going home actually,' she said briskly, and turned away.

'Going home? There is home, and then there is home. Some go home by short ways, and some go by long ways. Some go by . . . do I not know you?'

'No,' she said (too quickly), 'I don't think so. Goodbye.'

'Wait!' He uttered this lone word with such power that she stopped, turned, perched upon one foot, and put one hand over one eye to shut out the sun's rays and see him better.

'Ah, yes,' he breathed in a voice of roots under stones. 'Ah, yes, you may see me better that way . . .' and he leaned against the tree, his brown coat seeming to melt into its twisted stem, his head within the spiky lower branches oblivious to cuts or stabs.

The obvious conclusion was simply too ridiculous; she *knew* that this person could not be . . . 'Are you whom I think you are?' she whispered softly, thinking he might not hear.

'I am whoever you think I am,' he answered in a voice ground flat with time and lonely dreams.

'Well then, I want to ask a question . . .'

'Asking questions is less hard than answering them, as the fox said to the duck.' And with this a faint shadow-smile touched his face, half hidden within the branches.

'All right, then, here it is. Are you ready? Why is it always a girl that is to blame?'

At this, he edged away from her a little, almost moving behind the tree out of her sight. A distant ewe began to bleat for her lamb.

'Who taught you,' he whispered, 'to ask that question?'

'No one. No one *taught* me. It's in all the stories, the girls, the girl is always to blame. And then you are imprisoned. Why?'

'Ah, in the stories. Well there are stories, and then there are stories.' This was a most unsatisfactory, riddling sort of answer, and she walked half-way around the tree to see him better. He backed away from her, keeping his face averted as if he dare not look directly at her. The sun stopped still in the sky and it might be evening for ever.

'You are supposed to know so much,' she persisted, growing impatient with him. 'So much and yet a girl can keep you imprisoned in a tree. It sounds so silly to me and so unfair.' At the word *unfair* he hissed like a snake, or perhaps drew in a deep breath, and moved quickly away from her again. She took another turn, three steps around the tree, until the sun was behind her, shining fully in his face. He was both young and old at once, as if all the cares and visions of centuries had been seeded into a boy's dream, ageing him instantly from within. The black, stone eyes met hers and he whispered: 'You are walking against the sun.'

It seemed so absurd, a stupid thing to say, meaningless. All she had done was to follow him around the tree, turning all the while to the left. The sun was still far away over the hills, waiting to set.

'You must answer me,' she insisted, growing angry at last, and taking three steps towards him. He backed away again, yet stretched out his hand as if longing to touch her, but hating the thought of touching. 'I must know,' she cried, 'it's too wrong, too unfair, why me?'

'Why me?' he called back, and hopped around the tree like a bird. She jumped after him, tripped over a root, and sprawled hard upon the boney clay. As she lay there breathless after her fall, a shadow loomed over her, cutting out the long evening light. He looked down upon her, his grey hair falling over his face, hiding his eyes.

'A full circle, nine steps and a leap around the tree, and all against the sun. And *you* ask *me* why the girl is always to blame?' His voice filled with tears and longing, and he murmured, 'There is love, and then there is love . . .' and as he bent over her she was suddenly afraid. But as he bent, it seemed in her confusion that he grew younger, and coming nearer still grew younger still, until a youth with golden hair touched her lightly upon the cheek. Three warm tears fell upon her neck, right into the hollow of her throat. Unable to cope with this strangeness, she clenched her eyes tight shut.

There was a rustle of branches, and then the call of a raven flying home. When she finally opened her eyes, she was alone. She stood up, dusted down her dress, and carefully unpacked her last sandwich and the bottle of bright-red drink. She set them down upon the flat, worn slab of stone beneath the hawthorn tree. Then she turned and resolutely walked home to her parents without looking back.

4·wayland's smithy and the white horse

In the county of Berkshire, upon the ancient Ridgeway road that leads eventually to the great temple of Avebury in Wiltshire, is Wayland's Smithy. This is one of the best loved and most visited of ancient sites, and during the summer months a constant procession of walkers comes to the smithy. Some have walked the Ridgeway, treading in the footsteps of travellers upon a road truly thousands of years old, one of the great trading routes of the south of England, used as recently as the nineteenth century, but dating back to

The Vale of the White Horse.

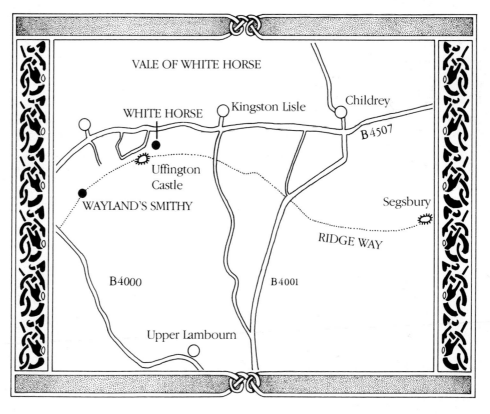

VALE OF WHITE HORSE

WHITE HORSE   Kingston Lisle   Childrey

B 4507

Uffington Castle

WAYLAND'S SMITHY

Segsbury

RIDGE WAY

B 4000   B 4001

Upper Lambourn

Wayland's Smithy. Surrounded by a circle of trees, this prehistoric chamber represents successive phases of sacro-magical burial.

prehistoric times. Others have come as sight-seers to the nearby Uffington Castle and White Horse, a vast hill-fort and ritual carving, to which we shall return shortly.

Wayland's Smithy stands within a circle of huge trees. It is a prehistoric burial site that has been extended and reworked through several phases. Today we see the remains of a huge barrow, with massive frontal stones guarding a tiny cruciform entrance chamber. The remainder of the barrow has collapsed, but archaeologists have found human remains dating back to prehistoric times. The function of Wayland's Smithy, like that of many burial chambers or mounds in Britain, was the veneration of ancestors. It was not a general burial ground, but a specific location for selected burials, perhaps connected to the widespread cult of the dead that permeated early cultures. It was certainly present at the earliest stages of the Ridgeway, and it is tempting to suggest that the guardian spirits of the road were originally buried here on this high downland site. Even today the remains of the tomb are impressive.

But how did a prehistoric burial site, present long before the Celts and the Saxons came to Britain, present long before the large complex of the White Horse and its nearby hill-fort (Uffington Castle) were built, come to be associated with Wayland Smith? The basic legend is simple: Weyland or Weland was a smith, a magical being, who would shoe travellers' horses if a silver coin was left in offering to him. Somehow the relatively later figure of Wayland, perhaps a Saxon deity of the fifth or sixth century in England, became attached to existing legends of the spirit-tomb, acting as a watcher or guardian of the way. Wayland himself is a fusion of several factors, for the smith was a sacred person to Saxons, Celts, and the pre-Celtic peoples, a motif dating back to the Bronze Age when metal was first worked in Europe. The earliest smiths were, traditionally, the swarthy people now called tinkers (from *tinklers*, or tinsmiths), who even today form a separate branch of the British and Irish

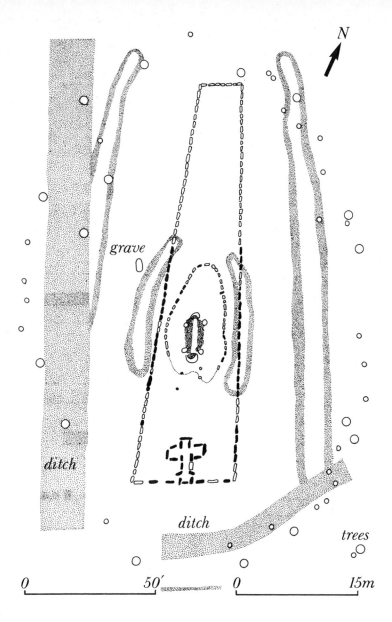

Plan of Wayland's Smithy.

grave

ditch

ditch

trees

N

0   50′   0   15m

people. This type of tradition is, in itself, a curious reflection of memories of ancient legends and races, and should not be taken too literally.

But it is the Anglo-Saxon traditions of Wayland, deriving from the Norse god-smith, Volund (called Volundr in the *Edda*), that are the strongest and best loved in England. The invading Saxons, fighting their way westwards along the ancient roads, saw the massive stones of the neolithic long barrow by the Ridgeway. Clearly these were the work of a god or giant . . . the work of Volund. We find a similar reaction to the Romano-Celtic ruins at Aquae Sulis, which were described in a Saxon poem, 'The Ruin', as the deserted works of giants. The ancient myths concerning smithcraft define a titanic figure, maimed in certain adventures or by those who keep his awesome power under control.

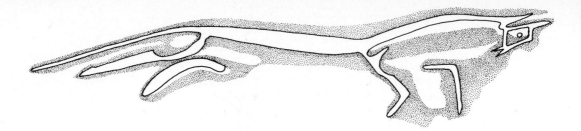

He struggles to break free of bondage and regain his true love. Eventually he flies forth on wings, having vanquished his opponents. There are elements in this legend shared with those of the Greek god, Hephaestus, and of Daedalus and Icarus. We find the motif of magical flight, linked to kingship and ancestral powers, in the tale of King Bladud, the British king who flew (see p. 68).

In the British Museum may be found a Northumbrian casket from the seventh century, depicting pagan Saxon and Christian scenes. The Franks Casket, as it called, gives the pictorial history of Volund and his smithcraft, combined with biblical and classical motifs. It is this figure, originally Norse, who came to be the Anglo-Saxon Wayland Smith.

Thus we have a curious sequence, in which a prehistoric burial barrow, built for certain revered persons, perhaps guarding an ancient roadway, becomes associated with a divine or magical smith. The maimed smith and his powers were a motif known to the Greek, Celtic, Saxon and Norse story-tellers: all such figures were originally powerful gods. Wayland partakes of the titanic nature of certain beings, personified by William Blake in his prophetic poem, 'Albion'. Wayland's bones were said to be the ridges and earthworks of the prehistoric people – he was a giant of the land, a guardian figure.

The Uffington White Horse.

The Ridgeway, one of the ancient prehistoric roads of Britain. On the horizon Wayland's Smithy may be seen. The view is taken from the outskirts of Uffington Castle, a prehistoric hillfort close to the White Horse.

THE WHITE HORSE AND DRAGON HILL

OT FAR ALONG the Ridgeway from Wayland's Smithy is the later site of Uffington Castle and the White Horse. These are large works, partly built into the naturally sculptured glacial landscape, and in the case of the castle, sited in a strong defensive or offensive position on the downs above. There is some dispute over the age of the complex, but it is likely to be an early Celtic settlement. The horse is the feature that has attracted most attention over the centuries. Like a number of similar chalk images, it was made by cutting away the topsoil to reveal the white chalk beneath, making the shape of a gigantic figure. The style of the horse is, nowadays, typical of Celtic art, but it has been through a number of changes. Until as late as the nineteenth century, great festivals or *scourings* were held in England to clean such images; nowadays the preservation is in the more staid and scientific hands of the Department of the Environment or English Heritage.

There are endless speculations concerning the origins of the horse, ranging from the simplest to the most wild and imaginative. Certainly, the Celts worshipped a horse goddess called Epona, the Mare, and the flat lands around the region are renowned even today for breeding the best racehorses in Europe. It is easy to imagine a kingdom of horse people, with their fortress upon the downland, and their goddess symbol marking out not only a site of worship, but a trading sign visible for miles around.

Slightly separated from the horse is the round hump called Dragon Hill, which has acquired legends of St George and the Dragon. This mound is said to be one of several sites in England at which St George defeated the Dragon . . . the entire theme being a reworking of the earlier legend of the archangel Michael, who was set by the first Christians to guard over sacred pagan hills, previously dedicated to the solar deity, Bel. There is some evidence that the St George story has been attached to this mound at Uffington fairly recently, but that does not detract from its dream-like association with the general flow of legend. We have ancient gods – Bel, Volund, Bladud – associated with kingship and guardianship, and with mysterious magical powers sometimes represented as dragons. The archangel Michael, and later St George, were set to control

such forces, yet we know from the prophetic or Underworld tradition that these very powers were preserved in legend as the source of seership and magic, as in the tales of Merlin, or the much later and historical figure of Thomas the Rhymer.

In time, the Saxon god, Volund or Wayland, became the giant smith, the keeper of the way. Her merged with the primal Underworld guardians, the ancient kings or ancestors that are the foundation of all religion. As late as the middle of the twelfth century, we find that Merlin (in Geoffrey of Monmouth's *Vita Merlini*) was offered rings and cups 'made by Wayland Smith in Segontium' if only he will return to the court and cease living the life of a wild man in the woods. Even at this late date, the treasure of Wayland was considered a poetic or worldly temptation.

When visiting the Smithy, we should consider a simple time-scale, in which a very early burial predates any of the later works. This first burial occurred before the development of the vast temple of Avebury, but the sacred site of the barrow was held in some reverence, for later additions were made, until the large structure that lies in ruins today was the last, formal stage of development. By this time Avebury, with its vast ranks and avenues of standing-stones, huge defensive earthworks, and astounding inner stone circles and alignments, had been completed. The Ridgeway, leading to Avebury, and the high downland, made the location close to the burial mound (later to become Wayland's Smithy) ideal for the Celtic builders of Uffington Castle, who probably carved the White Horse as their totem symbol.

The White Horse of Uffington. This gigantic chalk figure of a stylised horse may be seen best from a distance or from the air. It may have been the totem symbol of the people who lived in Uffington Castle, the large prehistoric hillfort nearby.

The Smith King,
or Three Rogues Underground

This tale is set primarily at Wayland's Smithy, but slightly in the future: the Waste Land, a fundamental feature of Arthurian legend, is found here in the twentieth or twenty-first century. But this is not an Arthurian tale, and like the legends of Wayland from the traditional past, it mixes Norse, Saxon and Celtic themes. This is not necessarily done as an intellectual or planned process — most British people are a mixture of the three branches, and it is not difficult to raise their legendary spirit. But a number of other good old British traditions are found also, such as the puppeteer (and the style of his show), and the three drunken men (a well-known British music-hall routine). Even these mask deeper motifs, for the puppeteer in his broad-brimmed black hat seems to be a secretly powerful figure, manipulating events while unnoticed; he is strangely similar to the Norse god, Odin, working in disguise among men. The heroes of the tale, if heroes they are, are typical of the 'man in the street' or the ordinary person suddenly caught up into a magical adventure. This motif is found particularly in connection with tales in which a labourer, shepherd, or drunk meets Merlin, or Arthur, or any of the other legendary sleepers. The crux of the tale is whether or not the individual understands the purpose of the meeting, or the meaning of what they see. This harks back, of course, to the initiation of Thomas the Rhymer, who had to see, understand, and after asking the right questions, remain silent for seven years. By the time this fragment of old bardic lore had devolved into popular story-telling, it became attached to the simple man who met Arthur and his knights sleeping in a cave, and foolishly woke them up at the wrong time.

The theme of the sleeping king, for they find such a king under the hill, is known not only through the legend of Arthur, but has also become attached to the quite historical emperor, Frederick I of Germany, known as Barbarossa because of his red hair and beard. He, too, is said to be sleeping beneath a mountain with a great hoard of treasure (see the author's *Barbarossa*, published by Firebird Books, Poole, 1988, for a short biography and summary of the Barbarossa legends).

One last detail must be mentioned before the story itself: the Old Woman. A standing-stone is described, into which seekers after treasure, or perhaps just wishers of wishes, must put their hands. This is not found at Wayland's Smithy.

This is a story of buried treasure and seekers after that treasure; if you have ever heard a tale about such matters before you will recognise some of the secrets, the parts that may not be flippantly spoken aloud, but that creep into your thoughts as you remember the original telling. For this is the effect of anything that deals with that which is underneath, the Underworld – it proliferates from hidden roots.

There were three drunken men sitting in a public bar one evening, listening to someone telling a story. This someone had started the evening quietly enough, but after he had absorbed sufficient beer, he produced two puppets from his pocket, and the puppets began to have an argument.

'It's there.'

'It's not there.'

'I say it is.'

'And I say it isn't.'

'What do you know, wooden head?'

'I know all and everything about it, because my head was *grown* there!'

'Your what . . ?'

'My head, grown right on the top of it!'

'What d'you mean, *grown*?'

'My head was a tree, when yours was still an old sock!'

'If your head was ever a tree it must have been an alder!'

'A what?'

'An alder . . . full of weak, yellow sap!'

'My head, I'll have you know, was once an oak tree. And it grew right on top, right on top of the . . .'

'No! Don't say it aloud, they're listening. *They* are listening!'

The three drunken men tried to look like men who were not listening, which is hard when you are sober, and impossible after a collective intake of more than three gallons. The puppeteer looked around slyly to see if anyone was watching him, a took a long swig by wrapping Sock-Head around the handle of his pint mug and lifting it to his mouth. Oak-Head leant forward to watch this action curiously, mimicking every move. When the puppeteer had closed his eyes and slumped back in his seat, the puppets began to speak in whispers to one another, gradually increasing in volume and agitation.

'It's bloody well there, I say, right there where I grew up!'

'Sphericals it is . . . if it was there, which it isn't, it wouldn't be there now, even if it was!'

'What d'you mean by all that?'

'Dug up!'

'Dug up?'

'And *spent*!'

The three drunken men looked cautiously at one another, for this was what they had been waiting to hear word of. In the south of England, after a long destructive war, poverty was the rule. Families lived on nettle soup and stale flour, shoes were made out of car tyres (there was no fuel without a military permit), and everyone dreamt endlessly of treasure. Wild tales circulated the villages, graves were opened, and houses robbed of their pitiful contents. Treasure-seeking had become a mania: large parties of men and women would drink themselves into a frenzy and go treasure-seeking before they collapsed for the night. The puppeteer was known to live out on the isolated downs, and he was reputed to dig successfully for ancient hoards of treasure, selling them to military officers in exchange for food and paper credits.

'But no one can get in,' said Oak-Head, 'without knowing the right way . . .'

'And no one knows the right way,' said Sock-Head.

'Except us!' they screeched together. Then they looked about, turning in opposite directions in a parody of caution and secrecy. They even looked under the table, twice. Both puppets avoided looking at the three drunken men. The puppeteer's broad-brimmed hat slipped over his eyes and he seemed to sleep.

The three drunken men nudged one another clumsily under the table-top, each wrapping his mouth around a pint of beer. The drink was made from dubious mixed yeasts, and coloured water laced with ethyl; it was not good for the health. The walls of the bar shook as heavy military traffic ground past through the night. The dim lights flickered and the puppets waited quietly until it was over, mimicking the other, silent, waiting figures in the room.

'So, what's the right way, eh?' whispered Sock-Head loudly.

'We know it already . . . why repeat it?' said Oak-Head.

'Just to be sure.'

'Just to be . . ?'

'Sure.'

'Well, all right. First you walk along the old ridgeway . . .'

'At night . . .'

'Then you get to the mound . . .'

'When the moon is full.'

'Yes, oh, yes!' Both puppets erupted into tittering laughter and flung their arms wide. No one paid them any attention; a few heavy drinkers lay slumped over their tables, the landlord listened half-asleep to propaganda bulletins on his headphones. Only the three drunken men seemed able to hear the puppets, with that great clarity of reception and perception that comes only with excessive alcohol. One of the men broke wind horribly, but the others hardly noticed. They were waiting desperately for the puppets to speak again.

'And then what d'you do?'

'Don't you know?'

'Course I know!'

'No you don't!'

'Oh, yes I do!'

'Oh, no you don't!'

'Do!'

'Don't!'

'Do too . . . you look for it!'

'Look for what?'

'The door! Look for the door!'

'Oars and rowlocks, you don't do that at all, you pull it out!'

'Well, that's nice I must say . . . pull what out?'

'Your token!'

'Me what?'

'Token, dummy, *token*!'

'Oh, that's what I thought you said — me token.'

'Anything will do.'

'Anything that is . . .'

'That's made of *silver*.'

The three drunken men eyed each other sideways; one of them pulled a silver chain — really just a fragment of a chain — out of his inside pocket and crushed it tight in his fist after showing it quickly to the other two. He had heard this much of the act before, but nothing more.

'Then you meet someone,' said Sock-Head, 'or you think you meet someone, don't you?'

'The Old Woman . . .'

'Who's not really old . . .'

'And not really a woman at all!' Sock-Head and Oak-Head both screamed this last line together, flinging their arms around one another and laughing madly.

'Why's she not really an old woman?' whispered Oak-Head scratching his chin with his hand.

'Because she's an old — '

'*Stone*!' they yelled together, collapsing upon the the table and drumming loudly on the wood. The three drunken men now knew exactly where the place was, for the Old Woman was a popular name for an ancient standing-stone that marked a burial mound. This site had been dug over countless times by treasure-seekers, and even the more-refined treasure-seekers of pre-war archaeology had found only burials. The puppets slowly rose upright, cast a few glances over their shoulders, and put their heads close together. Their voices carried clearly across the bar, even when they put their arms upon each other's thin shoulders in conspiracy.

'And you leave your bit of silver at her feet . . .'

'Oh yes, that's what you do.'

'And you put your hand — '

'Your what?'

'Your hand! You put your . . .'

'Hand . . .'

'Up her hole!'

'Ooh! You are naughty. Go on with you . . . put your hand up . . . ooh, I'm ashamed to be seen out with you . . .' Sock-Head pulled away from his partner

Wayland Smith.

and wrinkled up his face in disapproval.

'She's got a face there!'

'A face where?'

'There – right where her whatsit should be!'

'Her what?'

'Her chest . . . right where them bumps was . . . there's a face!'

'With an 'ole.'

'For a mouth.'

'Then what d'you do?'

'You put your hand in, like I said, and the door opens.'

'*Open sesame!*'

'Open says who?'

'Says me. I says, you put your hand in her hole and open says me . . .' Suddenly both puppets fell silent and looked around the bar. The three drunken men had left, rolling off into the wet, stinking night. The puppets nodded to one another wisely and continued their conversation.

'But it's dangerous.'

'Very, very, very, very dangerous.'

'That's why no one's ever found the treasure.'

'And that's why no one's ever come back from looking for it.'

'Not alive, at any rate.'

'Or sane – ' Sock-Head and Oak-Head burst into shrill laughter at this, pounding one another on the back and swaying back and forward in a mockery of drunkenness. Finally, the landlord came around from behind the bar and threw a bucket of ripe slops over the puppeteer. He merely pulled his broad-brimmed black hat down tight, and slept on. The puppets lay limp and wet upon the scarred table, just empty bags, one with a dirty sock and the other with a lump of wood as heads.

There are people, nowadays, who doubt the word of story-tellers. You yourself may doubt the simple fact that three rogues believed two puppets, or believed *in* two puppets (which is far more important). You may challenge the fact that they even listened to the puppets in that numb, smoke-filled, rotting bar. But drink and gullibility were only part of the recipe that set them staggering off into the curfewed night.

The three drunken men lived in the middle of a civil war. Ruin and fantasy beyond mere nightmare were their everyday surroundings. Britain was divided into small regions, governed by military or gangster factions, each forming and reforming alliance or feuds in a bewildering sequence. Most people, unable to find any relevance in the struggles to their immediate needs, were willing to grasp at illusion to lift them out of grinding truth. Children organised crusades to plunder relics of pop-stars from the pre-wars years; adults gathered in their thousands in disused football stadiums to watch battery-powered video projections of old television commercials. The perfect dream-home flickered in green and mauve and orange on the ragged screen. There was a cargo cult based on those vast silent lands across the ocean, from where no word had been heard for a long time. There was a football cult, though the game itself was banned unanimously by all-controlling powers, gangsters, or military; footballers met in small groups and replayed matches, taking it in turns to be television commentator. There was a strong revival of what might have been Christianity, except that its saviour was a long-dead immigrant who had lived in a London suburb.

So for three petty thieves to go a-seeking where no loot could possibly be found, inspired by a story told by a pair of waggling hands covered in rags, wood and socks, vocalised through a swozzle, is not so unusual. We might also remember that rampant yeasts in pseudo-beer, and old rye-ears in the bread ration, tend to create illusions.

The three drunken men waded out through deep, oily-green and rainbow mud, churned and lubricated by military traffic around the border region where they lived. The village had been on the borderlands for so long that no one worried which side they were currently on. All five factions in the Peace Programme ignored the village utterly. The women were not considered worth assaulting, there was no bean or yeast crop to speak of, and the men were too sodden and weak to recruit. So bread rations were only given out by two of the five factions, and those were both gangster-based rather than military. Such distributions were made only when the whim took the suppliers, or when a suspect batch needed testing for a few days before a major-city food-drop. Despite a national curfew, with five different sets of rules that all meant shooting without questioning, no one challenged the three drunken men as they rolled through the barbed-wire into an open, devastated field.

Like most of the surrounding land, little grew in this field. Long-lost agri-business had devoured the land before the war, sucking it dry beyond further growth or recovering; then defoliation and bombardment had taken its toll. The present, unknown landowner did nothing with the arid mush that froze in winter and turned to chalky dust in summer. Why bother? On that curfewed night, the main contents of the field were the three drunken men, and it was very large. It sloped gently upwards towards the ancient high lands, the downs where grasses still peeped forth. In deep darkness they staggered and splashed towards their destination, an ancient long barrow upon the hilltop. Far to the west a corona of multi-coloured lights played against the horizon, and a moment later flying machines growled high overhead, returning swiftly from whatever they had done to the city of Bristol.

As the rainbow lights coruscated then died away, it became impossible for the three drunken men to see where they were going. They leaned upon one another, feeling their way upwards with their feet, poking around with their boot-toes. Not one of them doubted for an instant that wealth lay ahead, though no form could be put to that imagined wealth, no plan made as to its use if it was not confiscated. The putrid dream was enough, the reality meant nothing.

More by luck — ill or good — than by pathfinding, they fell over together into a gritty hollow before tall stones. These monoliths marked the entrance to the barrow, sailing through time, oblivious to human wars. Slime-covered weeds crept from wet earth here, plants that survived and endured all pollution and poverty of soil. In places, a few tufts of hard, rasping grass with razor leaves shoved their way out from between great rocks.

The rogue with the fragment of silver chain took a candle stub from his pocket. With much fumbling and cursing he lit it from a grey, plastic cigarette-lighter that was unwilling to light and hardly made any flame. The candle, hoarded from his family ration, gave off thick black smoke and a greasy yellow flame. The three drunken men saw three tall rocks, flat, high pointed, supporting the ruined entrance.

'Where the hell is that old, old woman?' he muttered, swaying about; his muddy light revealed a hunched leering figure with her face dropped down to her chest. For an instant he gasped and almost dropped the candle. Then he realised that the night and the flickering flame had deceived him, and that it was only a stone. He threw his seven links of silver chain into the mud below, and thrust his arm into the open hole that looked like a lipless, grinning mouth. Nothing happened.

His friends shoved him aside, and with witty remarks about various holes that they had filled in their time, inserted their arms in turn. Each one felt around and drew back muttering. Each had felt damp, earth, gravel, and little lumps and whirling patterns in the rock. They then began to feel foolish, and wondered what might happen next. No one dared to be the first to make a suggestion.

One of the drunken men unzipped his fly, and urinated against the little hunched stone. For a moment he stood on tip-toe as if planning to reach the mouth, but something made him draw back. It was not such a good joke after all. He stood uncertainly for a moment, his limp organ dribbling over his trouser legs; then he zipped up and sat down suddenly in his own urine. His companions sat too, one against the dry side of the little stone, and the other against the massive upright that formed the front wall of the tiny, cruciform gate-chamber. Aware through their backs that they were in a place thousands of years old, separated from one another by only a few feet, the three drunken men became lonely people rather than a drunken crowd.

'There's nothing here,' said one.

'There never was,' said another.

'There never will be,' said the third.

They sat in silence for several minutes after this, their minds empty. Then, as people do, each one began to struggle within himself for a good suggestion to break the gloom.

'Let's get in out of this bloody rain!' said one.

'What, in there? Push off . . .' said another.

'At least it's got a sodding roof!' said the third. So over the shallow, fallen mound of earth they climbed, down behind the great facing wall of monoliths, taller than the tallest men, and into the tiny, stone chamber beyond. It had a massive single slab of stone as a roof, and two box-shaped side chambers. As they entered a toad hopped out in disgust.

The three drunken men leant upon one another in the stinking wet and listened to the rain falling faintly upon the stones. They wrapped their arms around one another's shoulders, and sang a bright, clever little song about Peace Corps officers crossing the line. No planes screamed overhead, no armoured cars ground along the road below the hill, no strange, lurid colours tinted the night. High above the thick capstone, through which they could not see, a few hazy stars crept across the polluted sky.

After a little while, each of the three drunken men seemed to re-live the moment when he had thrust his hand and arm into the rock hole. Suddenly it became a vision of terror, of a closing mouth, mangled, pulped flesh and bones. But each, in his imagination, drew out unscathed, knowing that he had endured some ancient test. Behind them an impossible door opened into the long barrow with the slightest murmur of many tons of solid rock easing through the mother earth.

They seemed to turn and to creep through into darkness. The candle burned low, but there were others in a niche beyond the door, flat brown candles with a sweet honey smell. Each lit his own from the original candle, and followed the narrrow passage down into the barrow, squeezing between great slabs of unhewn rock. Flown in this strange vision they forgot their lust for treasure, and walked the womb-way not because they might, but because they must.

The passage narrowed to a crack barely wide enough for a man to ease through. Far above their heads they heard and felt a drumming sound, one that men of an earlier age would have recognised as wild horses galloping. One by one the three drunken men wrestled through the narrow crack, painfully, nauseously, for it squeezed the false beer and rye-husk bread in their swollen bellies. They paused and looked upon a long, low chamber roofed with flat stones and dark untrimmed logs. A crude, low table ran the length of this chamber, and many men squatted cross-legged, leaning in against it without chairs. They all slept deeply, their long hair and beards growing right through the cracks in the rough planks.

But these assembled ancients were in shadow, and the three drunken men stared beyond them to where two great horns were mounted upon young, green tree-trunks, each horn holding a red burning flame that lit the far end of the chamber. There he was sitting upon a low chair of carved green stone and ivory, his head bowed in sleep. A broad, powerful man with bare muscular arms; each arm was enclosed with an elaborate golden serpent. His fingers, spread palm-flat upon the table, had heavy gold rings upon them. They were the hands of a smith – broad, flat tips, hard black calluses, lumped knuckles.

Even his hair was red and gold, shining in the torch-light like bright wire upon his arms, like copper upon his wild, lock-tangled head.

The three drunken men leant upon one another and gaped; one of them thanked God that he had only put his arm into that rock hole and not . . .

Again the hoofbeats rumbled overhead, and tiny showers of moist, rich earth fell from the stone roof-slabs. At this galloping, the massive man upon the low throne began to move, slowly, slowly raising his head. The light of the torches grew bright as he moved, seething into gouts of flame as he rose to his feet. The three drunken men turned grey with terror; one vomited as the giant smith-king's head touched the chamber roof.

In one continuous fluid motion, the king spread out his massive arms. One hand held a dull, black, T-shaped hammer, the other a bright silver horseshoe engraved with seven stars. Across his brow was a wide gold circlet, deeply etched with signs that moved, and writhed, and uttered power, as if about to burst into sound. The smith-king looked down upon the three drunken men, his eyes opening wide to reveal the roaring, green, deep oceans. He saw into their feeble hearts, and smiled the beginning of an endless smile.

A third time the ground trembled, a wild whinnying cry rang through the rock, and the giant king flung down his black hammer and silver horseshoe. He reached up to the key slab of the roof and tore it away, pulling the vault down upon the sleeping company. Bright stars shone through the ragged gap, and there was a flicker of horsetails. The three sober men knew no more.

In the morning they had hangovers, the runs, blurred vision, and swollen tongues. It was the usual beginning of a normal day. As they staggered down the hill, one of them clutching a fragment of silver chain that he had scrabbled out of a pool of urine, they heard the sound of motors. A convoy of light-armoured hovercraft skirted the edge of the huge field, spraying pink powder over the meagre leafless hedges. The three men stopped to watch this impenetrable action for a few moments, drawing breath from the long descent. One of them eventually said, 'If I see that puppet man again, I'm going to beat the shit out of him!' They all agreed.

5·aquae sulis: temple of the underworld, home of the flying man

The modern museum and leisure site of the Roman Baths, at Bath in the south-west of England, is one of the most famous and extensively visited places in Britain. It forms the heart of the modern but essentially Georgian city, a location that began at least three thousand years ago. The origins of Bath are popularly believed to be Roman, but this is untrue: the site undoubtedly had a British or Celtic presence long before the Romans occupied the region.

It would not be unreasonable to date the significance of the hot springs as an

Bath.

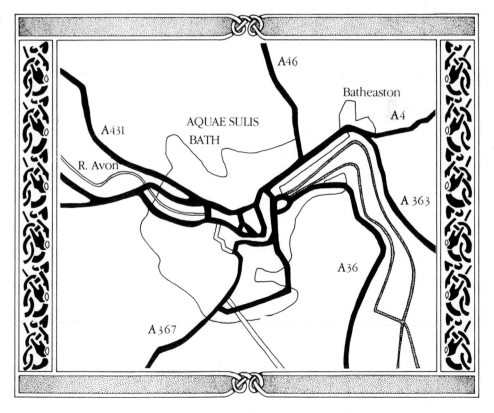

important site of settlement and worship to at least the first millennium BC, though there are very few early remains in evidence for the pre-Roman period due to the nature of the site itself, which is flooded daily by millions of litres of hot mineral water from an unknown source. We shall return to this mysterious hot-water source repeatedly in this chapter, as it is the very heart of the site and of its legends. Modern scientists now think that the water falls as rain on the Mendip Hills to the south of Bath, and gradually percolates over long periods of time through the rock strata to become heated. It emerges along a faultline that extends from the east of the city (where hot springs occasionally emerge in open country) and expands westwards opening out into the famous Avon Gorge, where the defunct Victorian riverside spa of Hotwells, part of the city of Bristol, testifies to the presence of the same hot water that emerges so dramatically at Bath.

Today, tourists are drawn in large numbers to the beautiful city of Bath, its many facilities, and most of all to the Georgian Pump Room and Roman Baths. Yet none of this remarkable historic city might exist without one vital feature: the hot springs. It was the copious flow of hot water that drew the conquering Romans, and much later caused the English gentry of the eighteenth century to establish a fashionable resort in Bath, ostensibly for taking the healthy waters but actually as a centre for gambling and other activities that were banned or frowned upon in London.

But beneath this well-known and superficially satisfying historical thumbnail history of the city of Bath, lies a deeper mystery. The Celtic or early British inhabitants seem to have held the hot springs in reverence: the Temple of Sulis Minerva, which has now been excavated by archaeologists, was by no means a solely Roman building. Even the name of the goddess, Sul or Sulis, is a Celtic language word, meaning eye, gap, opening or orifice. Thus the Latin name, Aquae Sulis, means literally 'the waters of the gap' or the water of the goddess of the gap, Sul or Sulis being an eponymous deity found only in connection with the hot springs of Bath.

The invading Romans undertook the building of a significant temple and associated bathing facilities in the first century AD, and many structures still lie undiscovered below the busy city centre. The temple style was a fusion of native British or Celtic symbolism and Roman State religion; furthermore, there were various Greek deities clearly identified by carvings and dedications. It seems likely, therefore, that a sacred spring or shrine to the local goddess, Sul or Sulis, was radically redeveloped by the Romans, both for religious and political reasons. In keeping with many of the late imperial worship sites, Aquae Sulis had an intentionally pan-cultural pattern of worship, based upon a local native goddess, State deities, and a mixture of minor local and classical powers. This may seem random to the modern observer, but to the ancients the harmonic relationship of these groups of gods, goddesses, and attendant minor powers was an organic part of daily life. Once we grasp the central concept of the goddess and her springs, the rest relate or perhaps revolve around her. Although there were formalised pantheons in both Celtic and Classical civilisation, they were never rigid or exclusive. This important concept has often confused archaeologists, researchers and scholars, especially if they come from an authoritarian or dogmatically religious background.

As a general rule, the Romans did not suppress native deities in the Empire,

The goddess, Luna, from the remains of the first-century temple.

but tended to amalgamate them within Roman worship. This tolerance was not necessarily philosophical or humanitarian, however, for at the height of imperial power and influence the Romans used religion as a political tool. Curiously, the two proscribed and oppressed religions within the Empire were those of the Hebrews and the Celtic Druids.

Thus, although Druidism as a movement had been banned by the Romans throughout Gaul and southern Britain, they took care to merge the sacred site of Sulis, which would have originally had a Druidic presence and associations, within a Roman structure and religious ambience. This must have been a curious situation, for there were still active Druids upon Anglesey in North Wales, while the Romano-Celtic temple at Bath (neatly deprived of Druids but retaining priests of the goddess, Sulis, as we know from inscription) was in its major stages of construction.

The political statement of Aquae Sulis is on a fairly large scale, and suggests that it was a major worship site for the Celts or Britons of the south-west. It also served, as we know from the inscriptions and curious nature of some of the construction, as an oracular shrine. It is this last, or perhaps we should say first, function of the site that is its most important: all other factors such as baths, theatres, state temples, and other buildings and services derived from this sacred quality of the oracular spring.

SACRED SPRINGS AND WELLS

O COME TO an understanding of the legendary and magical nature of Aquae Sulis, we need to consider the major factor of sacred springs and wells in Celtic culture, which was, to a lesser extent, paralleled in other European cultures. To the Celts, springs and wells were the entrances to the mysterious Underworld, the potent realm of power in which life and death originated; the Celts located the powers of procreation, destruction and creation beneath the ground. It is in this Underworld tradition that we may find the closest links between the Celts and the pre-Celtic inhabitants of Britain, descended from those same ancestor-worshippers and star-watchers who built the thousands of megalithic alignments that cover the British landscape.

One of the major Celtic concepts of Paradise or the Otherworld, was of a realm across the sea, upon a magical island, or under the ground, in a land that formed a counterpart or reflection of the upper world. Strictly speaking, we should say that this concept was the reverse of our modern interpretation: the upper, daily world was seen as a weak reflection of the potent Underworld, and it was sometimes considered essential by the early Britons to relate to and, if necessary, appease the beings who lived beneath the earth. Having said this, we must be cautious and not presume that they were ignorant savages making foolish sacrifices out of fear.

The clear evidence and subtle indications of sophisticated philosophy, metaphysics, psychology, and religion in the ancient cultures are considerable. The entire subject of 'sacrifice', so central to both ancient sites and their legends, has not been given sufficient unbiased attention or research, possibly due to religious prejudice or conversely to excessive reliance upon a behaviouralist viewpoint of human development.

At Aquae Sulis, as at many ancient sites, the original imaginal or spiritual powers were those of the Underworld. These Underworld beings took various forms: in the simplest sense they were the ancestors of the tribe or race; they were also regarded as powerful semi-divine beings, from whom the later legends regarding fairies (in the true sense of the word) were derived. Each gateway to the world below, each spring, lake, cave or well was peopled and guarded by Otherworld beings. Certain forms acted as gatekeepers, while others dwelt deep within the mysterious Otherworld below.

We know from both literary and archaeological evidence that the Celts paid considerable attention to such physical locations: vast treasures were deposited in lakes and springs, and Llyn Cerrig Bach in North Wales (Anglesey) has yielded many rich finds for modern archaeology. The Romans were also aware of this deeply religious practice of making substantial offerings, for they auctioned the Celtic lakes publicly, prior to actual conquests of proposed regions of invasion.

Apart from the mysterious inhabitants of the Underworld, who still feature strongly in later legend and folklore, the early Celts peopled the environment with beings who were generally related to specific features. Thus a hill or forest would have its own personality, a type of Otherworld or spiritual entity with a

Roman monument to the ancestors, from Aquae Sulis *c.* first century AD, part of the widespread cult of the dead that permeated European culture for millenniums.

particular name: springs and wells had their own deities, usually female. We know of many of these from Romano-Celtic inscriptions, of which there are a large number.

THE GODDESS SULIS

 MAJOR COMPLEX of hot-water springs like those at Aquae Sulis (unique in Britain) would have been regarded as one of the great gates to the Underworld. From these gates the ancestors or deities could issue, and the spirits of the dead were enabled to pass through such gates to other worlds. The actual springs were presided over by a local goddess, who, as we know from inscriptions, dedications and prayers, was called Sul or Sulis in the first century, a name that means gap or orifice in various Celtic dialects.

Localised powers, such as the goddess of a spring, or the god of a hill, were often aspects or lesser reflections of greater powers, those gods and goddesses (nowadays known generally as archetypes) of primal energies, concepts, and natural forces. Thus Sul or Sulis, when considered in the light of her location, her inscriptions, and the general evidence of the physical temple site, is a localised version of one of the mother goddesses, known as *Matres* in the Roman Empire.

More significantly, Sulis was a localised manifestation of the Great Mother Goddess known throughout the ancient world. But we have to be careful not to generalise – although all such goddesses relate in one way or another to the overall concept of the Great Mother, they are not by any means all identical to one another. Sulis, as we know from the inscriptions found within the temple area, was concerned with blessing, cursing, prophecy or augury, therapy, and possibly childbirth. Other dedications on the site suggest that she was also concerned with the spirits of the dead, or at least that ancestral spirits were revered at Aquae Sulis in the temple or in the surrounding baths and lesser shrines.

Sulis does not, on the strength of the known evidence, seem to have been a harvest goddess, or a spring goddess. Nor was she a cultural goddess, patroness of arts and sciences: this aspect is focused through the Roman Minerva, who was amalgamated with the original goddess Sul or Sulis when the Romano-Celtic temple was built. One of the most famous finds at Bath is a finely made bronze head of the classical Minerva.

The head of Minerva, who was amalgamated at Aquae Sulis with the Celtic goddess, Sul or Sulis. While Sul seems to have been a goddess of prophecy, blessing, and cursing, Minerva was the Roman patroness of order, arts, and sciences, and cultural development.

It is just possible that Minerva replaced a Celtic goddess, known to us today as Briggidda, and still found in Irish Celtic-Christian tradition as St Bride or Brigit. This important goddess had many Minerva-like attributes. She was the *sister* aspect of the Great Goddess who appears in triple form: maiden or sister, mother or lover, and crone or destroyer. When we consider these three aspects of the goddess, they are nothing more nor less than three major phases of all existence – Sul or Sulis seems to relate to the third and dark goddess of this ancient trinity.

The visitor today can see many remains from the Romano-Celtic period, and these are examined in detail in various books published on the archaeology of the site. But the unique atmosphere of Aquae Sulis is difficult to rationalize, for it is an experience rather than a description.

The Victorians, who first excavated and developed the remains, built a chamber giving access to the Roman period containing the wall and outflow arch of the sacred spring. This chamber, known locally as the Hot Box, originally had an impressive pair of bronze doors, but nowadays powerful extractor fans draw away the steam, and the arch is open to view as the visitor approaches the chamber. It is here that we may approach the heart of the place, a force the ancients knew as the goddess, Sulis. Close to the water pouring from the archway, standing in the steam, feeling the presence of the hot spring, that is how Aquae Sulis may best be understood. The Romans built a special access for this very reason, for to both Roman and Briton alike, this would have been an especially sacred area.

There is some evidence that a platform was constructed over the spring, and it may have been upon this structure that a priestess sat, like the Pythoness at Delphi, to utter prophecies.

KING BLADUD

 NCIENT GODDESSES ARE often associated with specific heroes, and these heroes are, in turn, manifestations of a god. Mother goddesses have divine sons . . . this relationship is perhaps more common than the simple concept of gods and goddesses acting as consorts. The truth of this matter of divine relationships is actually cyclical rather than linear, and was originally related both to the turning of the seasons and to longer time-cycles defined by stellar motion and by observed stellar patterns.

At Aquae Sulis there is little evidence of a consort god given equal status to the goddess Sulis: she is, after all, amalgamated with Minerva who was a virgin. Other attributes of the virgin warrior-goddess are found, such as the owl (originally the bird of Athena and the Underworld crone, Hecate, in Greek myth) and inscriptions to Diana, the virgin huntress.

There is, however, a curious legend referring to Kind Bladud. From the twelfth century or earlier, chroniclers refer to King Bladud in connection with Bath, and they are certainly drawing upon an older, oral substratum of British legend, as is evident from the tale they tell. Briefly, Bladud is described as ruler of the land, as a necromancer or magician, and as guardian of the hot springs. He is credited with spreading esoteric arts throughout Britain, and as founder of the original universities of the land. Finally, in his pursuit of arcane arts and sciences, he fashioned wings for himself and flew through the air, as had the Greek Icarus. Bladud, however, crash-landed upon the Temple of Apollo in Trinovantum (New Troy, which was a synonym for London), where he was dashed to pieces.

We might be tempted to assume that writers such as Geoffrey of Monmouth were merely fabricating upon classical tradition, but the myth of the Flying

Outflow from the hot spring. This small but impressive arch was built by the Romano-Celtic engineers to emphasise the mystery and sanctity of the spring beyond the enclosing wall. There is no structural need for its design, and it may have served a ritual purpose, as an approach to the primal goddess of the springs.

Man reflects certain Celtic Druidic characteristics, and is likely to be a reworking of bardic tradition, preserved in the medieval period by tales or verses from Wales or perhaps Brittany. In such traditions ancient poems concerning the magical and literal genealogies of kings were preserved: certain kings were mythical, others historical, while some were a curious fusion of both myth and history. This fusion is reflected in *The History of the Kings of Britain*, Geoffrey's major and highly influential work written around 1135.

Bladud is a mythical king – he is a type of Druidic, tutelary deity of Britain, and particularly associated with the hot springs of Bath. The arts of prophecy, necromancy (magical communion with the dead or with ancestors), and magical flight are frequently found relating to Druids in early texts. Indeed, the Celtic religion was firmly based upon an ancestral and Underworld or Otherworld mythology and cosmology. Kings were the sacred vessels or manifestations of ancestral and Otherworld powers, made flesh within one person for the benefit of the people and the land. Bladud is an archetypical god-king embodying not only Druidic practice or belief, but some of the attributes of a solar deity. Who else but the sun flies through the air and lands at the Temple of Apollo? In the *Vita Merlini*, set into Latin verse in around 1150, we find that Bladud has a consort called Aleron, which is a typical pun by Geoffrey of Monmouth upon the Norman-French word for wings, *aileron*. Furthermore, a priestess called Morgen appears in the same text, and she too has the power of flight, of shape changing, and she acts as patroness of all arts and sciences, practising therapy. If she begins to sound similar to the ancient goddess, Sulis Minerva, this is no coincidence.

But we must remember that medieval chronicles written out by Geoffrey and others, and reworkings of classical mythology and bardic lore such as the *Life* and *Prophecies of Merlin*, were circulated for centuries *after* the temple at Aquae Sulis had been buried under the accumulated silt and mud of the hot springs. The Roman-period inscriptions, statuary, and dedications to Minerva, Sulis, Diana and Apollo were quite unknown to the medieval writers, for they had been buried a thousand years before. Yet legend and tradition seem to be partly vindicated by the hard factual findings of archaeology.

THE LEGEND OF THE PIGS

 HIS CURIOUS DETECTIVE story is not yet finished, for in the seventeenth century, before the Roman-period remains had been excavated, a local physician, Robert Pierce, collected the following story concerning King Bladud for his book *The History and Memoirs of the Bath*:

Bladud, eldest son of *Lud-Hudibras*, (then King of *Britain* and eighth from *Brute*) having spent eleven years at *Athens* in the Study of the Liberal Arts and Sciences (that City being in those Days the chief Academy, not only of *Greece*, but of this part of the World also) came home a *Leper*, whither from that hotter Climate he had conversed in, or from ill Diet, or Infection, it doth not appear, those unletter'd times giving down little or no Account of things (though of greater moment) then transacted; but a *Leper* he was, and for that reason shut up, that he might not infect others. He, impatient of this Confinement, chose rather a mean Liberty than a Royal Restraint, and contrived his Escape in Disguise, and went very remote from his Father's Court, and into an untravell'd part of the Country, and offers his Service in any common Imployment; thinking it (probably) likelier to be undiscover'd under such mean Circumstances than greater. He was entertain'd in Service at Swainswicke (a small Village, two Miles from this City) his Business (amongst other things) was to take Care of the Pigs, which he was to drive from place to place, for their Advantage in Feeding upon Beachmasts, Acorns,

70

and Haws &c. the Hills hereabouts then abounding with such Trees, tho' now few, of the two first, remain. Yet there is a Hill, close upon the *South* Part of this City, that still retains the name of *Beachen Cliff*, tho' there is scarcely a Beach-Tree left upon it.

He thus driving his Swine from place to place, observ'd some of the Herd, in very cold Weather, to go down from the Side of the Hill into an *Alder-moore*, and thence return, cover'd with black Mud. Being a Thinking Person, he was very solicitous to find out the reason why the Pigs that wallow in the Mire in the Summer, to cool themselves, should do the same in Winter; he observ'd them farther, and following them down, he at length perceiv'd a Steam and Smoak to arise from the place where the Swine wallow'd. He makes a way to it, and found it to be warm; and this satisfied him that for the Benefit of this Heat the Pigs resorted thither.

He being a *Virtuoso*, made farther Observation; that whereas those filthy Creatures, by their foul Feeding, and nasty Lying, are subject to Scabs, and foul Scurfs, and Eruptions on their Skin, some of his Herd that were so, after a while, became whole and smooth, by their often wallowing in this Mud.

Upon this he considers with himself, why he should not receive the same Benefit by the same Means; he trys it, and succeeded in it; and when he found himself cured of his *Leprosie*, declares who he was; his Master was not apt to believe him, at first, but at length did, and went with him to Court, where he (after a while) was owned to be the King's Son, and after his Father's Death succeeded him in the Government, and built this City, and made these *Baths*.

(Printed for Henry Hammond, 1697)

This theme is not found in the medieval chronicles, yet it reflects certain typically Celtic mythical motifs. Bladud is suffering from leprosy, a wasting disease; he is associated with the rights of kingship and the theme of exile and restoration; he is led to his cure by pigs. These three elements are typically Celtic: the wounded or wasting king is found repeatedly in Grail legends and in earlier Irish legend; the theme of the once and future king is inseparably associated with Arthur in the popular imagination, but derives from sacred kingship concepts in the ancient world. Finally, the pig is a major totem beast of the Underworld goddess, who in her Welsh manifestation as Ceriddwen takes the shape of a black sow. These elements, therefore, may come from a localised tradition, heard by Pierce in the Bath area. A folk-tale, concerning Bladud, who was already established in general legend from the twelfth century onwards through the widespread use of chronicle histories, may contain further legendary motifs from ancient oral tradition. This tale, with so many hallmarks of Celtic myth, is not found in any written version or chronicle, but appears fully fledged as reported by Pierce in the eighteenth century. If we grant that the tale is not a forgery, and there is no evidence that Pierce was a Celtic scholar or antiquarian forger, it must be taken as a typical folk-tale or legend, such as is found in many areas of the Celtic world, where localised stories preserve variants of ancient myth for centuries within a fairly limited geographical region.

The village names of Swainswick and Bailbrook in the Bath area are sometimes proposed as further evidence of local legend (i.e. 'Swine's-wick', and 'Bal's' or 'Bladud's brook',) but this type of etymology is suspect. Bailbrook, however, is on the lower slopes of Solsbury Hill (perhaps derived from Sul or Sulis Barrow) where a hill-fort and prehistoric remains testify to the early settlement of the area.

THE FLAMING HEAD

HEN THE ROMANO-CELTIC temple was excavated in the nineteenth century, the most striking item was the huge relief carving of a mysterious male deity (originally described quite inaccurately as a male gorgon). This typically Celtic face, in a style sometimes associated with Celtic metal working of the period, echoes, or rather predates, the elements described in the chronicles concerning King Bladud. The following summarises these directly from the carving itself:

1. He is a Celtic male character, with typical long hair and moustaches as described by classical historians.
2. He is also a solar disc, for his hair is stylised into flames, and he is surrounded by the classical victor's wreath that Roman mercenaries or regular soldiers would have associated with the theme of Sul Invicta. The supporting figures that uphold the disc are rather crude renderings of classical Victories, which strengthens this implication.
3. He has the power of flight, for a clearly defined set of wings sprouts from either side of his neck.
4. He has staring eyes and very prominent ears, which imply attributes of supernatural sight and hearing. Such attributes – all-seeing, all-hearing – are traditional to solar deities.
5. There appears to be a pair of serpents coiled around his chin. These may be a neck torc (symbol of both royalty and divinity) and they may further be echoes of the Apollonian myth of the oracular serpent of Delphi, Bath being in many ways the western or British oracular site. The oracular implications are further supported by an altar to Apollo from the site, and by a statue base dedicated by a *haruspex* – a high-ranking state augurer from the city of Rome itself. It is unlikely, to say the least, that a *haruspex* would visit Aquae Sulis casually or be posted there, and his dedication implies that the Goddess answered his request.

The Flaming Head. Carved in the first century AD, this guardian head was the central figure of the Romano-Celtic temple pediment. Its typical Celtic style suggests that it represents a local god, perhaps the same figure that appears in later legends from the medieval period onwards as King Bladud, the traditional founder of the site. Bladud is associated with many Druidic attributes, such as magical flight, and necromancy. These abilities are rationalisations of what we now know to be Celtic religious beliefs and practices.

This relief carving, of a Celtic solar deity, seems remarkably similar to the attributes of King Bladud, preserved by the medieval chroniclers from tradition, who was firmly linked to Bath in the chronicle histories, and in the *Vita Merlini* that is the major repository of Celtic Druidic lore, mythology, and cosmology.

We might add one last, earlier item of archaeological evidence, which is a Belgic coin from the first century BC. It shows a man with flowing hair, a neck torc, and a pair of wings sprouting from his neck. The inscription is VLATOS ATEFLA, and the coin was struck by a Belgic war-leader or king, one of the Celtic mercenary kings used extensively by the Romans.

The word *Vlatos* is a literal rendering of the Celtic pronunciation of the word Bladud, which (allowing for variant spellings such as Blaidydd, Baldudus, and Beldud) would have been said as *Vla-duth*. The fundamental elements of this curious name may be *bel*, or *bla*, meaning bright or light, and *dud* meaning dark. Thus the name, Bladud, is actually a descriptive title, just as all Celtic god and goddess names were derived. His name is Light-Dark.

THE FLYING MAN AND THE RIVER AVON

 LTHOUGH BLADUD IS traditionally associated with Bath, there are indications that he was a god associated not only with solar powers and the hot springs, but also with the River Avon, which flows around the site of the springs and receives their copious hot water. Upriver from Bath, 30 Km (20 miles) or so by road, but many more along the meandering Avon, is the abbey town of Malmesbury, founded by the Saxons upon the site of a Celtic hermitage. The town and abbey are perched upon a steep prominence, which briefly divides the Avon into two. The Abbey of Malmesbury was one of the great centres of learning in medieval times, and even today the ruins are impressive.

Curiously, one of the earliest names for Malmesbury (in the British tongue) was Caer Bladon, a name also used for Bath, and commonly assumed to be connected to Bladud. But in Malmesbury the name is usually associated with the river. The chronicler, William of Malmesbury, related, in the twelfth century, the local story of one Guilmerius (Oliver), a monk of the abbey. He, it seems, made wings for himself and launched forth boldly from the high abbey-church tower. Regrettably he broke his legs upon landing, but used to swear that if he had only made a tail as well, he might have improved upon his flight and survived intact.

William relates this tale as a joke, a local folk-story, but he would not have been unaware of the tale of the Flying Man, Bladud, in other chronicles. If he was recounting a local tradition and dressing it in monastic garb for his readers, it is possible that it reflects the old theme of the Flying Man, an ancient British god, and his relationship to the River Avon.

Malmesbury Abbey. The remains of this great medieval abbey stand upon a hilltop site, which was once a Celtic hermitage and later developed into an important Saxon burgh. Here, as at Bath, there are legends of a Flying Man, possibly associated with the River Avon that connects the two ancient settlements. Both sides were called Caer Bladon in early records, meaning the castle of Bladon or Bladud.

The Goddess Speaks

King Bladud tells his own story next. The setting is a low drinking den or guest house some time or other before the first century BC. The Romans have not yet reached Britain, and the hallowed customs of Druidism and kingship still persist unchecked. So when the crippled ex-king (did he really fly and fall out of the sky?) tells his youthful audience of prophecies in order to win more wine, many of the enigmatic utterances refer to the forthcoming Roman period. But others reach forward in time to the Saxon period, the Georgian, and even into the present day. I shall leave it to the reader to decipher for his- or herself which are which, but must say that, like all worthwhile prophecies, they are not necessarily in proper chronological order.

You may well sneer, young man, but I was not always like this. In my day a youth would not mock a cripple, but help him. Yes, I can see you turn up your nose, but this is good, honest dirt from tending pigs; as in the beginning, so it is at the end. After such injuries I could hardly be king any more, now could I? What do you say? Oh yes, I most certainly was king, and most of the great works that you see throughout the land were mine . . . well, some of them anyway. Be a good boy and pass me that flask again; blessings upon you.

You turn up your nose and sniff, but have you been to the Goddess Springs? Ha! I can see by the look of fear on your green face that you have. And did she answer you? No? Well she answered me – and then did a little more. I built that temple you know, ordered the withy-and-stone enclosure for the hot waters, planted the sacred grove, and set up the eternal fire. It burns magic stones, black as black, bright as bright, grey as ash. That's the secret. Was it burning when you were there, or were you too stupefied by the Druids' potion to see? Yes, that's got your attention . . . you thought I was a smelly old pigherd with twisted arms and crooked legs . . . thought that because I dribble out of the side of my face I was simple. Oh, I know what you think, my lad, you think I'm a sot, blessed of that Greek god of wine, whatever his name is. But I can tell you things that will make your hair stand on end and your moustache stiffen without clay. I have been in the temple of eternal fire, I have been in the waters of the gap, I have been a bird in the air!

Sorry, I didn't mean to shout at you. There, we can mop it up in an instant. Yes, you may shrink back in your innate youthful superiority and cleanliness, but one time you would have shrunk from the blazing light of a king! Yes, I was a king once. My life is a circle, you see: exile, pigherd, king, pigherd, exile. A perfect circle. Ah, I can see from your trembling lip that you know the story now. Ah, yes, well might you make the holy signs between us . . . but they won't do you any good, or rather they won't be necessary, for my power vanished long ago. It was a long, long fall out of the summer sky, and after that, nothing. Well, nothing but pain for a long time, then exile.

So what do you want to ask me? They all ask something when they realise who I am, or rather who I was. Of course, there is a new king now, but he is forbidden to answer most questions. No such ban on me. Who believes a silly old drunken pigherd? Yes, you will ask some fragment of dross from me, such as will your true love be faithful, or how can you tell true gold from false . . . they all ask nonsense like that from the old king, as if he was a travelling showman pretending to be a seer. What's that? What did who say to me? Aah! What did *she* say to me in the swamp on my first day there? Hmm, yes, well that is certainly a good question. You have hidden depths, young man, perhaps you should enter one of the schools that I founded so long ago, there are tests, of course, but I could help you there with a few little hints. What? Of course I'm not avoiding the question, I'm merely wondering if you will really understand the answer. Very well, as you have another flask of this nasty resinous Greek stuff, I will try to answer you. Sit back and listen, and I will tell you how I became king – the true story, that is, and not the legend, though they are close enough for most purposes.

I had been exiled due to a skin disease, little white marks on one hand and a constant itching. As the chosen twin and successor to the king, I had to be without blemish, so you can imagine how badly everyone, including myself, took the appearance of this skin problem. They sent me to Greece, of course, where they are less fussy about such things, being merely bucolic cousins who inherited the Sun God from us. And there I stayed for several years, learning some of their curious new ways of thinking, basking in the sun, and sporting with girls who didn't mind a little scab on one hand in the slightest. I was, after all, of the royal blood of Apollo (as they call him), and they stood a good chance of bearing children by me. Some of them certainly did just that, but eventually I became bored with it all, and slipped away in a cargo ship bound back for the Island of the Mighty, back to Britain.

Now my return had to be secret, for if I was found it would have meant instant death, followed by heroic laments by the bards, praises for my lineage, and a final removal of my verses from all genealogies. I made my way inland from the marsh port near the barrow of Gwynn ap Nudd, which they call the Summer Land in that region (as if there were no other Summer Lands all around Britain), and eventually came to the area of the hot springs. There was already a shrine there, of course, dedicated to a dark and terrible goddess, so fierce that they called her the Kindly Sow and blessed her name daily between every breath and before every action. It was, as you might imagine, rather unlucky to be a swineherd in that region, but as I was a beggar and had no true lineage to boast of (for I dared not tell the truth), I was allowed to tend the pigs in return for my keep, and the use of a little mud hut not far from the edge of the swamp.

Now it is often said that I watched the pigs bathing in the mud, and that this gave me the idea of curing my skin disease by the same method. This is nonsense, for cautious people came to dip themselves in the warm mud almost daily, mainly to ease the joints that swelled each winter or stiffened with endless labour in the fields. So although I was cured, it was not really an inspiration, and in any case when I went into the swamp it was not cure but curiosity that led me on . . . that and a black pig.

I had been sleeping, you see, beneath a hawthorn that grew upon some dry, rocky ground. Not a good start to the afternoon, but swineherds are not afflicted by tree magic – and I had forgotten, in my idleness, that I was of the blood. The hawthorn leant over me, and I was awakened by the sound of angry squealing from the herd. To my amazement they were milling around a perfectly black pig that had appeared out of the wild forest beyond the open ground, grunting and squalling with excitement. As I stood to brandish my staff, this pig looked over her shoulder at me, and then scurried off into the swamp. The entire herd trilled with joy and splashed in after her. I knew for sure that if I did not get them back it would be a good beating for me, and possibly the end of my position as swineherd. Below pigman there is no other rank, so naturally I ran straight in after them.

They headed into the steam and mud, ploughing straight for the three tall rocks and the bare, leafless tree that housed the good, kindly, friendly, noble, generous and smiling goddess. I almost wet myself with terror when I saw where they were headed, and fell against the tallest stone, sobbing with exhaustion, just as they scampered off into the thick foliage beyond. There was a strange radiating carving upon the stone, like a face surrounded by flames, but I hardly noticed it as I fell, and fetched my head a strong blow upon the rocks beneath. For a while I was drowning in darkness, but when I came back to the light I could feel my hand itching terribly and the cold rocks beneath me hurt my side.

It was only when I stood up that I realised that the rocks should have been warm and damp with the hot mud of the springs, and that I was standing upon a perfectly flat, jointed stone floor, the like of which I had never seen before. The workmanship of that floor was superb, better even that the crafts of Greece or Persia . . . and just a few arm's lengths away was the black pig, waiting for me. She scuttled off, squealing loudly, and I gave chase again without thought. My staff had gone, and so had my ragged clothes, but I had been so used to wandering around naked in Greece that I hardly noticed.

As I ran clouds of steam began to build up around me, until I could hardly see where I was: there was a great rushing, roaring sound of waters, and suddenly the pig darted through a high cavern entrance. Or at least I thought it

The Temple of Sulis.

was a cavern, till I realised that it was a work made by men – or perhaps by the gods themselves. High, perfectly shaped columns of smooth rock rose before me, leading away like the trunks of trees. These columns stood flanking a floor inlaid with the most brilliant and dazzling colours and patterns that I had ever seen. At the far end of the chamber, for chamber it surely was, stood a tall bronze tripod, filled with dark lumps of rock that burned with a rich yellow flame. The smoke from these rocks mingled with the steam that floated in clouds around the chamber roof. I fell over in astonishment, and lay there scratching my arm.

I thought I was in the Halls of the Dead, the Blessed Isles, or the Chambers of Dis. As I lay there, there was a rustling sound, and I sat up thinking to see the pig. But no, a dark figure emerged from between the smooth rock columns, a sinuous female figure with a hood pulled far over her face. I began to sweat with fear, and watched in utmost terror as she revealed a glowing white globe from within her long sleeves. She put one finger to her unseen lips, or rather to the front of her hood, in the ancient gesture for silence, and held up the white globe. It filled my vision like a sky full of snow or moonlight, and a cool musical voice spoke deep within my head:

'This is the temple that you will build, though you will not build it. Invaders will build it but they shall be at home. The mother will bless it and it will be accursed. You will be king like the sun and fall into the shadow. You will found great schools of ignorance. The dead will speak to you and live forever. You will be the highest of the low and above the highest. On the temple of the sun you will be broken until you are made whole. You will burn stones here perpetually and they shall never burn away to ash. Giants will have made it and monsters guarded it when the strangers come in ships and make your people into strangers. The waters will bring blessing and cursing. The powers of a great empire shall here be cast down into the depth before they are arisen. And in time the healing waters shall bring death but only to fools and liars. Get up now and stop scratching, the king your uncle is dying and awaits your presence . . .'

And with these last words I found myself at the foot of the sun-stone in the centre of the swamp; a large crow sat over my head on the withered tree, and cawed loudly. I knew then that I had to return to the dwelling of the king and declare that I was ready to take his place. My skin disease had vanished, and to this day it has never come back, not that it would make any difference now . . .

So there's your tale, young man, and make of it what you will. Some of those prophecies I've seen come true, made come true myself, but others are still dark to me. What was that great chamber, why did she say that I would built it? Eh, pass the wine again will you – slowly, slowly, it takes my hand a while to uncurl . . .

6·the island
of glass

FORTRESS OF THE HOLY GRAIL

LASTONBURY IS A beacon. One sees it from afar wherever one goes in the area of the Somerset Levels. The tower of St Michael, all that remains of a fifteenth-century chapel that fell down in an earthquake in the seventeenth century, rises above the vast bulk of the Tor – a landmark for voyagers from every point of the compass.

Here, according to local tradition, Joseph of Arimathea, a rich Jew with connections in the tin trade, often came, on one occasion perhaps bringing with him the boy Jesus, his 'nephew'. Later, after the fateful events in Palestine and after many miraculous adventures on the way, Joseph returned, bringing with him perhaps the most sacred and most sought-after relic in Christendom – the Holy Grail, a cup believed by some to have been used to celebrate the first Eucharist at the Last Supper, and subsequently to catch some of the Sacred Blood that flowed from the wounds of the young Messiah as Joseph watched the body being prepared for interment in his own tomb.

Such are the few scarce details that form the kernel of one of the great stories of all time, and one of the great mysteries. The existence of the Grail, never proved nor disproven, unacknowledged by the Church, has remained a tantalising puzzle, leading men and women from all walks of life to search for the truth it embodies.

For the Grail is much more than an object – it is the embodiment of an idea, a vision, that is so completely a part of the human psyche; its quest is of supreme importance to each and every one concerned with the search for their own identity, and ultimately perhaps with the future of human kind itself.

It is this dream that brings pilgrims to Glastonbury in their thousands, the numbers growing year after year. Not that very many of them expect to find the Grail there, they are simply drawn to the place that has been called 'this holiest earth', and that seems to call out to the seekers after the infinite, as though it were somehow a gateway to that elusive state of being. Certainly

79

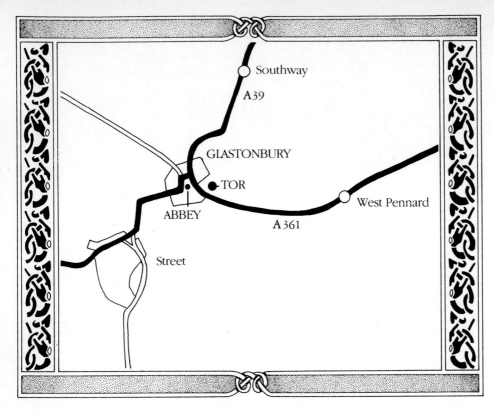

Glastonbury.

there is some evidence to suggest that one of the earliest Christian communities (if not *the* earliest) was established in or near Glastonbury. Tradition speaks of a 'church of wattles' built by Joseph of Arimathea and consecrated by angelic hands. Later foundations, including the elaborate medieval splendour of the abbey, were built upon these foundations.

Elsewhere, in the landscape around the Tor, investigators as varied as the Elizabethan magus, John Dee and, in the twentieth century, Katherine Maltwood, have claimed to have found the remains of another mystery – a vast terrestrial zodiac shaped from the land itself and following the lines of ancient trackways, medieval field-boundaries, and even modern roads. These shapes, which seems to be very much in the eye of the beholders, may perhaps stand for another kind of Round-Table fellowship, originally twelve in numbers, who in some way inscribed their presence on the countryside where once they lived and hunted and fought. Whatever the reality, the Glastonbury Zodiac is very much a part of the legendary landscape of Glastonbury – and of the mystery that draws people in.

More recently, the terraced sides of the Tor itself have been recognised as forming the outline of an ancient processional maze, and this has in turn revived memories of an ancient Druidic or priestessly foundation at the foot of the hill with its sacred temenos at the top. It is not hard to imagine a torch-lit procession winding around the great bulk of the hill on sacred occasions, though what rites were carried out on the summit cannot so readily be guessed. Certainly, if there ever was a standing-stone or circle on the Tor, no

Tower of St Michael's Church. Dominating the landscape for miles around Glastonbury, the remainder of the church fell down in an earthquake in the seventeenth century. Its dedication to St Michael marks it as a site of especial importance.

trace of either now remains, though the presence of the tower of St Michael suggests that an earlier, pagan site may have lain beneath, for it is a well-attested fact that wherever churches or chapels dedicated to this particular angel are to be found, there is usually some form of more ancient resonance close by.

The story of Joseph and the Grail has left a more profound signature. Wearyall Hill, to the south-west of the Tor, still bears the scion of an ancient thorn tree, believed to have sprung from Joseph's staff, which he planted on the hillside and which at once burst into flower in the dead of winter. The original tree was cut down by a follower of Cromwell, as a symbol of 'papist idolatry', but below in the ruined abbey a larger tree still supplies the table of the reigning monarch with a cutting on every Christmas Day.

Wearyall Hill. Here, tradition has it, Joseph of Arimathea climbed for a view of the surrounding land, and liking what he saw, planted his staff in the earth, which then took root and flowered. The scion of the thorn may still be seen to this day.

Nearby lies Chalice Well, set amid beautifully tended gardens in a sheltered trough between the Tor and Chalice Hill. There an ancient spring rises that had long been attributed with healing properties. It is of the kind known as chalybeate, and the iron in it stains the rocks all round a rusty red – giving rise to all kinds of associations with the Grail and Holy Blood. The well-head is lined with massive stones of unknown origin, and a fine nineteenth-century cover with the symbol of the *vesica piscis* adorns its rim. A sense of peace and tranquillity is to be found here, where for a few moments the need to theorise about Arthur and the Grail seems unnecessary and an understanding of the deeper significance of the stories becomes clear.

Chalice Well Gardens. A modern site that has become something of a pilgrim centre for visitors to Glastonbury. The nineteenth-century well-cover depicts the *vesica piscis*, a symbol of the overlapping worlds of which Glastonbury is a nexus-point.

A GRAVE FOR ARTHUR?

T GLASTONBURY THE stories of Arthur and the Grail come together. An incident found in the *Chronicle* of John of Salisbury (*c.*1159) tells how Arthur had a vision telling him to go to the hermitage of St Mary Magdalene on Beckery Island (a site, it is believed, of a foundation dedicated to St Brigit). While Arthur was deciding whether or not to go, his squire visited the chapel and stole a candlestick, receiving a mortal wound from an unseen hand. Arthur then decided to visit the chapel and there witnesses a miraculous mass in which the Virgin Mary offered her Child as the Host. At the end of the mass, Arthur received a crystal cross, which he later presented to the abbey. It was still said to be part of the abbey treasure in the Middle Ages.

This story, retold in a more elaborate form, becomes the starting point of the Quest for the Grail in *Perlesvaus*, a thirteenth-century romance that may have been written at Glastonbury. It was a study of this text that led Katherine Maltwood to her rediscovery of the zodiac imprinted in the landscape around the Tor.

The earliest church at Glastonbury, a suggested reconstruction. From Sir Henry Spelman's *Consilia,* 1664.

Today, the ruins of Glastonbury Abbey – like the thorn a victim of anti-Catholic sentiments, in this instance those of Henry VIII – crouches in the lea of the Tor. The abbey church was once the largest foundation in the country, stretching some 180m (590 ft), with a Lady Chapel that was the pride of Britain. Like the rest of Glastonbury, it has attracted its share of legends. Even its archaeological history is unusual, much of the current foundations having been discovered by means of psychic investigation carried out by Bligh Bond in the early part of the century. Saints seem to have been attracted here like bees to a flower – the list of those believed to have dwelt there including SS Brigit, Patrick, Collen and Dunstan. Dunstan at least was definitely Abbot of Glastonbury soon after Arthur's day, and traditions of the rest remain strong. You will, however, look in vain for memorials of their presence. The site of St

Bridgit's well is lost forever beneath a sewage works, and the rest are only names.

Gildas, the irascible chronicler of Arthurian Britain, also spent time at Glastonbury and was, according to another local legend, instrumental in settling a dispute over the ownership of Guinevere, Arthur's oft-abducted Queen, who was carried off on this occasion by Melwas, the sixth-century 'king' of Somerset. Besieged by a justifiably outraged Arthur, Melwas appealed to Gildas, who was able to prevent outright warfare between the two kings. Guinevere was returned, unharmed, and the story went into legend as a colourful and romantic tale in which the evil knight Melyagraunce (Malory's version of Melwas) kidnapped the Queen and was subsequently slain by the dashing Sir Lancelot (see *Warriors of Arthur*, Blandford Press, London, 1987, by the present authors, for another version of these events).

The name Melwas probably disguises a much older figure, an Otherworldly king of the Summer Country, a region not found on any map. And

Glastonbury Abbey. Once the finest abbey in all Britain, enough still remains of the once-imposing building to give an impression of its size and granduer. It contains the supposed grave of Arthur, discovered in the Middle Ages but since proved of doubtful authenticity.

Glastonbury Tor itself is said to be a gateway to the faery court presided over by Gwynn ap Nudd, whose encounter with St Collen is recounted in the story that follows. The name Glastonbury itself may have given rise to its association with the Otherworld and its rulers. Several attempts have been made to interpret the name so as to make it fit various theories. As the 'Isle of Glass' it is part of Celtic myth, which has numerous references to islands inhabited by strange beings that are walled about with glass or crystal. As Glaestinga-burgh it becomes the foundation of a British chieftain named Glaesting, who once chased an escaped pig across the marshes until he finally recaptured it on high ground beneath an apple tree.

This tale, not recorded until the thirteenth century, may have given rise to the subsequent identification of Glastonbury with Avalon (*aval* means apple, hence Isle of Apples, Avalon). Pigs, of course, were sacred to the Celts, and there is still extant a poem in which the seer Merlin addresses his 'Little Pig' beneath an apple tree (see also pp. 28–38).

Avalon was long known as a name for the Celtic Isle of the Dead, and it was here that Arthur repaired 'to be healed of his wounds by Argante, Queen of Faery' (Layamon). In the thirteenth century the monks of Glastonbury added still further to the already prestigious role of honour of those buried in the grounds of the abbey by claiming to have unearthed a massive oak coffin containing some huge bones and a hank of golden hair that fell to dust when touched. Attached to the underside of the sarcophagus was a leaden cross bearing the inscription:

Cross marking Arthur's grave at Glastonbury (from Camdem's *Britannica*).

HIC JACET SEPULTUS INCLITUS REX ARTHURUS
IN INSULA AVALONIA

(HERE LIES THE RENOWNED KING ARTHUR IN
THE ISLAND OF AVALON)

This cross and its inscription has been the subject of debate ever since. It was last seen by the antiquary, William Camden, in the eighteenth century, though subsequent and so far unsubstantiated claims have been made for its more recent recovery.

In effect, the bones discovered in the monk's graveyard were probably those of a prehistoric burial, and modern scholarship has tended to dismiss the Latin and the lettering with which the leaden cross was inscribed as too late to have been executed in the sixth century, and therefore as almost certainly a forgery. Certainly the discovery was to the advantage of the abbey, which needed money for restoration, and to the ruling Plantagenet monarchy, who felt more secure with Arthur's death clearly established beyond reasonable doubt. As a sleeping lord, Arthur might return at any time to raise rebellion in Wales and oust them from the throne of Britain. Safely dead he could offer no real threat.

The legend outlived all such partisan needs. Arthur continues to sleep beneath various hills across Britain, his deeper contact with the land assured. Signposts outside Glastonbury welcome visitors to 'the Ancient Avalon', and pilgrims continue to flock there in search of their personal grails. The reality, as ever, remains elusive, buried within the maze-like layers of mystery and romance that have always surrounded this remarkable spot.

The Struggle for Spring

Glastonbury has many other legendary associations besides those of Arthur and his men. One of the strangest figures whose story connects him with the Tor is Gwynn ap Nudd, a King of Faery and a wily and resourceful adversary of St Collen in the story that follows.

Gwynn is traditionally associated with the area of the Vale of Neath in Wales, which derives its name from Gwynn's father. Nudd was a foster-son of the goddess Don or Danu, which implies that he was of human origin, though nothing more is known of him.

Another theory identifies Gwynn with the Irish hero, Fionn mac Cumhail. Both were warriors and huntsmen whose prowess was legendary; but while Fionn is of purely mortal stock, there is a wildness in Gwynn that marks him out as an Otherworld being. A poem in the early Welsh *Black Book of Camarthen* puts words into Gwynn's mouth that ably describe him:

> I am called the enchanter
> I am Gwynn the son of Nudd
> The lover of Creiddylad, daughter of Ludd.
> This is my horse Carngrwn,
> The terror of the field; he will not
> Let me parly with you; when bridled
> He is restless; he is impatient
> To go to Drum, my home on the Tawe

The most famous episode concerning Gwynn, alluded to here, is his love for the maiden Creiddylad, and his age-long battle, fought out year after year, with Gwyther ap Greidawl. Every spring they meet and fight, and can find no supremacy over each other; nor will they, it is said, until the end of time. Commentators have seen in this echoes of a most ancient tale in which the gods of summer and winter battle for the Maiden of Spring. Such myths are as deeply buried in the human psyche as any known to us, for there was always the fear that once winter took hold, spring would never return and life would cease. Deeper still, perhaps, is the idea of sovreignty, an embodiment of the land for whose favours succeeding generations of kings fought.

In Gwynn ap Nudd, then, we have a figure of ancient lineage and mighty stature, found harrying the souls of the departed over the hills and levels of Somerset, the Summer Country; or accompanying Arthur in the hunt for the great boar, Trwch Trwth, with his pack of white, red-eared hounds — the hounds of Annwn; and the Otherworld, over which he ruled, to which entrance might, just possibly, be gained from the steep-sided bulk of Glastonbury Tor . . .

Gwynn ap Nudd had ruled over the People of the Mound for more than a thousand years, for longer than he could remember, and the doings of the folk Outside had never troubled him before. From time to time he heard of new kings who came to rule over the Lands Above, and sometimes Heroes (an annoying race) found their way into the Lands Beneath and caused him some slight trouble – but by and large he remained careless of Men and their ways. That is, until the day when he noticed that there were fewer of his own folk at the court under the Mound, and that there were several inexplicable cracks in the roof of his palace: cracks that should not have been there since the fabric of the place, like all the works of the Lands-Beneath-The-Land, was intended to last forever.

Now, being filled with years and wisdom, it did not take Gwynn very long to discover that the cause of these two things had something to do with the race of Men. So he sent for his wiliest and most trusted adviser, who was at least as old if not older than himself, and demanded an explanation.

What he heard was so profoundly disturbing that it caused Gwynn to feel seriously perplexed for the first time in several hundred years. It seemed that a new breed of Men had come to live in the Lands Above who were followers of a new God. There had been such before, of course, but a surprising number of people had taken up worship of this particular deity and as a result had begun to question the existence of Gwynn and his kind. Not many, it was true, took this at all seriously, but enough shrines and wells were being neglected to cause some of their encumbents to fade – in some cases to vanish utterly. This was also the cause of the cracks that had appeared so ominously in the roof of the great royal chamber.

Gwynn thought about what he had been told for several days, then he heard how one of his people, a friendly and unassuming marsh-sprite, had met with one of this new breed of priests – they called themselves monks – who had actually knocked the sprite into a nearly bottomless mud-pit when he had attempted to prevent the building of a new causeway across his part of the march.

Gwynn was so angered by this that he decided to summon one of the monks to answer for his crimes, and forthwith sent word by a trusted messenger to a place only a mile or so distant in the Lands Above, where a community of the unpleasant fellows had set up a dwelling of some size.

The man he picked upon for this confrontation was named Collen. He had a reputation for wisdom and holiness surprising in one as yet still young, for such was the strength of his personality and the quality of his purity, that many believed he would one day be acknowledged as a saint.

Collen, of course, refused even to hear of any such a possibility, and persisted in living his life independently of all those who kept trying to persuade him to take higher office in the Church. But he could not prevent the people from bringing their problems to him in spite of his humility – indeed he knew it would have been wrong to try, and so he was not surprised when a rather curious-looking fellow appeared in the entrance to his cell and asked if he would come to see his master and help settle a dispute.

Collen immediately got up and followed the man along the path that led away from the monastery towards the Tor. It was only when they had been travelling for some little time that Collen realised they were actually climbing the side of the ancient hill. Then he stopped and asked the man who his master was.

Next moment there was a quivering and shaking in the air and Collen found himself standing in a vast hall roofed with a golden canopy held up with fantastic pillars and with brilliant tapestries hanging from its walls, while on every side were rich ornaments and treasures such as any man would find it hard to believe.

Collen stood, leaning on his staff and looking around in mild amazement. And when he looked harder at the place he saw that it had a slightly insubstantial look about it, as though it were not really there and might fade or vanish at any moment. The pillars, though beautiful, were formed from naturally striated rock; the walls, where they showed through the ornate tapestries, were of rough-hewn stone. And when Collen raised his eyes to the roof he saw there not only the glimmer of stars — somehow *under* the earth — but also the dark and heavy earth that covered the place.

So busy was he in looking at all this that Collen was not at first aware of the people. But gradually it dawned upon him that the great hall in which he stood was filling up with strange and beautiful beings, the like of which Collen had never even dreamt. Tall and stately women, whose raiment seemed made of tree-bark or leaves or even of living water; whose hair stirred as though to an unfelt breeze; and striking men with a greenness about their skin like loam, their clothing seemingly of earth and moss and still-growing leaves. And in all their eyes a kind of glow that spoke of a life-force so strong as to make most humans seem like dead things.

And as Collen stared, so they stared back: seeing a small, solid man with once-black hair now pied with grey; dressed in a plain white robe and leaning on a rough-hewn staff. Bright black eyes regarded them steadily and without fear . . . . something most there were unaccustomed to in Men.

Collen's scrutiny was broken by a great voice that suddenly boomed out, 'Welcome, child of the Lands Above, to the Lands Below!'

Collen turned and saw a tall splendid being seated on a golden throne that was carved all over — back and arms — with a hundred laughing, smiling, grimacing, snarling faces. The being was dressed in a great cloak of animal skins, and under his fine garments rich-red gold glittered at neck and wrists. His wild hair and beard had a hint of green about them too, and gleamed with energy; his eyes were well-springs of ancient knowledge and delight in life.

Collen visits Gwynn ap Nudd.

Two hounds crouched at his feet, each one as white as light save only for their ears, which were red as blood, and they looked upon the visitor from the world of Men with bright intelligence.

'Welcome, Collen,' said the personage on the throne, 'to my kingdom. Let us sit and eat together, and afterwards talk for a while.'

'I will be glad to talk with you,' answered Collen, 'but first I would know with whom it is I speak.'

The King of the Lands Beneath threw back his great head and laughed. 'I have many names, and one is as good as another. In your world I am known as Gwynn ap Nudd, or Avallach, or the Fisher.'

With this Collen had to be content, as a table was set before him and rich food and wine laid upon it. But of these he would have none, having a good enough idea where he was and knowing the prohibitions about eating the food and drink of that place. Instead, he asked simply for some water; and though Gwynn frowned at this he made no move to force his guest, but bade the table be removed and called for music. When the strains of a harp filled the hall, he bade Collen's chair be brought close to him and said, 'I would learn something of your ways. Tell me of your life in the Lands Above and of the new God you follow.'

If Collen was surprised he did not show it. With a smile he launched into an account of the birth, death, and return to life of the one whom he called the Son of Light, who had dwelt among men as a man but who had shown by certain wondrous deeds that he was more than a man.

Gwynn ap Nudd listened without interrupting and with great attention, and afterwards asked several questions. Then at last he said, 'You profess to follow your God in loving all things and all Men – yet you and your kind make war upon me and mine. How do you explain this?'

Collen said, 'We make war upon no men. You are not men at all, nor are you part of my God's creation. Therefore we have no need to acknowledge you. As far as we are concerned you do not exist.'

And though this was said politely and without anger, the Lord of Annwn rose abruptly to his feet, spilling wine from the rich golden cup he held. 'It is as I thought!' he cried. 'You seek our ending. We who were here before your foolish race were spawned upon the earth, we who have guarded and tended the Lands Above since the beginning. You seek to hasten our passing. Yet when we are gone there will be an end to many things that you would as soon not lose. The power of earthly kings will wane and the land itself will grow sick.'

'Better that I should so do,' answered Collen mildly, 'than that men should continue to worship false gods or the spirits of river and tree.'

The King of the Otherworld snorted in disgust. 'We have nothing to say to each other, mortal. Whatever you may say or do, we shall be here when you are all long since dust, you and all your kind. Now go!' He waved his hand in dismissal and at once Collen found himself standing alone on the summit of the Tor in a keen wind. Collen addressed the empty air: 'All this world is beautiful,

King of Annwn, and it is all God's Creation, with or without your help.'

The only answer was a faint tremor in the earth beneath his feet as of a great door slamming shut in the Lands Beneath.

This was not to be the last that Collen saw of the Lord of Annwn. A year passed in the Lands Above and the seasons went by until once again winter held the land in thrall. Collen continued to work in the fields around the monastery and to walk the countryside speaking to any, who would listen, about his God. And the little community grew slowly until it held as many as twenty monks and gave shelter to travellers who passed that way. Then one morning as Collen sat deep in meditation in his small cell, there came in at the window a wren that cocked its head on one side and addressed the little monk in a bright, hard voice: 'Collen, the Lord of Annwn bids you visit him again.'

Collen looked at the bird and said, 'Tell your master I will come – but in my own time.' When the messenger had flown away Collen finished his orisons and took his staff and a flask of holy water and set out across the frozen fields and water meadows towards the Tor.

When he stood at last on the summit he knocked with his staff on the hard earth and called, 'Lord of Annwn, I am here.'

At once there was a swirl of movement in the air and then once again Collen found himself standing in the great underground hall with its pillars and tapestries and crowds of brightly garbed folk. And there as before was the imposing figure of Gwynn ap Nudd with his two, red-eared hounds at his feet.

This time he did not offer Collen food or drink but spoke directly of the matter that had caused him to summon the little monk again. 'Once, long ago – as you measure time in the Lands Above – there were wise and unbiased judges upon whom any creature could call for any reason. Now it seems that all such Men have departed and there are none to be found who will make peace between those who seek it. Therefore I have called you, Collen for – despite the differences between us – I believe you to be an honest man without fear. Will you therefore act as judge in a matter that troubles me greatly?'

Collen answered, 'If there is anything that I can honestly do, that will I do.'

'Then listen, and observe,' said Gwynn ap Nudd, and told Collen how there lived a girl of surpassing beauty named Creiddelyadd, daughter of Llud Silver-Hand. And she was loved by Gwythyr, son of Greidyawl, the Lord of Summer, and by Gwynn himself who, because he was the stronger, raised an army against Gwythyr and had taken him prisoner, along with the maiden.

Now all this had been in the time of the Emperor Arthur, whose wife Gwynhyvar was the sister of Creiddelyadd. And when he heard of the matter he went with his own warriors and took back Gwythyr and the girl, whom he sent back to her father. And there the matter stood. 'But I was unable to forget the beautiful Creiddelyadd,' said the Lord of Annwn, 'and it seemed to me right that she should go to myself, who was the strongest. Therefore I have summoned Gwythyr ap Greidyawl to fight with me once every year on May

Day ever since. And ever since then we have fought and neither have won the victory.'

While he listened it seemed to Collen that he saw all that was described: the beautiful maiden, the Lord of Annwn on a horse as black as the blackest night with armour that seemed to absorb the light, in combat with Gwythyr who rode a horse the colour of sunlight with armour of gold – two mighty champions who fought with primal strengths but could not overcome each other . . .

As the Lord of Annwn finished his tale Collen was suddenly back again in the hall of the Lands Beneath and blinked in the subtly shifting light.

'How say you to this matter?' demanded Gwynn ap Nudd.

'I am no Druid, Lord of Annwn, nor have I any right to judge such as you. Yet, I will give my opinion as to how this matter may best be resolved.' Collen drew himself up. 'It may be that I am a foolish mortal who has no understanding of such things, yet I believe I see a greater parable here than the lust of two mighty beings for the love of one woman. Fair indeed is the lovely Creiddelyadd, and mighty indeed are you, my Lord of the Lands Beneath. And so too is the might and strength of the Lord Gwythyr ap Greidyawl. But in your striving I see a pattern – for you are like the winter and your opponent is like the summer, and you each strive for possession of the Lady of Spring. Perhaps you each desire lordship over the rest of the year, for I have heard such things are sometimes so in the Lands Beneath. But all of this is merely a tale to me, and you are no more real than the shadow cast by a tree at midday. And I say to you, Lord of Annwn, that there are laws immutable to such as you; and that the most immutable of all is the law that says that season must be followed by season, according to the pattern of Creation. And I see now that I was wrong to say that you were not a part of my God's making, for you are so indeed, even though you do not really exist, and as such you are subject to certain laws yourself. This then is my judgement, for which you have asked me. You shall struggle for victory in this fight every year as you have already striven until the coming of Doomsday. Only then shall it be resolved, though how I cannot say . . . And now I would be gone from here, and may the blessing of the Son of Light be upon you and upon all here.'

So saying Collen took out his little bottle of holy water and sprinkled a few drops on the ground, at which there came a crash like a great door slamming shut, and the little monk found himself standing again on the summit of the Tor with the great voice of Gwynn ap Nudd ringing in his ears. 'Farewell, Collen, until we meet again. Your judgement is wise, though harsh, but you have shown me that there may yet be peace between the followers of your God and those of the old way, despite all that is between them.'

Collen smiled as he walked away, back down the sloping sides of the Tor, along the old path that men still called the Maze, and back to his little cell in the monastery that men were beginning to call Glastonbury. And he sang a hymn to his God that told of the beauty of the world and of all Creation.

7·Robin hood
and the green men

WHO WAS ROBIN HOOD?

ENERATIONS OF CHILDREN have grown up with the tales of King Arthur and his knights; but alongside these popular legends are those that tell of the life and adventures of another hero, the outlaw, Robin Hood. No one knows for certain whether such a person ever actually existed – though there are several contenders for the title – but he is generally assumed to have lived during the reign of Richard the Lionheart and his brother, John (though this, as we shall see, is a comparatively recent idea). From his hideout deep within the impenetrable reaches of Sherwood Forest, Robin led a band of famous outlaws whom legend swiftly transformed into champions of the poor and down-trodden and, more specifically, of the Saxons against their Norman overlords:

> No man must presume to call me Master
> By name of Earle, lorde, baron, knight or squire;
> But Robin Hood, plaine Robin Hood
> That honest yeoman, stout and good.

So says one of the ballads that relates the stories of Robin's exploits. The reality underlying these tales reflects the harshness of the times. The Normans kept the peasants of England under a stern rule. Knights and barons held their lands from the king, and the people who happened to live upon it were considered part of their property, also held in thraldom and unable to move to any other part of the country. Those who did so, or who hunted any of the king's deer that roamed the wide woodlands, were branded as 'wolves' heads' – outlaws who could be hunted down and killed on sight without benefit of trial or judgement.

Reaction to this ruthless treatment found expression in the songs and stories of Robin and his Merry Men, who became the heroes of the peasant class in the

93

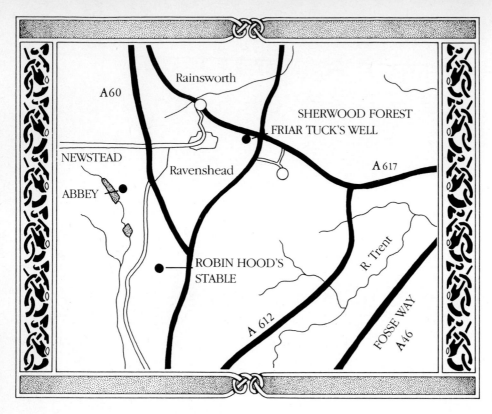

Sherwood Forest.

same way that Arthur and his knights were the favourite subject of courtly narrative. Robin's archetypal enemies, the Sheriff of Nottingham, Sir Guy of Gisborne, or Prince John, represented the most obvious enemies of the people. The sheriff administered the law and extorted prohibitive taxes; the knights helped him with ready swords; and the greedy monarchs grew fat on the proceeds while the people starved.

These are archetypal figures and Robin himself is something of an archetype, whose likeness is to be found in most parts of the world where people have suffered under a powerful ruling class. William Tell is his Swiss counterpart, as is Till Eulenspiegel in Germany and Riu Blas in Estonia.

But Robin acquired more than the status of a local hero; he became a national figure, with his own cycle of songs and stories, which seem to have begun to be written almost from the time in which he may actually have lived, and which continued to be sung, and eventually written down, into the seventeenth century. *The Little Geste (Life) of Robin Hood,* published by Wynkyn de Worde in 1495 (just ten years after Malory's *Morte D'Arthur*) is the most famous. It contains most of the best-known stories and all of the heroes who became part of Robin's band: Little John, his giant second-lieutenant; Friar Tuck, the fat monk who was as handy with a quarterstave as with a rosary; Will Scarlet or Scathlock; Much the Miller's Son; Alan-a-Dale, the minstrel (perhaps a memory of one of the first balladeers to sing of Robin Hood); and many others.

Also present, of course, was Robin's 'wife', Maid Marian; and it is her

Wood engraving from the first page of *A Gest of Robyn Hode*.

Robin Hood and Little John (Roxburghe Ballads, 1600).

character that gives us the first clue to a deeper reason for the continued popularity of Robin and his men.

GENTLE ROBYN:
THE MYTHOLOGICAL ARGUMENT

HROUGHOUT THE BALLADS are continual references to Robin's devotion to the Virgin Mary. This might strike one as odd in a character generally portrayed (however altruistically) as an outlaw. The real reason lies in the fact that in almost every instance of extreme Marian devotion, this stems from the presence of an earlier deity. (Thus is the Magdalen seen as a deposed goddess figure in certain parts of the world.) Robin, who — as we shall see — himself inherited the dimensions of an ancient pre-Christian figure, required a suitable consort. Hence, by a subtle play on words, this became Maid Marian, the eternal Maiden of the Wood, whose form disguises that of a far older and more formidable goddess of woodland and stream – perhaps Ceriddwen or Creuddilad (see p. 86) – who, in Arthur's day or earlier, held similar positions in the traditions of the first-born of Britain.

In the ballads, Marian may be described in more sober terms, but one may still see glimpses of something more:

> As Robert was ranging in the Earl's wood
> He espeyed a pretty maid,
> Her gait it was graceful, her body was straight
> And her countenance free from pride.
>
> Her eyebrows were black, and so was her hair,
> And her skin was as smooth as glass,
> Her visage spake wisdom and modesty too,
> Said Robin, Oh, what a fine lass.
>
> (Ritson, *Robin Hood*)

But if Marian was once a goddess, who or what was Robin? Behind the merry tales of the outlaw band and their charismatic leader lurk the shadows of much older figures: the ancient spirits of the greenwood, the denizens of field and stream, hill and valley, who once populated most of Britain and who continued to linger on in the folk-memory of the people long after the coming of Christianity to British shores. The Fairy Folk, the Good People, the Mothers – they had many names and faces, some of which we know better than others. Shakespeare made famous the character of Puck or Robin Goodfellow, and the name Robin or Robyn itself seems to have been attached to one of the oldest spirits of the woodland.

Throughout the fifteenth and sixteenth centuries, Robin featured largely in the entertainments that accompanied the great medieval fairs held throughout the country. The midsummer festivals and May Day games, where Morris Men danced, plays were performed and peddlars plied their wares, were often referred to as Robin Hood's Games. That they were later condemned as 'lewd' by puritan writers indicates the presence or memory of pagan memorials enshrined in these gatherings, and points still further to the older aspect of Robin o' the Wood (or sometimes Hood, hence the Hooded Man).

Even the colour of the outlaws' clothing, referred to again and again in the ballads, is another argument in favour of the mythological interpretation. Although Lincoln Green was a famous cloth in its own right, the colour is always associated with faery, and echoes the ancient vegetation cults that once flourished in the land.

Add to this the presence of stones, boulders, trees and other natural features that still bear the name of Robin Hood, and one has an even stronger reason for believing that he was once a mighty figure of myth and magic. Such figures as Arthur, Wayland Smith, or Gwynn ap Nudd left their marks on the landscape in the same way – often indicating that these places were once the sites of worship or cultic activity. Heroes as much as gods became part of the landscape in this way, and passed into the realm of the legendary. Robin, in his turn, assumed the mantle of an ancient Lord of the Woods, donning the green clothing of the faery race and gaining a new dimension for himself and his men.

THE GREEN MEN OF SHERWOOD

T IS IMPOSSIBLE to read about Robin Hood without encountering another figure from the native, pre-Celtic past. He is the Green Man, and his face, peering out from between the leaves – which are perhaps an actual part of his face – is to be seen both inside and outside churches the length and breadth of the land. These multifoliate heads, as they are commonly known, have long been recognised as symbols of the relationship of ancient humanity with nature, personified as an actual figure.

In the Middle Ages he appears as the Green Gome (or man) in the Arthurian poem, *Sir Gawain and the Green Knight.* Gawain (significantly) like Robin is said to have a special devotion to the Virgin, but is in fact the Knight of the Goddess (see *Gawain: Knight of the Goddess,* by John Matthews, Aquarian Press, Wellingborough, 1989). The description of his adversary, the Green Gome, is nowhere more vividly described than here:

The Green Man, from Auxerre Cathedral (thirteenth century).

> Very gay was this great man guised all in green,
> and the hair of his head with his horse's accorded:
> fair flapping locks enfolding his shoulders,
> a big beard like a bush over his breast hanging
> that with the handsome hair from his head falling
> was sharp shorn to an edge just short of his elbows,
>
>   . . .
>
> his glance was as lightning bright,
> so did all that saw him swear;
> no man would have the might,
> they thought, his blows to bear.

(Lls. 179–84, 199–202, trans. J. R. R. Tolkien)

Here, as in the rest of the poem, the symbolism is precise. The Green Gome is a spirit of nature with all the power of the seasons in his train. His alliance with Morgan le Fay in the same poem also signifies his part in the endless dance of nature and time, for Morgan is herself a goddess and but a single aspect of sovereignty, the tutelary spirit of Britain whose enclave is all of the legendary land (see *Arthur and the Sovereignty of Britain by Caitlín Matthews,* Arkana, London, 1989).

And, as Robin is himself identified with the Green Man of the Wood, so his men become Green Men also, their carved faces peering between the leaves of Sherwood Forest with the light of ancient magic in their eyes.

There is a famous and often-quoted scene at the end of *Sir Gawain and the Green Knight,* in which Gawain finally re-encounters the Green Giant in his secret enclave deep within a valley where lies a cave or mound known as the 'Green Chapel'. This title has been applied, in one form or another, to more than one ancient sacred site, and 'the chapel in the green' is well known to students of paganism as a probable sacred *locus* for the Great Goddess. It would clearly be right for one of her servants, such as the Green Knight most certainly is, to be found at such a place.

Aside from this, several attempts have been made, with varying degrees of success, to identify the site of the Green Chapel. One of the most convincing – as well as interesting – of these is in Staffordshire, not far from the ancient Roman city of Chester. Here, on the Staffordshire moorland, in a valley where the Hoo Brook runs into the Manifold, lies Wetton Mill, also known as Nan Tor, or Thurshole. The latter name gives an immediate clue: it is really Thor's Hole, after the Norse god, and it accounts for the local name, Fiend's House, also attached to the site.

The scholar, Mabel Day, was the first to spot the similarity between this ancient natural cave-site and the description as it appears in the Middle English poem. Nearby lies Lud's Church, which Professor Ralph V. Elliott has suggested as a contender for the Green Chapel. This is a deeply delved cave with a truly fearsome entrance hole that seems to lead down into hell itself. Lud again is an ancient name associated with the fertility of the land and its sovereign goddess; but it seems to fit the description in *Sir Gawain and the Green Knight* less precisely than does Wetton Mill. Lud was one of the legendary kings of Britain, a descendant of Brutus and the one who gave his name to London, Lud's Town. The name still remains in the city's Ludgate Hill, near Fleet Street.

The Green Knight is as strange and terrible a personage as one should ever wish to meet, and it is perhaps unnecessary to seek for an actual site at all for one of the best-described encounters between a mortal hero and a lord of the

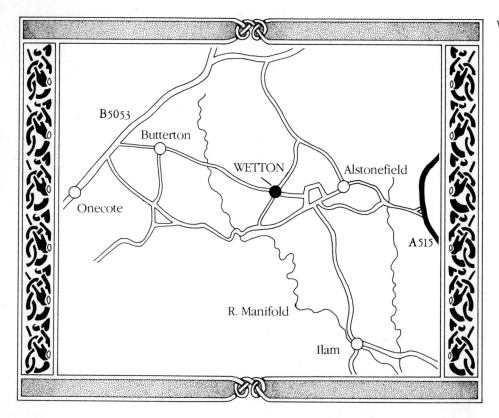

Wetton.

Wetton Mill. The traditional site of the Green Knight's Chapel, where Gawain encountered the fearsome, green-clad giant and played out the Beheading Game.

Otherworld. Wetton Mill is still worth a visit, though, as it is full of atmosphere and one certainly feels as close to the ancient mystery – whether of the Green Man or of Robin Hood – than almost anywhere else in this part of the land.

THE GOOD YEOMAN: ROBIN HOOD IN HISTORY

HATEVER THE NATIVE people of Britain saw as Robin's true significance, they were aware of him also as a very real figure: someone who was stronger, more cunning and resourceful than their enemies – whether these were the Normans or simply their overlords in a later time. For the period in which Robin is supposed to have flourished varies sharply according to which tradition or literature one accepts. The reigns of Richard I, Edward II, and Edward III, and even Henry VIII, have been put forward at various times in Robin's long history. The first, most generally accepted, really stems from Walter Scott's famous novel *Ivanhoe*

(1819), which introduced the story of Robin of Locksley and made him a Saxon nobleman, despite the fact that all the ballads persist in making him a 'stout yeoman'.

Among the more reliable contenders for the identity of the 'real' Robin Hood are Robert of Huntingdon, who may be a totally fictitious figure, and Robert Hood who was born in the time of Edward II (1307–27) and died during the reign of Edward III (1327–77). Opinions differ as to the exact placing of the stories, and while Sherwood Forest remains the better known and most popular choice, the area around Wakefield and Barnsdale in the West Riding of Yorkshire has also yielded some remarkable evidence concerning the person of Robert Hood who, with his wife Matilda, took to the life of the forest after following his liege lord, the Earl of Lancaster, in rebellion against the king.

A study of the court rolls for the area in the thirteenth and fourteenth centuries reveals the existence of this personage, born about 1290 in Wakefield to yeoman parents. Adam Hood was a forester in the service of John de Warenne, Lord of the Manor of Wakefield. His son, Robert, received education at the local school run by John of Wakefield, clerk to the earl, and in time became a householder in the manor and married his Matilda, a local girl of whom nothing more is known.

When, in 1316, Edward II began gathering an army to subdue rebellious Scots along the Borders, we find Robert Hood mentioned as being fined for failing to answer the summons of his liege lord. Soon after this, the same John, eighth Earl of Warenne, became involved in the abduction of the wife of the Earl of Lancaster with whom he was in love. Subsequently the manor of

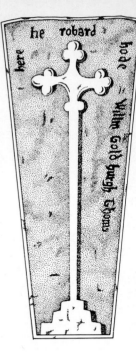

Gravestone of Robin Hood at Kirklees Priory (from a drawing made in 1665).

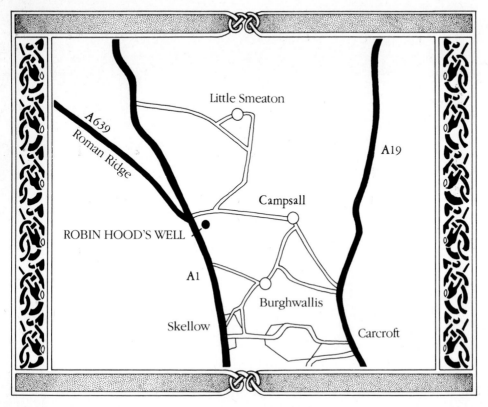

Robin Hood's Well.

100

Robin Hood's Grave. Here, in what was once part of the great forest of Barnsdale, is the supposed grave of Robin Hood. As with Arthur, it is perhaps unwise to seek an actual resting place for the heroes of legend. This site is of doubtful provenance.

Wakefield changed hands when the same John de Warenne granted it to the Earl of Lancaster in reparation of the wrongs done to him. Thus Robert Hood became liegeman to a new lord.

Then, in 1322, Lancaster was the centre of the rebellion against Edward II and his favourites, Piers Gaveston and the Dispenser family. In a battle at Boroughbridge on 16 March he was defeated and subsequently beheaded. Robert Hood, who seems to have answered the call to arms on this occasion, forfeited his house and plot of land as a result, and either chose or was forced to become an outlaw from that time onward. Matilda, it is said, went with him; and from this point the legends began.

Whether this is the man who became Robin Hood, whether he changed his name (or had it changed by the balladeers) to align him with the more ancient woodland sprite, we shall probably never be able to say. The point that emerges is that the stories of Robin are part of the *legendary* history of Britain. They are for all time and belong to no single race or class of people, and they transcend mere literary fashion or pseudo-historical interpretation.

The Major Oak. According to tradition, Robin and his Merry Men used often to meet and camp beneath the tree. It is certainly one of the oldest and most imposing still-standing trees in the once-mighty groves of Sherwood Forest.

Robin Hood's Well. Now known as St Anne's Well, this site is traditionally associated with Robin Hood, in an area rich in legend of the famous outlaw. Its present impressive cover was designed by Sir John Vanburgh in the eighteenth century.

THE LANDSCAPE OF ROBIN HOOD

AS TO THE places associated with Robin, they are many and widespread. Like Arthur he would have needed to have sprouted wings to be in all the places mentioned in the ballads or in the local traditions at the times specified. The earliest tales show him living in the forest of Barnsdale, south of Pontefract. From the seventeenth century, for no known reason, he became associated with Sherwood Forest, and this is where the greatest number of sites associated with him are still to be found today. Notably, the Major Oak in Sherwood itself is popularly believed to be the place where Robin and the Merry Men met for feasting and to plan their latest attack on some unsuspecting knight or churchman. St Ann's Well, still within the bounds of present-day Sherwood, was known as Robin Hood's Well in the sixteenth century, though it is less interesting than the identically named site in Barnsdale that has a cover designed by John Vanburgh for the Earl of Carlisle in the eighteenth century.

As with Arthur there is no known grave for Robin. The story of his death is told in the story that follows, though in a speculative manner. The legend itself is as strong as ever, as the popularity of the recent TV series, *Robin of Sherwood,* testifies. Robin is perhaps an idealised form of *all* outlaws, transformed from someone outside the law into a hero of the people.

The Death of Robin Hood

Like all true heroes, Robin Hood's death is mysterious and his grave unknown. In the light of his identification with the Otherworldly character of the Green Man of the Woods, the story of his poisoning by the Prioress of Kirklees Abbey, while apparently healing his wounds is of particular interest. A very similar event takes place in the Arthurian legends, where Morgan le Fay – Arthur's arch-enemy who was herself brought up in a nunnery – takes the king away to heal him of his wounds. Within the shadowy world of legendary and myth, one may glimpse here further echoes of an ancient pattern in which the Lord and Lady of the Woods were both ally and mortal foe in the struggle for mastery of the seasons. The fact that Morgan is also seen as ruling the Green Gome in *Sir Gawain and the Green Knight* should not be forgotten, any more than Robin's frequent attacks on churchmen – themselves regarded as legitimate targets since they were as notoriously corrupt and greedy as their secular counterparts. The story that follows attempts to suggest one possible interpretation of Robin's part in the mystery of the land, which is the theme of most – if not all – the stories in this book about legendary Britain.

Robin came awake with a cry, sitting upright in the narrow cot, then gasping as weakness flooded over him, making the world turn over. He sank back with a groan and struggled to gather his scattered wits. A dream it had seemed, long and dark and without ending. The effort of shaking free of it had drained him. He saw again the face of the Prioress, lips drawn back from her teeth in what might have been a smile but that seemed to Robin more of a grimace. They had told him she was no friend to him and he remembered other strange tales of Kirklees Abbey and its mistress.

Slowly he set himself to remain still, to breathe, to think, to piece together the fragments of that day's events . . .

Sickness he had known enough of in his life. One could not live an outlaw in the greenwoods of England without agues and fevers and the swelling of joints. But of late he had felt the onset of age, a slowness in the sinews that strung the great longbow and loosed the clothyard shaft, a reluctance to wake in the morning – all the more so now that Marian was gone.

That thought drew him back to the present with a shock. Now instead of the Prioress's face it was Marian's that hovered above him, lined and solicitous. He saw, with a start, that there was grey in the russet locks that showed beneath her linen coif. Marian grown old! Worse: a cloistered nun. These things were not to be contemplated. Where was Marian's youth? Where indeed was youth itself? Again he groaned aloud and clutched the sides of the cot in desperation.

Scenes from the past then returned to him, bright days in the sun-dappled wood, the laughter of men at meat, the cheers as John or Alan or Will brought home another of the king's deer. The faces of his enemies also came to him: the sheriff, Sir Guy of Gisborne, Owein of Clun – he would have welcomed the sight of any one of them at that moment. But the sheriff too had grown old, fat, and gouty and too indolent at last to care about his old adversary. And Sir Guy was dead in the Holy Land and Owein by Robin's own hand, long years since . . .

A fragment of a ballad, sung in marketplace and fair throughout the land, drifted into his mind:

> Robin was a proud outlaw
> Whyles he walked on ground,
> So courteous as he was one
> Was never one I found . . .
> So courteous as he was one
> Was never one I found . . .
> Robin he took a full great horn
> And loud he gan to blow:
> Seven score of strong young men
> Came ready on a row . . .

Already they sang about him as though he were dead. But the song put him in mind of his own horn and he forced himself to open his eyes and focus them on the far corner of the room, where he had laid his bow and quiver and horn before he lay down to let the Prioress search his body for ill humours.

After a moment the walls of the room stopped advancing and retreating and Robin was able to take in his surroundings: a small bare room containing only the cot in which he lay and a small chest against the wall. On the top of that lay a basin and ewer, the use of which he knew only too well, and his horn. She had left it there, not expecting him to have the strength to blow it.

Perhaps there was truth in that. The mere effort of sitting up set the walls and floor of the room in motion again, but this time Robin fought back against the dizziness, and was rewarded by some small clearing of his head. None the less, it took him an age to rise, and holding on to the wall all the time, to fumble his way the three steps to the chest.

His fingers closed on the smooth curve of the horn and he set it to his lips with a tembling hand. The sound he then produced was scarcely that which a child might make, and the effort it cost was such that he was forced to seek the safety of the cot once more. From there, patiently now that he had a purpose, he drew together the last reserves of his strength, and tilting the horn towards the narrow window, blew one great blast and two short – an old code that any one of the outlaws who heard would answer as soon as they might.

Spent, Robin lay back and closed his eyes again, feeling the darkness advance upon him. Then he heard the rattle of a bolt and the creak of a door opening:

too soon to be John, or Will, or Tuck. He forced himself to look and gasped at what he saw.

'Marian, she . . .'

Finger laid to her lips, Marian entered the room. Behind her the Prioress stood, her face now unreadable. As Robin struggled to speak, to rise, Marian gently restrained him.

'Have no fear, Robin. She means only good.'

Then she pressed a cup to his lips and he drank, weakly, all the while staring at the Prioress, who made no move to do him hurt, but merely stood, hands hidden in the sleeves of her gown, staring down at him with something – pity? – stirring in her eyes.

The drink was like fire and swept through Robin, pushing back the shadows and the weakness for the moment. At once he struggled to rise, but again Marian restrained him with a gentle pressure on his breast.

'I don't understand . . .'

'Be still, my love, listen to what she must tell, then all will be made plain.'

Robin's eyes sought those of the Prioress. That Marian seemed to know made it harder to be certain of anything. Was he wrong, had the potion she had given him been other than deadly poison? Yet if not, why had he felt so weak?

'In all your years in the wood, have you never wondered why you have been spared any kind of wound?'

The question took him by surprise. Considering it, he realised the truth of what she said. Countless dangers and escapades, escapes, captures, chases – yet never once, in all those years, had any sword or knife drawn blood. Bewilderment seized him.

'Why?'

'These woods are old, far older than you know. They were here in the Foretime when the First-Born walked the earth. In that time many laws were laid down that will last as long as the land itself. You will know of the old kings who gave themselves for love of the earth, that it might bear fruit. Now there are strangers here, men who care nothing for the old ways, whose blood is not of the land. Other ways must by found. Robin-o'-the-Hood is one such way.'

The words had an ominous ring, as did the title, which Robin himself had never taken, for all that the people might use it behind his back.

'I know nothing of these things,' he said at last, sullenly. Fear and anger stirred within him and he looked at Marian. 'What is your part in this mummery? Have you turned against me?'

'Oh, Robin, Robin, say no such words to me. It is your Marian who speaks, and I was ever so.'

'Part of the pattern also,' said the Prioress inexorably, 'for ever did the Robin

Robin Hood and the Spirit of the Wood.

have his Marian, and ever was she named so for the Lord of the Wood.'

'What foolishness . . ?' Robin began.

'No foolishness, man. Look within yourself, call upon your deepest self and you will see!'

Her eyes flashed fire and beneath their power Robin fell back. Strange sensations began within him. The weakness, held at bay by the fiery liquid, returned – and this time he could do nothing against it. The faces of Marian and the Prioress swam before him, changing, shifting, until they were no longer there. The walls, too, all that he knew of the real world, seemed to melt, and he was once again in the greenwood, striding forth with all the vigour of youth returned to him. Gladness rose within him and he ran as he had not run for years, joyful in the strength of his limbs and the beating of his blood.

Down the forest rides he raced, drawing ever nearer to the heart of the greenwood, and the great oak whose heart had been beating for more than a thousand years. Then as he reached the clearing where the ancient tree stood, it seemed as though some part of himself became separate, so that he was able to watch himself walking towards the tree and placing his hands on its gnarled trunk. Oddly shy, as though watching something private of which he had no part, Robin watched.

He saw a tall man, clad in the green of the forest, his face shadowed by a hood, his great longbow at his side, standing next to the tree as though waiting. And, with the strange detachment that held him, Robin sensed rather than saw an aura, perhaps a shadow, falling away from him. No, not one shadow, but two, a smaller part of the greater shadows that seemed as he watched to take on substance and grow solid, until he could see a smaller figure who stood, or crouched, by – his own? – thigh. Beneath the gloom of the trees, where the sunlight grew dim, he should have seen nothing. Yet in some way his sight, the sight with which he watched himself as though watching a stranger, was enhanced, so that the outlines of that other figure became gradually clearer.

He saw a small man-shape, ancient it seemed as the tree itself, gnarled and weathered as a nut. A fringe of white hair clung to his head, which was otherwise bare. His clothing seemed to be made of bits of hide stitched roughly together, and his limbs – bony, thin, and yet somehow filled with strength – stuck out of the gaps in the rough skins.

But it was his eyes that drew Robin. Deep they were, and filled with life that burned so strongly it seemed to have no ending. Centuries of knowledge, of sorrow and wisdom and laughter mingled in his gaze. It seemed to the watcher that he knew all things, and that all things had come to amuse him greatly, save one, and that was his greatest pain . . .

Then, as Robin watched, he saw the little man take out a tiny silver knife, sickle-shaped like the paring of a finger-nail. With this he made a wound in the tall man's – in Robin's – wrist, from which blood began to well.

The pain brought Robin back to himself and to the cell in Kirklees Abbey. There he saw the Prioress bending over him, his arm outstretched above a basin, the tiny silver knife in her hand, his own blood welling forth into the bowl.

Fear now leant him strength to sit upright, but it was not enough to bring him to his feet.

'Peace, man. Do you *still* not understand? The colour of your own clothing is like the raiment of the greenwood. You are the Man of the Forest, the land's king. Let be what must be.'

The words rang in Robin's fevered brain like a horn call. He saw Marian, her eyes dark with sorrow and love, watching him as he fought with the terror of realisation.

And then suddenly all fear left him, and with it any anger at what seemed betrayal. He lay back in the cot and felt a peace that he knew would outlast his life begin to steal over his limbs. The world about him grew dim, and as though the walls of Kirklees Abbey grew transparent again, he seemed to be lying in the greenwood with the sunlight falling upon his upturned face . . .

Thus John Little found his old comrade when he came at last in answer to Robin's desperate horn-call; and thus were the three oldest and dearest friends able to share the last hours together, speaking of other and happier days, as Robin's blood, shed at last and sacredly, took him away from them all.

At the last he called for his great longbow and knocked a last arrow to the string. Then supported in the arms of the giant outlaw, he leant in the narrow window and let fly his last arrow, bidding them lay him to rest where it fell.

Marian marked its flight and later that day John Little dug a grave in which he laid the mortal remains of the greenwood's greatest outlaw. And when he had done, shouldering the spade with which he had turned the dark earth, and taking Robin Hood's great bow and his silver-mounted hunting-horn, he set out for the heart of the forest, where he knew he would find a small man clad in skins, whose claim was greater than any on these things.

8·thomas the Rhymer in the eildon hills

The Eildon Hills are situated on the Scottish Borders, and in their shadow the ancient town of Melrose grew. This region of Scotland has many vivid historical associations, due to its sensitive position close to the north of England. It became a debated and often lawless zone in the long wars between Scotland and England, and was harassed for many centuries by border raiding, robbing and feuding. The present Abbey of Melrose is a grand and beautiful ruin, the resting place of the heart of Robert the Bruce, the great hero of the

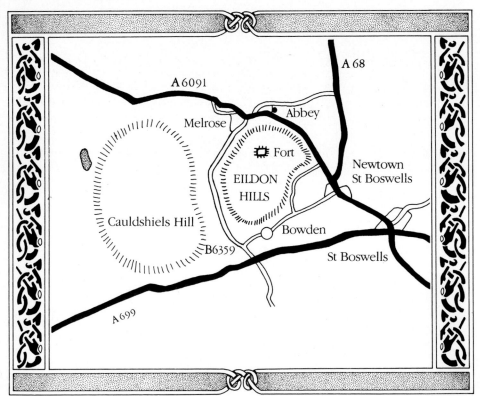

The Eildon Hills.

110

Melrose Abbey. With the Eildon Hills in the background, this massive yet elegant abbey holds the heart of Robert the Bruce, for whom the historical Thomas the Rhymer may have been an agent in the Scottish fight against English invasion.

Scots. Yet, ironically, the abbey represents the increasing Anglicising of medieval Scotland, for it was part of the continuing ecclesiastical building and reformation programmes deriving from English sources originally commenced in the eleventh century by Margaret, the English wife of King Malcolm Canmore. The old Celtic Church, founded centuries before upon Iona by Saint Columba (see Chapter 9), was replaced by Roman Christianity, which in Britain – as elsewhere in Europe – was a State religion tied inseparably to power politics.

It was into this rich yet hazardous region that Thomas of Erlstoun or Erceldoune was borne in the thirteenth century, when terrrible wars and disputes arose between Scotland and England with Edward I (of England) ravaging and destroying ruthlessly. Thomas was a member of a landed family, and there are documents still in existence that refer to his estate, and may indeed bear his signature. The estate was eventually donated to the Church by his son, also called Thomas, though there is some confusion over this matter.

This simple factual history may seem ordinary enough to the modern reader, but there are two accounts of the end of Thomas's life. The first is that he was murdered by followers of the Earl of March, having accurately foreseen and predicted his murder. The second is that Thomas vanished into Fairyland, where he had previously served the Fairy Queen for seven years. Thus Thomas is sometimes said to live on in the hollow hills of Eildon, waiting like other national heroes until a time of great need calls him forth. It is perhaps significant that he was also reputed to be a nationalist agent, in his role of travelling poet and seer, during the war with the English. We can detect a similar mingling of legend and history here to that found on a far larger scale with Merlin and Arthur, both of whom also feature in legends from this same region of Scotland.

When Thomas returned from his seven years of service in Fairyland, he wrote a number of prophetic verses, which still exist, and which refer with apparent accuracy to local and sometimes national events. Thomas is also

111

credited with the authorship of a long romance poem describing his adventures in Fairyland, and as the first formal author (in the sense of producing a written text rather than reciting oral tales or verses) of the story of Tristan and Isolt, which is featured in Chapter 1. His curious adventure into the Otherworld is also celebrated in one of the classic, Scottish, traditional magical ballads, which bears his name. We do not know if Thomas was the author of this ballad, but we do know that the song was circulated widely as part of genuine oral tradition for some centuries — later becoming formalised in a more literary revamped state during the nineteenth century (see pp. 115–117).

It seems that Thomas, in the thirteenth century, represents the same tradition as Merlin in earlier medieval literature that drew upon bardic sources. At least one historical Merlin seems to have lived in the sixth century, and the tradition is repeated as late as the seventeenth century with the enigmatic figure of the Reverend Robert Kirk of Aberfoyle, another Scot who vanished into Fairyland. Kirk did not return, though local tradition preserves the method of his potential release and several tales of attempts to bring him back to the human realm. The fusion of historical persons with a tradition of prophecy, the Otherworld or Underworld, and the fate of the land or people, is an enduring theme.

THE EILDON HILLS

HE DISTINCTIVE, ROUNDED mass of the Eildons, which form sister hills (of the kind sometimes called 'paps' in Ireland and reminiscent of the shape of a fruitful earth goddess) are said to be hollow, containing the way to Fairyland. Whereas in Glastonbury, in the south-west of England, we have the specific residence of Gwynn ap Nudd, Lord of the Otherworld and the Wild Hunt (see Chapter 6), Eildon hides the entrance to an entire world or dimension. This detailed cosmography is described in Thomas's adventures, both in the traditional ballad and in the long, elaborate romance. It is one of the most

The Eildon Hills. As seen from near the Memorial Stone to Thomas the Rhymer.

Memorial Stone, dedicated to Thomas the Rhymer and standing at the foot of the Eildon Hills.

significant sources of information regarding Otherworld beliefs in British and, in the wider sense, European or Western tradition.

From the town of Melrose, we see the Eildons looming over our heads, but on the opposite side of the hills, a long walk leads up gently into the lower slopes. It was down this slope that Thomas the Rhymer was said to have walked when he emerged from his seven years of service to the Fairy Queen. Today a stone by the roadside marks the site, though this has been moved slightly in recent years to allow for road widening.

A flowering hawthorn tree.

THE HAWTHORN TREE

HOMAS IS ASSOCIATED closely with the hawthorn tree, traditionally the tree of the Fairy Queen and in earlier times of the Great Goddess. In the ballad and associated legend, it was a hawthorn tree under which he fell asleep. Hawthorn has a curious role in British folklore, for it is associated with death and is considered unlucky if brought into the house. Yet during certain ceremonies thorn-tree blossoms such as may or hawthorn are used freely as symbols of joy and rebirth. This spectrum of folklore is widened by its Celtic-Christian associations, such as those at Glastonbury, where a flowering thorn tree is central to the apocryphal legends surrounding the followers of Jesus, and the arrival of Joseph of Arimathea in Britain.

Originally the hawthorn was sacred to the Great Goddess who, in various aspects, was universally worshipped in ancient Europe. The Fairy Queen of legend is this same goddess in a traditional but hardly less daunting and powerful form. She has powers over life and death, transformation, blessing and cursing, and rules a mysterious and wonderful realm that extends far beneath the upper earth.

Just as Merlin aroused the primal dragons within the earth, and uttered far-

The Otherworld Tree, traditionally said to be half of green leaves and half of flames. In the vision of Thomas the Rhymer, the Otherworld was reached through rivers of blood and tears.

reaching prophecies as a result of those energies, so did Thomas, a historical person whose literary works remain in existence today, pass into the Otherworld or Underworld, to emerge with prophetic powers. Thomas's gift was known as the Tongue That Cannot Lie . . . a two-edged gift, as we might think today. The Eildon Tree, an aged hawthorn, remained in existence until as late as 1814, when it was blown over by a storm. The villagers of Earlston attempted to revive it in true Scottish fashion by pouring whisky over its roots (we are told), but to no avail. One of Thomas's local prophecies had declared, almost six hundred years before the storm, 'As long as the Thorn Tree stands/ Erceldoune shall keep its lands'. Following the collapse of the ancient tree in 1814, a chain of financial disasters struck the community, and their common land was sold to pay off debts.

THE UNDERWORLD INITIATION

HOMAS'S EXPERIENCE OF sleeping under the sacred tree, meeting an Otherworld queen, undertaking a magical journey, seeing wonders, and serving for a set period of time, are all recollections of an ancient system of initiation. This initiation, which took place within the Underworld, was the essential experience of the bard or poet, and of the prophet. After his harrowing and deeply transformative experiences, the bard is given mysterious gifts: a harp (the power of music), clothing of green (the power of the land), and the Tongue That Cannot Lie (a power of insight and prophecy). Anyone seeking to follow Thomas, therefore, into Fairyland, should think long and hard upon the possible results!

A Celtic harp.

114

MERLIN'S GRAVE

NOTHER OF THOMAS'S thirteenth-century prophecies stated 'When Tweed and Powsail meet at Merlin's Grave Then England and Scotland shall one monarch have'. When James VI of Scotland became James I of England, in 1603, following the death of Elizabeth I, the Tweed and Powsail flooded, and met together to form a new junction at the ancient block of stone known as Merlin's Grave.

This stone still stands at Drumelzier, where the Tweed is joined by the much smaller Powsail; it is possibly an ancient altar stone. Whatever its origins, Merlin's Grave is traditionally the site where the aged prophet was buried in the sixth century. He had fled to this region following the battle of Arthuret (now just across the English border, but then part of Scotland) in 573, in which great slaughter drove him mad with grief. Merlin was eventually stoned to death by angry pagans upon his acceptance of Christianity at the hands of St Kentigern. This tale is mentioned in early sources, and forms a curious counterpoint to the broader traditions on Merlin; it is, of course, a monastic rationalisation of the emergence of the Celtic Church from Druidism during the fifth and sixth centuries. More subtly, it may restate the important pagan sacrifice known as the Threefold Death, which was undergone by kings and sacred or inspired persons for the benefit of the land. Local people in Drumelzier say that Merlin's Grave was long marked by a hawthorn tree . . . yet another indication of the bardic or Underworld elements to the tale.

THE BALLAD OF THOMAS THE RHYMER

OTE: IN THIS text some of the Scottish dialect words have been Anglicised for the general reader. Detailed texts in the Scottish vernacular are found in F. J. Child's collection, *The English and Scottish Popular Ballads*, reprinted in paperback facsimile by Dover Books, New York, NY.

I

True Thomas lay on a grassy bank,
And he beheld a lady gay,
A lady that was brisk and bold,
To come riding o'er the ferny brae.

II

Her skirt was of the grass-green silk,
Her mantle of the velvet fine,
And on every lock of her horse's mane,
Hung fifty silver bells and nine.

III

True Thomas he took off his hat,
And bowed low down to his knee,
'All hail thou virgin, Queen of Heaven,
For your like on Earth I ne'er did see.'

IV

'Oh no, oh no, True Thomas,' she said,
'That name does not belong to me;
I am but the Queen of Fair Elfland
That has come for to visit here with thee.

V

'And you must go with me now, Thomas,
True Thomas you must go with me,
And you must serve me seven years,
Through good or ill as may chance to be.'

VI

She turned about her milk white steed
And took True Thomas up behind,
And aye whene'er the bridle rang,
The steed flew faster than the wind.

VII

For forty days and forty nights
They wade through red blood to the knee,
And he saw neither sun nor moon,
But heard the roaring of the sea.

VIII

Oh they rode on and further on,
Until they came to a garden tree,
'Light down, light down, you lady fair,
And I'll pull off that fruit for thee.'

IX

'Oh no, Oh no, True Thomas,' she says,
'That fruit may not be touched by thee,
For all the plagues that are in hell
Are upon the fruit of this country.

X

'But I have bread here in my lap,
Likewise a bottle of red wine,
And before that we go further on,
We shall rest, and you may dine.'

XI

When he had eaten and drunk his fill,
She said, 'Lay your head down on my knee,
And before we climb yon high high hill,
I will show you wonders three.

XII

'Oh do you see that broad broad road
That lies by the lily leven?
Oh that is the road of wickedness,
Though some call it the road to Heaven.

XIII

'And do you see that narrow narrow road
All beset with thorns and briars?
Oh that is the way of righteousness,
Though after it few enquires.

XIV

'And do you see that bonny bonny road
Which winds about the ferny brae?
Oh that is the road to Fair Elfland,
And together there you and I will go.

XV

'But Thomas you must hold your tongue

Whatever you may hear or see . . .
For if one word you chance to speak,
You will never get back to your own country.'

XVI

And he has gotten a coat of woven cloth,
Likewise the shoes of velvet green,
And till seven years were past and gone,
True Thomas ne'er on earth was seen.

The stark ballad of Thomas the Rhymer was preserved in oral tradition for at least six hundred years, sung as part of family education and entertainment. But the thirteenth-century ambience of the ballad and the historical nature of Thomas merely absorbed something even older, the Underworld or Otherworld vision. When such ballads were sung in later centuries, they provided picture sequences to open the imagination and were, in a very real sense, active parts of a magical tradition. When a magical ballad is sung, the *incantatory* quality is far greater than when we merely read the text upon a printed page.

Within oral tradition, particularly in Scotland, there were a number of such magical ballads, describing Otherworld adventures, loves, curses, and transformations. Though there is no suggestion that such matters were preserved *consciously*, as this would be nonsense, they were preserved on a dream-like or unconscious level. The strictness of traditional poetry and song was such that verse remained virtually unchanged for generations. (For analyses of magical ballads, see the authors' *The Underworld Initiation*, Aquarian Press, Welling-borough, 1989, and *Where is Saint George?*, Blandford Press, London, 1988.)

It is increasingly difficult for modern people, thoroughly conditioned to television, to relate to the culture of past centuries, when people generated images through song and stories. We can only hope that this magical power, of image-making through simple verses and spoken words, common to us all, does not finally vanish away completely, back into the Otherworld from which it was said to have originally appeared.

The Tongue That Cannot Lie

It has always seemed to me that many parts are concealed in the story of Thomas the Rhymer; not missing, but inherent in the stark imagery and progression of his Otherworld journey and visions, as they are preserved in tradition. In this tale, we hear from Thomas himself some of the details of his experiences beneath the earth, and at the close we gain some hints of the adventures that he was forbidden by the Queen of Elfland to describe, on pain of never being able to return home. The story is compressed, in part, from my forthcoming novel, *The Adventures of Thomas Rhymer*, where by a subtle trick we are allowed to hear that which Thomas was originally forbidden to tell.

It is hard to be always telling the truth. By this I do not mean that it is hard not to tell lies, but exactly what I say . . . that it is hard to always be telling the truth. The truth is sharp, and it stabs. But that is only part of the problem, for the worst is when people declare the truth to be a lie. That is the most stabbing blow of all.

Having gained some notoriety as both a lady's man and a staunch patriotic fighter in my younger days, it seemed quite natural to meet a beautiful, dark-haired woman beneath the hawthorn tree. And what followed after was natural also, but of a different order of nature. To most people it merely meant that when I returned my verses had changed, and that I was no longer the great laird and lover roaming the Borders. There can only be one great love in a man's life, or many lesser ones; for some men it is God, or perhaps the Church itself, while for others there may, if they are lucky, be a wife, or more painfully but no less sweet, someone else's wife as in the tale of Tristan that I have written of elsewhere. She whom I loved precludes all such lesser rivals. But I am married to a good wife, a shrewd and well-arranged marriage as is the custom, and I have a son. He will leave all my estates to the Church, but the hare will dance upon our hearth-stone soon enough and houses and barns are not always home. Even the sacred hawthorn tree will fall in time, and a forest will conquer an unconquered castle that no army has entered before.

That was a mild example of truth-telling, by the way, though you may not have noticed it. That is really what people prefer, simple truths that pass unnoticed until after the event. They do not want to be told what will occur, merely what has already occurred. There are plenty of daft old biddies roaming the Lowlands who will tell your fortune, so do not ask a bard for such pointless nonsense. But what I would tell of is that which is assumed to be the lie, or at the best (which is a poor best) the poet's dream. But it is truth, and reality, and more true than I dare express.

We travelled for a long, long time under the earth. The stallion passed straight through the side of the hill, and where I had expected a tunnel or a cave there was a wide flat plain. Although it felt like a wide flat plain, at least as far as the flatness of the ground and the speed of the horse, I could see neither to the right nor left, nor above, and it was impossible to measure any space in that place. The stallion seemed to move with great speed, and I saw that the silver bells upon the bridle were in fact tiny silver skulls. I knew fear then, such a fear of death as I had never felt while wielding a sword against the barbarian English.

And because there was no measure of space, there was no measure of time: I held to that slim waist and felt her dark curls scented with white blossom blowing into my face. When the terror ceased I swore to myself that I would never idly court a woman again if this was what it led to. But at that stage in my journey I hardly knew her, and had not become fully her servant. After some time, immeasurable, the silver bells no longer made me shiver; I foolishly began to wonder how one measured time in a place with no distance, no sun, no moon. With that thought I became aware of a faint, deep, roaring sound that grew and grew more rapidly as the stallion galloped on. With the roaring came a sound as of flowing water, and the hoof-beats, at first dry and hard, began to splash. Soon the horse slowed and seemed to be struggling against the flow of a great river.

Yet he never faltered nor stumbled, and as the roaring increased until it seemed to fill the vast emptiness through which we travelled, I knew it to be the sound of a great ocean. I looked down, for hearing the sea I expected to find water all around us. To my horror I realised that the liquid rising up, reaching to my knees, was as red as blood. As I heard the ocean, and saw the blood, I discovered that a faint night sky with many brilliant stars had opened out overhead. It was as if we had travelled through a void, but were now reaching a defined place at last. It was then that she told me that the roaring sea was an ocean of suffering, and that two rivers, one of blood and one of salt tears, flowed through that land. But all of that seemed commonplace when we came to the tree.

In the song I called it 'a garden green' or sometimes 'an apple tree'; there seemed no point in describing it fully, and it was, in truth, a green tree bearing apples set in a garden. In recent years some literary poet, who perhaps heard me talking late one night before the fire, has made a great complex poem of my journey, and he describes a tree of many different fruits.

> Sche led him in-till a faire herbere,
> Whare frwte was growand gret plentee:
> Pere and appill, bothe ryppe thay were.
> The date, and als the damasee.

Thomas the Rhymer meets the Fairy Queen.

> The fygge, and alsso the wyneberye,
> And nyghtgales byggande on thair neste.

The nightingales were his own invention, of course, because he could not imagine a magical tree and a beautiful woman alone in the company of a poet without nightingales.

If I told you the type of winged creatures that sang in that tree, you would call me a liar: they had wings taller than the height of a man, of coloured flame that moved with great speed, and their claws and beaks were of pure flashing gold. Each one had seven eyes that turned, each eye was of a different primary colour and radiated the light of each of the seven planets; their voices were as the blowing of a mighty organ, of harps, of flutes, of deep, booming drums and the sweet timbre of viols. And they were the least of the inhabitants of that tree. I said, truthfully, that you would not believe me.

But when we reached the tree, before I saw into its branches, I had a sudden rush of romantic ardour come upon me again – I suppose it was the joy at being somewhere defined at last, and being out of the blood. Indeed, I must tell the truth and say that I could not see the tree fully. It was surrounded by haze or golden mist, and I did not, at first, notice that it was not a normal tree in a green garden. The garden – well, it was a small plot of grass, quite ordinary grass, set within an irregular, circular stone wall. A good old farmer's wall, such as we have all over the Borders. It was the garden plot and the dry stone wall that fooled me.

The stallion leapt over the wall, for there was no gate. As he leapt the garden seemed to grow larger, for we galloped through rich pasture approaching the tree for a long time without ever reaching it. Eventually she bent over the horse's neck and whispered to him, and he slowed to a walk. Immediately we were at the foot of the tree. It grew far above us, surrounded by a glowing mist, and there, right in front of my nose, was a simple apple branch with a ripe fruit upon it. Naturally I leapt from the horse, made my best bow, opened my mouth and offered to pick it for her; no gentleman or poet could have done less.

She dismounted, or rather she suddenly stood by my side, her long white fingers gripping my wrist with terrible strength. She forbade me to pluck the fruit, offering me instead bread and wine from a little sack that was slung across the horse's neck. I never believed, even then, that all the ills of the world were in that one apple . . . but I am glad to this day that I did not pluck it. We sat beneath the tree, and I ate the moist golden bread and drank the rich dark wine. Then she caused me to look up into the branches, and I saw the tree truly for the first time.

Up and up it rose: I saw crystal fruits burning with inner light, and the glowing haze thinned to reveal the winged creatures, for it had been the motion of their wings that created the mist. Higher in the branches were beings that looked back at me, with eyes that stripped me bare beyond my deepest, secret heart; and if I described their faces to you, you would not think me a man of truth. The leaves of that tree were of silver with golden veins, and some were of flames that burned silently, giving off light instead of heat. I saw the sun and the moon holding hands as man and woman, and the Blessed Child sitting in a fork of the branches above them, but when he looked down and saw her who was with me, he struck the living wood a great shivering blow with his tiny hand, and a many-voiced chiming sound, like a chorus of bells, vibrated the length of the tree. The winged creatures folded their pinions about the fruit; sun and moon and the crystals and flaming leaves turned black as the night.

Suddenly we sat under a gnarled old apple tree, and she told me to lay my head in her lap and sleep. This I did, for the long journey, the bread and wine, and the sight of that tree had made me very sleepy.

When I awoke we seemed to be in open country again, and far away upon the horizon a huge stone wall rose up, marking some distant boundary that ran as far as the eye could see, both right and left. There was neither sun nor moon visible in the sky, but there were many brilliant stars, and the land itself seemed lit from within by a green vital light. I felt rested and energetic, and lay for a while with my head resting upon her lap, though she knew I was awake. It seemed absurd that this woman had been my lover under the ancient tree at Erceldoune; she was a great queen, and I was merely a humble poet.

She bid me rise and look about me. I stood at the foot of a tall standing-stone, such as we have in many parts of Scotland. I was sure that there had been some kind of tree in that place before I slept. Doing as she commanded, I turned a full circle to spy out the land. The great wall, on the far horizon, seemed to run on for ever, but there were places where it was hidden from sight by hills, both high and low. It was impossible to tell where north was, as there was no sun, and none of the stars were familiar. No more than one Scottish mile from the standing-stone was a high mountain, rising into the sky. Far beyond this solitary mountain I could see the wall, and immediately before us was a path leading from the upright stone where we stood, and eventually branching into three.

These were the three wondrous roads that everyone sings about; one led off to the left up the steepest side of the mountain through a thorny thicket – the Road of Righteousness, she called it. The other was broad and well paved, and meandered gently through a great field filled with lilies. This, she said, was the Road of Wickedness, known in my land as the Road to Heaven. The third road was the middle one, leading off into a sloping ferny brae, and eventually curving and meandering away out of sight around the other side of the great mountain. This, she said, was the Road to Elfland that we would take.

The horse had gone, and we set off down the middle road, our feet hardly seeming to touch the path. There were no shadows, and only the faintest breeze blowing. As we came around the side of the mountain, the wind increased; I heard deep horns blowing, and to my astonishment saw before us a great entrance-way carved out of the mountainside, with tall towers bearing long green banners that snapped and streamed forth. The flowing air was warm, and issued out of the mountain from between lofty bronze gates that stood wide open.

Within the mountain, beyond the gates, I could see a vast cavern, with many fair buildings in it. There were great halls of shining marble and crystal and brass, tall wooden spires carved with rich patterns; every window was open and brimming with light, every door was flung wide and uttering music. There was a great feast being held in that city, and the sound of laughter came to me in the warm scented wind, mingling with the deep rumbling of horns and the booming of bass gongs. I stood in wonder and astonishment, for she told me that I was to spend seven years in this place, learning, watching, serving. Then she turned to look upon me in her full power, and I sank to my knees in awe, in terror, in joy. She laid a vow of silence upon me before we entered those lofty bronze gates, so I may tell you no more of what came to pass in that place.

But when I emerged or, I should say, when I was ejected, for suddenly one morning I awoke and found myself in the ferns on Eildon side, I brought three gifts out with me. The first was a harp, richly made of red wood shot through with golden and black markings, inlaid with polished stones and always tuned, no matter what the weather or the heat of the hall in which I play. That was the first gift and the easiest to win, for those people are renowned as great lovers of music, and I was, in my way, not unskilled. The second gift was a pair of green shoes of a skin that not even the most skilled leather-worker can identify; they were the second gift and much harder to win, though in my youth I was renowned as a runner. The third gift was a great velvet cloak, woven into a pattern of green leaves and golden-red flames, with a deep hood that sheds rain water. That cloak never lets the wearer become wet or cold, or even over-warm in summer; he who wears it may blend in with the forest shadows and touch the shy wild deer, or walk unnoticed down the filthy streets of Edinburgh at noon, casting only the thinnest of wavering shadows behind him. And that was the hardest of all to win, though I was known as a hardy warrior when I was young.

Well, I knew that you would believe none of this, so I will tell you the greatest gift that she gave me, one that I did not even know of until I returned to the outer world . . . it was the Tongue That Cannot Lie.

9·iona and the sacred isles

Iona is a tiny island off the coast of the large island of Mull in the Hebrides, off the west coast of Scotland. There is nothing upon the map to show that this is one of the great spiritual centres of Britain and Europe – but from this speck in the sea the Celtic Church expanded into Scotland, England, and extended its influence for several centuries through Europe. There are indications that before it was a Celtic Christian settlement, the island was a Druid sanctuary; the first Celtic Christian priests were often Druids or members of noble Irish

Iona.

families; tradition tells us that the Druids knew of the coming of Christ before the first missionaries appeared in their land. Whatever the truth of this matter, we do know that the original Celtic Church predated that of Rome, and that the evangelising of pagan Britain was not initiated by St Augustine (as is frequently stated) but by various preaching movements and monasteries that can be traced directly back to Iona. Later missionary work, such as that of Augustine, was more concerned with control of existing Christians and encouraging or enforcing them to conform to Roman practice.

Iona is visited by thousands of people annually, for in the last fifty years it has once again risen to command attention as a spiritual centre, after several centuries of quiescence. The island is reached by a short ferry trip from Mull, which in turn is reached by a longer ferry trip from the mainland fishing port of Oban. It is a remarkable tribute to Iona, and to its heritage and power, that people travel from all over the world merely to walk, rest, and pray or meditate in this insignificant speck of rock emerging from the sea, isolated from all the major events of the world.

But what are the origins of this power? We can only make half-educated guesses at the Druid past from the little general evidence available to us, but there is more evidence of the Celtic Christian roots of Iona. A combination of the two traditions will help to define Iona's unique quality and its historical and spiritual importance in Britain.

PAGAN ORIGINS

HERE IS SOME evidence from Iona place-names that Druidic associations were retained upon the island for many centuries. In addition to this, we find some curious half-propagandist accounts of Druidism in the early texts that recount the founding of the Christian community upon the island. The over-all evidence from both classical and native Celtic accounts shows clearly that islands were regarded as the locations of, or gateways to, the Otherworld. Druid colleges were located upon western islands in Britain and Ireland. Perhaps the most famous one was destroyed by Suetonius Paulinus and his troops in the first century AD, when they attacked the college upon Anglesey off the north-west coast of Wales. The Hebrides and Orkneys – off the west and far northern coasts of Scotland – each have special legends and attributes as sacred islands, particularly as locations of the Otherworld. The island of Skye held a school for warriors, where they were instructed by the warrior-queen, Scathach, according to the *Cuchullain Saga*. Many other figures in legend, including Merlin, are associated with offshore islands, while the mysterious Fortunate Isles, the archetype of this theme, were ruled by the priestess or goddess, Morgen, who held all arts and sciences in the control of herself and her Nine Sisters.

Thus it comes as no surprise that Iona, with its great spiritual heritage from the Celtic Church, should have an undercurrent of Druidic and Otherworld tradition. In a region where the word *druíd* is still used in Gaelic, and associated with many Hebridean and western Scottish place-names, where the second sight and the lore of the fairies still persist even today, we would expect to find such sacred islands as were venerated and inhabited by the Celts, their Druids, and perhaps by the pre-Celtic population also.

CELTIC CHRISTIAN ROOTS AND THE ARRIVAL OF ST COLUMBA

St Columba's Bay. The site of the first landing of Columba and his twelve followers on their evangelical mission to Scotland. There had, in fact, been some previous Christian presence in the Dalriadic west of Scotland, but from Iona, Celtic Christianity spread through Scotland, England, and Europe long before the ascendancy of the Roman Church.

 HE MODERN HISTORY of Iona begins with the arrival of St Columba from Ireland on 12 May AD563. This date marked the beginning of one of the greatest spiritual movements ever known across Britain and Europe. But there is some evidence of an earlier Christian settlement in the region, for the Scots of Argyle, the Dalriadic Scots, were of the persuasion of St Patrick, who died in 458 after evangelising Ireland. This early Christian influence is supported by a reference in the *Litany of Angus the Culdee* in which seven bishops of Iona – or Hii, as it was then called – are mentioned. The earliest saint known in the region is Oran, perhaps the same person as Oran of Latteragh, Tipperary, in Ireland. His name is given to the Relig Oran upon Iona where the Scottish kings are buried, to a burial ground on the island of Colonsay, and to a district in

Mull known as Tir Oran or the Land of Oran. This particular Culdee or Celtic saint died fifteen years before Columba arrived in Scotland, though he also appears in a curious tale of human sacrifice at Iona as a contemporary of Columba, and we shall return to this motif shortly when we examine the founding of the great abbey upon the island.

Columba was born in Ireland on 7 December AD521, at Gartan in Donegal. His father and mother were both members of the Irish and British Dalriadic royal families, and he was christened Colum (Dove) by his foster-father and spiritual mentor, Cruithnechan. It is most significant to note that while he was brought up within the Irish Celtic Church, he also studied bardic lore, which at this time was virtually inseparable from Druidic lore, under Gemman, bard of the province of Leinster. Druidism had been proscribed and shattered by the Romans five or six centuries earlier in Europe and southern Britain, but flourished untouched in Ireland and many parts of Scotland. Thus the early Irish Celtic Church spread its gospel directly into a Druidic pagan culture, rather than into a post-Roman one in which many religious cults were fused together as a result of the imperial presence.

Columba, of royal lineage, with bardic and Christian upbringing, eventually rose within the Church, and by 553 he had founded the great Monastery of Durrow. The famous *Book of Durrow*, which survives from this period, is sometimes ascribed to Columba as its copyist. It is a set of gospels in the vernacular language of the time, ornamented in the early Celtic style. The more elaborate *Book of Kells* housed at Trinity College, Dublin, is called – in the *Annals of the Four Masters* – the *Great Gospel of Columba*, though it is not certain how accurate this traditional ascription may be. Between 544 and 562, he founded a number of churches in Ireland, and was clearly a tireless and devoted follower of Christ in the active monastic tradition of his day.

COLUMBA IS EXILED

T SEEMS THAT Columba may have been exiled from Ireland for a very modern-sounding dispute: infringement of the laws of copyright. If this tale is true, he copied a psalter, and the original owner demanded judgement from the King of Ireland upon the rights of ownership of the copy. *'Le gach bo a bionenn agus le gach leabhar a leabrhan'*, was the judgement: 'to every cow belongs her calf and to every book its copy'. As the king was a member of the southern O'Neills, Columba incited the northern O'Neills (to whom he was kin) to avenge this judgement in battle. Although the northern O'Neills won the battle of Cuildremhue in 561, Columba was charged before a great assembly with inciting such bloodshed, and was banished from the land and ordered to convert as many souls as he had caused to be slain in the dispute over the book.

This curious tale may be a rationalisation of the battle that occurred around the time that the saint left upon his missionary work, though we should not underestimate the pride-and-honour code of the Irish nobility and dismiss the entire tale out of hand. The Celtic Church was an active missionary movement,

128

dedicated to spreading the gospel among all people and, incidentally, offering it in their native tongues rather than in exclusive and inaccessible Latin – though this was also widely used in the Church and learned circles. It seems most unlikely, therefore, that Columba's missionary work would have been a penance or a punishment. Furthermore, he is recorded as having returned to Ireland on several occasions, and his body was taken there for protection from Viking raiders and returned to Iona . . . none of this fits with a sentence of exile for inciting warfare.

His main biographer, Adamnan, simply states that 'Columba, resolving to seek a foreign country for the love of Christ, sailed from Scotia [i.e. Ireland] to Britain [i.e. Scotland]' (Adamnan, Bk II, Chap. 42). On 12 May, when forty-two years old, Columba landed with twelve followers at Port-a-Curach. The name simply means port of the currach, a currach being a leather-hide boat such as was widely used for centuries by the Irish and Scots. A small cairn called 'arn cul-ri Eirin' (the hill of turning one's back to Ireland) upon the hill west of the port, marks the spot where Columba searched the horizon for his homeland, and discovered that it could no longer be seen.

THE FIRST MONASTERY

Iona Abbey. This ancient worship site, probably one of the oldest in Britain, is now restored as a working religious community through the efforts of dedicated Scots.

HE PRESENT-DAY CATHEDRAL is a restoration of the last great medieval church to be built upon Iona. Its modern presence is a tribute to the vision, effort and dedication of many Scots who worked towards its completion in the twentieth century. But the original monastic settlements, as described in retrospect by Adamnan, was very different in style and concept. It consisted of a simple circle of huts around a central green. Worship was conducted in a mud-and-wattle church with an adjoining sacristy, and a refectory and

kitchen served the communal needs of the members. There was, additionally, a guest house and the abbot's hut, which was set slightly apart from those of the brothers.

The pattern is almost identical to the descriptions of the Celtic monastery at Glastonbury far to the south, and follows the standard early Irish monastic design. The entire settlement was enclosed by a rath or earth-and-stone rampart with an exterior ditch. If we divorce the settlement from its religious context it is essentially a typical Celtic settlement or village, with the important distinction of being dedicated to religious purposes and having a central church. The concept of the grand cathedral was not to develop for several centuries. The monks lived by fishing and farming, combining the disciplines of manual work, meditation and prayer with the arts of worship such as chanting, copying texts and stone or wood carving.

From this humble centre, Scotland and northern England were converted to Celtic Christianity. So great was the force of this missionary movement that by 574 Columba could crown Aidan King of Scots upon Iona. Here we find an indication that Iona was previously a sacred isle, for Aidan is said to have been crowned upon the Destiny Stone, which was sacred to kingship. This stone is reputed to be part of the English Coronation Chair today (visible in Westminster Abbey), and certainly a sacred stone was carried off by the conquering English King Edward I in 1296. By this time the stone had become

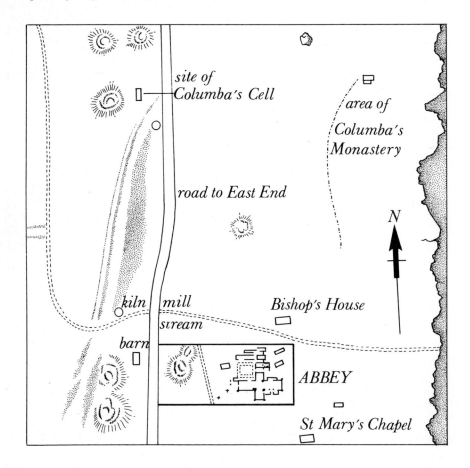

site of
Columba's Cell

area of
Columba's
Monastery

road to East End

N

kiln | mill
stream

Bishop's House

barn

ABBEY

St Mary's Chapel

Plan of the ancient and medieval monastery locations, showing that the original site was to the north of the later stone-built Cathedral (from the 1898 guide-book).

130

lodged at Scone, the traditional election site for Scottish kings, and was a totem or sacred object of great importance and significance to the Scots . . . and, of course, to the English, who would not otherwise have taken it.

DEATH OF COLUMBA AND THE FATE OF IONA

OLUMBA DIED ON 9 June 597. Knowing in advance of his death, he had ascended a little hill overlooking the monastery and uttered these famous words:

Small and mean though this place is, yet it shall be held in great and unusual honour, not only by Scotic kings and people, but also by the rulers of foreign and barbarous nations, and by their subjects; the saints, also of other churches, shall regard it with no common reverence.   (Adamnan, Bk III. Chap. 24)

St Columba's Shrine. By the main entrance to the abbey, this small chapel commemorates the great saint of the Celtic Church. The shrine does not mark Columba's tomb, and his relics were moved more than once to avoid plundering Vikings. Nevertheless, the atmosphere of this simple shrine is impressive.

The position of Abbot of Iona was retained for several generations among the *coarb* or extended family of Columba. It was an hereditary appointment, with what might be regarded as mystical or magical undertones, similar to those of the Irish kings or sacred priest-kings of the classical and ancient world.

By the eighth century, however, the Roman Church began to extend its grasp towards Iona and the other, established, Celtic settlements, seeking to bring them under its power. The ensuing disputes, which were eventually won by the Roman Church, greatly weakened the power of the original order. Within a hundred years, however, disputes over papal authority and the date of Easter were hardly relevant, as the plundering Danes burnt the ancient monastery, and around 802 killed all sixty-eight members of the remaining Iona community. The remains of Columba were removed to Ireland, though they were later returned to Iona in 818. In 829, Abbot Blathmac was killed by Danes when he refused to tell them the place of Columba's shrine. From this period onwards Iona slowly declined in importance as head of the Celtic Church in Scotland, and the focus of power moved to the mainland. By the eleventh century, the undermining of the independent Scottish Celtic Church was partially completed by Margaret, the English wife of Malcolm Canmore.

Later ecclesiastical buildings, including the elegant nunnery ruins still visible today, date from the period of post-Celtic monastic development.

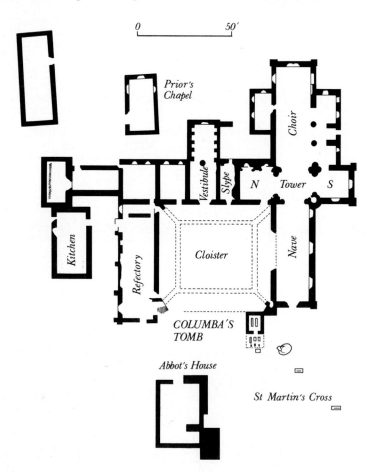

Plan of Iona Cathedral (redrawn from the 1898 guide-book by Rev. Archibald Macmillan).

132

THE RELIG ORAN, BURIAL PLACE OF KINGS

 NE OF THE most interesting sites upon Iona, seeming to bridge the pagan and Christian heritage of the island, is the ancient burial site of the Relig Oran. The custom of carrying kings and nobles to sacred islands for burial is typically pagan, and is summarised in the legend of King Arthur, who was carried to the Fortunate Isles for his eventual cure, awaiting a time to return to his people. The magical islands of the Otherworld were often identified with actual sites, places where the barrier between the worlds is thin. Iona is undoubtedly one such place, and this is well attested by the ancient custom of burying Scottish kings and nobles on the island.

Nor was the custom limited to the Scots, for an early account tells us that there were originally three communal tombs, 'formit like little chapels' (Monro, Dean of the Isles, 1594). The tombs were in a north-south line, surrounded by a wall, and contained, respectively, kings of Norway, Scotland, and Ireland. By far the greater number were Scots, but the presence of Norse and Irish rulers strengthens the ritual practice of burial upon the sacred isle. It is interesting to note that Macbeth and his wife, Gruach, were buried on Iona, giving us an insight into the character of this much-vilified king, who was, historically, a good ruler. His killer and successor, Malcolm Canmore, however, was not conveyed to the sacred isle, perhaps due to the deliberate attempts of his wife, Margaret, to destroy the old Celtic Church power.

The name Oran refers to a Culdee or early Celtic saint, who may have preceded Columba into the west of Scotland. It hints that the burial site is connected to early religious practices. We also have a very curious tale, in which Oran is made into a member of Columba's original band of twelve. The *Leathar Breac,* an old Irish text, contains an account of Columba's life, and describes the founding of the first church as follows:

The Relig Oran. The chapel commemorates Oran, who is possibly a pre-Columban Celtic saint. The burial ground of the Relig Oran holds the remains of Scottish, Irish, and Norse kings and lords, and was for many centuries a sacred location for the interment of kings.

Colum Celli then said to his people, 'It is good for us that our roots should go under the ground here,' and he said to them, 'it is permitted to you that one of you may go under the clay of this island to consecrate it.'

(MacMillan, A., *Iona*, 1898)

Oran volunteered to be this human sacrifice, and Columba stated that no prayer would be answered at his own grave after death, unless it was asked first of Oran. But the story does not end here, for after the third day of interment – for Oran was buried alive – the tomb was opened. Oran still breathed, opened his eyes, and said to Columba, 'Death is no wonder, nor is Hell as it is said.' Columba made haste to cover the saint again, with the words that passed into Gaelic folklore as a widespread proverb: 'Earth, earth upon the mouth of Oran, lest he talk more'.

Here we have a curious tale indeed, for the historical Oran seems to have died fifteen years before Columba came to Iona, and may have preached the gospel in the isles before the settlement of Iona was founded, yet the tale itself has many resonances of pagan Druidic tradition, and need not be discarded as fantasy. It represents the traditions that predate the advent of Columba . . . those of sacred earth, dedicated souls seeking the Otherworld through sacrifice, and the function of the dead as prophets and communicators. The key to the entire tale is perhaps found in the curious statement that no one could have a prayer granted by Columba unless they first asked it of Oran: the new order is founded upon the old. Thus the burial site of the kings is traditionally connected with the Otherworld or Druidic cult of the sacred land, prophecy, and spiritual mediation.

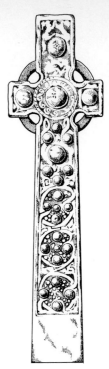

St Martin's Cross, Iona.

IONA TODAY

AT ONE TIME the remains visible upon Iona in and around the monastic settlements and the Relig Oran were considerable, and even today the remaining carved stones and crosses are of great skill and beauty. The modern visitor sees only a fraction of what once stood upon this sacred isle, but the spiritual power of the restored Cathedral, and the various ancient locations around the island, are still evident. The visitor can obtain several excellent guide-books and there are guided tours available in the summer, but it is the lone walker who is best able to grasp the spirit of Iona, which comes through peaceful meditation. Two traditional sites are of interest in the context of Celtic legend and monastic history. The first is a tiny spring called the Well of Eternal Youth, situated upon Iona's highest hill. Such names reflect a very ancient heritage, deep in Celtic myth, for a sacred spring or well of youth and wisdom lies at the very heart of the Celtic mythos.

To the west of the island may be found the ruins of what is now called the Hermit's Cell, a circular structure of uncertain age, with a large stone enclosure built into the cliff nearby. These mysterious remains form the setting for the story, *The Hermit*, which follows this chapter.

Well of Eternal Youth. A tiny spring on the summit of Iona's highest hill, this natural water-source may have Druidic associations, though there is no way of proving such connections historically.

Hermit's Cell. These ruins, on the western uplands of Iona, are traditionally said to be the dwelling of a hermit.

134

FIONA MACLEOD AND THE
ISLAND OF THE GRAIL

T IS NOT possible to deal, even briefly, with Iona without mentioning the remarkable work of William Sharp, a nineteenth-century mystic who wrote under the pseudonym of Fiona Macleod. Sharp was steeped in Celtic tradition, and recreated many of his works from genuine sources, though with a leavening of creative or poetic imagination. To conclude this chapter on some aspects of Iona (for it would take a large book to deal with its entire history and legendary tradition), we can quote the words of Sharp, which to this day have not been improved upon:

A few places in the world are to be held holy, because of the love which consecrates them and the faith which enshrines them. Their names are themselves talismans of spiritual beauty. Of these is Iona.

The Arabs speak of Mecca as a holy place before the time of the prophet, saying that Adam himself lies buried here: and, before Adam, that the sons of Allah, who are called Angels, worshipped; and that when Allah Himself stood upon perfected Earth it was on this spot. And here, they add, when there is no man left upon earth, an angel shall gather up the dust of this world, and say to Allah, 'There is nothing left in the whole earth but Mecca: and now Mecca is but the few grains of sand that I hold in the hollow of my palm, O Allah.'

In spiritual geography Iona is the Mecca of the Gael.

It is but a small isle, fashioned of a little sand, a few grasses salt with the spray of an ever-restless wave, a few rocks that wade in heather and upon whose brows the sea-wind weaves the yellow lichen. But since the remotest days sacrosanct men have bowed here in worship. In this little island a lamp was lit whose flame lighted pagan Europe, from the Saxon in his fens to the swarthy folk who came by Greek waters to trade the Orient. Here Learning and Faith had their tranquil home, when the shadow of the sword lay upon all lands, from Syracuse by the Tyrrhene Sea to the rainy isles of Orcc. From age to age, lowly hearts have never ceased to bring their burthen here. Iona herself has given us for remembrance a fount of youth more wonderful than that which lies under her own boulders of Dûn-I. And here Hope waits.

To tell the story of Iona is to go back to God, and to end in God.

But to write of Iona, there are many ways of approach. No place that has a spiritual history can be revealed to those who know nothing of it by facts and descriptions. The approach may be through the obscure glens of another's mind and so out by the moonlit way, as well as by the track that thousands travel. I have nothing to say of Iona's acreage, or fisheries, or pastures: nothing of how the islanders live. These things are the accidental. There is small difference in simple life anywhere. Moreover, there are many to tell all that need be known.

There is one Iona, a little island of the west. There is another Iona, of which I would speak. I do not say that it lies open to all. It is as we come that we find. If we come, bringing nothing with us, we go away ill-content, having seen and heard nothing of what we had vaguely expected to see or hear. It is another Iona than the Iona of sacred memories and prophecies: Iona the metropolis of dreams. None can understand it who does not see it through its pagan light, its Christian light, its singular blending of paganism and romance and spiritual beauty. There is, too, an Iona that is more than Gaelic, that is more than a place rainbow-lit with the seven desires of the world, the Iona that, if we will it so, is a mirror of your heart and of mine.

(*Iona*, Floris Books, Edinburgh, 1982, pp. 93-5)

These words are as true now as then, for they describe an ever-changing place that can transport the willing visitor into other dimensions. They touch upon an aspect of Iona that has seldom been noticed.

The thirteenth-century romance known as *Sone de Nausai* is unique among texts dealing with the subject of the Grail in that it introduces actual places and historical events into its narrative, which is otherwise a straightforward historical romance of the Crusades. There are several episodes of a fantastic nature, of which the following is one.

Sone, who was possibly a real historical personage from Alcase, takes service with Alain, the King of Norway, whose lands have been invaded by Irish and Scots. Having killed the King of Ireland in battle, Sone undertakes a single combat with the giant champion of the Scots. In order to ensure divine favour in this battle, Sone and King Alain visit a certain island where there is a monastic community and a number of extraordinary relics.

The description of the island and its community is so like that of Otherworldly palaces found within the pages of Arthurian romance that we are quite clearly in the realm of wonder. The effect of this is reinforced when the Abbot takes Sone and Alain on a tour of the abbey and shows them the relics. These include the body of Joseph of Arimathea and his son Adan (Aidan?) together with the Grail and the Spear that wounded Christ. All this is described in terms familiar to students of the Grail myths.

What is interesting to us here is the siting and description of the island. In the romance it is presumed to be somewhere off the coast of Norway; but 'Norway' here is a misnomer. In Geoffrey of Monmouth's *Historia Regum Brittaniae (History of the Kings of Britain)* where Arthur is said to rule over Scandinavia, Norway is sometimes translated as Llychlyn, which is a name also applied to the Otherworld. In *Sone de Nausai* we are also told that 'Norway' was once called Logres, and that it was protected by the magical sword of Joseph of Arimathea. Logres is the name for Arthur's Britain in the romance, and there is an historical tomb of Norwegian kings on Iona.

There are echoes here of several Otherworldly islands off the coast of Britain – in particular Grassholm where Bran the Blessed entertained the Company of the Noble Head in a manner similar to the abbey's hospitality of Sone and Alain (whose own name is, of course, the same as the Grail King in several texts). But it is the similarity to the great Chrisian communities at Lindisfarne and Iona that springs to mind as one reads the story of Sone. The spirit of Celtic Christianity they represented has long been recognised as Grail-centred, and many of the beliefs taught by the wandering Celtic monks in the fifth to eighth centuries gave fuel to the growing impulse of mystical Christianity that was to blossom forth in the romances of the Grail.

We make no excuse, therefore, for setting this story of the Grail and the Waste Land on Iona. Although it cannot be proved nor disproved that there was ever such a community as described here, anyone who visits the beautiful and haunted island cannot fail to recognise the atmosphere of mystery and wonder that is the hallmark of the Grail and Arthurian legends.

The Island of Sorrow and Joy

It is often wrongly assumed that only men went on quests or had adventures in the Arthurian world. In fact, women played an extremely important role in the whole of the Arthurian mythos and one in particular, Dindraine, the sister of Perceval, sacrificed herself for another lady and thus enabled the three Grail knights to achieve their quest on behalf of the whole realm of Logres. Dindraine's body is carried with them to the holy city of Sarras and she is buried there along with Galahad, after the achieving of the mysteries – the first man and woman of earthly lineage to be interred there.

There is a sense in which Dindraine represents Guinevere, Arthur's queen, in the same way that the wounded king stands as a surrogate of Arthur himself. The relationship of king and land, as discussed elsewhere in this book and in the forthcoming *Arthur and the Sovereignty of Britain* by Caitlín Matthews (Arkana, London 1989) is one of the deepest themes of the present book. This story, in a way, complements *Drustan's Ghost* (pp. 10–15). There we saw how the planned marriage of king and land was hindered by the love of Drustan and Isolt. This was one of the causes of the Waste Land, as was the later wounding of the Grail King. In this story, set on the island of Iona, we see a kind of solution in which Dindraine/Guinevere offers a sacifice for the sake of the king and the land.

You will all have heard of the Waste Lands; how in the time of Arthur there came a day when nothing would grow, no new seeds sprouted, no fresh leaves grew on the trees, the rivers ran dry and the streambeds were cracked and empty. Many tales are told of how this came to be, and of how it ended. Many record how the wondrous Grail passed through the land at that time, and what happened because of it. This is one such tale, but it has not been told before.

There were two brothers, and their names were Bran and Sgeolan. They eked out a living as fishermen on the inhospitable western coast of the Island of the Mighty, and though it was a hard life, it was less so than formerly, before the Irish raiders were driven away by the warriors of Arthur. So the brothers were content enough, until there came upon them the events that were to change them both forever, and change the history of the Island of the Mighty. This was the way of it. One morning, at the end of summer, there came a knock at the door of the bothy where Bran and Sgeolan dwelt, and when Bran opened it there stood a figure muffled deeply against the cold, who when it spoke had a woman's voice. And that surprised Bran as much as anything, for it was not often even in those times that one saw a woman unattended, especially not one who spoke like a noble. But he bade her come in to the fire, and when she pushed back the hood of her cloak he saw that she had a fine pale face with great dark eyes in it, and a look upon her of one that had come far with little food and less shelter.

So Bran got her some bread and some of the soup from the cauldron that hung by the fire, and when some of the pinched look had gone from her face he asked her politely enough what brought her to that lonely place. And she said: 'You and your brother are fishermen. You have a boat. I would take passage with you.'

Bran was so surprised at this, and at the strange way the woman talked, that he quite forgot to notice that she knew he had a brother, though Sgeolan was at that moment away working at the nets down by the shore. But he nodded anyway and said cautiously, 'Where might you wish to go, lady?'

'To the island,' said she, and Bran grew pale as she spoke, for though there were many islands off the coast, yet he knew somehow that she meant but one of them, and that had a grim history that kept most men away from its shores. When he made no answer, the woman spoke again. 'I must get across to the island. You are the only ones who can take me. Please!'

'I must ask my brother,' said Bran

The woman sat still. 'He is coming,' she said, 'ask him now.' And before Bran could say more, the door opened and Sgeolan came in with a gust of chill air, beating his hands against his sides to warm them. He stopped in surprise when he saw the woman, and looked a question at his brother.

'This lady wishes us to take her to the island,' said Bran carefully. 'What is your word, brother?'

Sgeolan said, 'That is something I would not wish to do.'

The woman said again, 'Please!' with such desperation in her that Bran and Sgeolan looked at each other, and when Sgeolan shrugged, Bran said, 'Very well, we will take you. But do not expect us to wait for you.'

'That you will not need to do.'

'Then let us go,' said Bran, and took his cloak from where it hung by the door.

The woman did not speak again as they walked the short distance to the shore. Bran and Sgeolan pushed their small craft into the sea and helped her aboard. And she remained silent as they pulled away from the shore. Once out of the shelter of the land, the water was rough, a strong swell running before an easterly wind; but Sgeolan plied the oars steadily, and Bran steered the craft with a firm hand on the sweep, while the woman sat in the prow and stared forward as though she was hungry to see their destination.

It was not a long journey to the island, but the weather worsened steadily as they drew near. Soon they could see the shoreline, and grim and forbidding it seemed, as was always the case to those who looked upon it from the

The Island of Sorrow and Joy.

direction of the land. Bran and Sgeolan had lived within sight of the place for many a year, and its outlines were familiar. Yet they never looked that way without a shiver of fear, for it was said that the island was a place of spirits and wonders, where perhaps the old gods themselves still lived – even Bendegeid Vran himself, whose name the fisherman bore. And more than once they had seen strange lights on that distant shore, before hastening to look away and make the sign of the horns against evil.

Yet now, as they neared a line of rocks, against which the waves beat thunderously, Bran suddenly pointed ahead with a shaking hand, and when Sgeolan paused in his rowing and looked over his shoulder he gave a gasp of fear.

The whole island seemed wrapped in a ghostly shawl of light, as though a curtain stretched between the place where their frail craft rode the churning sea and the shore of the island. There, where none had been before now, showed the outline of a small stone chapel, and from its narrow door – and even narrower window – spilled light of such intensity that it seemed as though the sun was rising within.

And yet, though the brothers were shaken by what they saw, they did not hesitate for more than a moment. Sgeolan began to row as though his very life depended upon it, while Bran clung to the sweep for dear life. Only their silent passenger showed neither fear nor astonishment, but clung to the sides of the craft with white hands.

Then, when it seemed the craft must be dashed in pieces against the cliffs of the island, the wind dropped and the sea became flat calm – calm as it seldom was along that bleak and barren coast. Sgeolan sculled into the lea of the island and the brothers beached their craft easily on a shelving lip of sand. Bran helped their passenger on to dry land and was about to push the boat off again and leap back aboard when his eyes caught those of his brother. Sgeolan was staring fixedly at something behind him. Fearful of what he might see, Bran turned to look, but there was nothing there except a narrow path that climbed inland, and the smooth sand that stretched away on either hand. The woman had already vanished from sight, having not even waited to speak her farewells.

Bran turned back to Sgeolan with a question on his lips, but before he could ask it his brother stood up and leapt ashore, and without a word began to hurry inland. Bran called his name to no avail and when he received no answer followed him, all the while looking over his shoulder and to either side in fear and apprehension of what he might see.

The climb was easier than it seemed, and in no time Bran stood for the first time on the summit of the isle and looked across towards the mainland, and what he saw there caused him to stare. A dark cloud seemed to hang over the Island of the Mighty, but it was no ordinary cloud such as might bring stinging rain or battering winds. This was a deep midnight smirch, rank and bitter as the smoke of burning thatch, and it seemed as impenetrable as a shield of ancient power.

Terror overcame Bran and he turned about and called out to his brother. But there was no sign of Sgeolan, or of the woman. Both had vanished as though the earth has swallowed them, although there were neither trees nor rocks to shield them from sight: only the narrow stone cell that they had both seen from the water and that no longer gave off a brilliant light. Then Bran saw that away to his right lay a small huddle of buildings, built like beehives around a taller structure of the same shape. There Bran could see figures moving, and though his teeth rattled in his head with the fear of the place, yet he would not depart until he had found Sgeolan and so he turned that way and hastened towards the buildings as swiftly as he might.

As he neared the little collection of huts he heard singing and then he saw a strange procession coming towards him. In the front came several men in white garments who carried tall candle-sticks, and they sang as they walked. Behind them came others carrying a litter of their shoulder on which lay a woman deathly pale and thin, covered in heavy drapes against the cold. By her side walked the woman whom Bran and Sgeolan had ferried to the island. She had taken off her cloak and Bran saw that she was clothed like a princess with gold at wrist and throat. At the end of the procession came several simply dressed men and woman, and among them was his brother.

'Sgeolan!' he cried and hurried to his side. Sgeolan beamed at him but laid a finger to his lips.

As Bran joined him, Sgeolan leaned close and said softly, 'We go to heal the Queen.' Bran stared at him in bewilderment and was about to ask what he meant and to tell him to come away when Sgeolan laid a finger again to his lips and taking Bran's arm, pulled him into step with the rest.

For a moment, Bran thought of pulling his brother physically away and back to the boat, but then something, curiosity perhaps, made him pause. For all their strangeness, these folk seemed to mean them no harm. With some reluctance, he allowed himself to be borne along with the procession, which he now saw was making for the chapel.

As they drew near, light once again beamed from within, and the singers fell silent as though at a signal. Then the front of the procession passed through the doors and the woman on the litter was carried within, the other walking still at her side.

The chapel was small and the rest of the party, including Bran and Sgeolan, had to remain outside. By craning forward they could see inside and Bran looked with curiosity to see what was happening . . .

Afterwards he was never quite sure of what he saw, and though he told the tale many times, he never really understood it. I tell it merely as it has come down to me, without comment, though I have heard many different reasons for what took place.

As he looked into the small chapel, Bran saw that the woman in the litter had been laid before a rough-hewn altar-stone on which had been stood a cup that blazed with light so bright that he could not look at it directly. Also present was the woman they had brought from the mainland, seated in a great, carved wooden chair, like a throne. By her side stood a man in rich robes, embroidered with wondrous designs in many colour. The white-robed ones were ranged upon either side.

Then as Bran watched, the Great One by the altar took up the cup of light, which somewhat modified its glow, and in the other hand a little silver knife. And the woman on the throne held out her arm, bare from the shoulder, and the little knife flashed once and red drops of blood began to flow from the woman's arm into the cup. Though she made no sound or sign of pain, Bran saw that she grew paler at every moment, and her dark eyes seemed ever larger.

But at length the cup seemed to be filled, and the man in the rich robes then bent over the body of the woman in the litter and, raising her up, seemed to offer the cup to her. Bran remained unsure of the order of events, which seemed to merge into one another. He recalled the woman rising from her litter and that she seemed younger than before, though perhaps it was only that she was in some way healed. And he remembered that the other, she who had but lately sailed with them, had slipped quite to the side of the great chair, and that her eyes were closed.

Then things became even more confused as he stood aside and watched the newly healed woman emerge with the cup in her hands and, walking to the edge of the cliffs, empty what it contained into the sea. It seemed that he also heard words, though what they were he would never recall: something about the Waste Land and the sovereignty of the island of the mighty. Then the whole group began to wend its way back as they had come, leaving Bran and Sgeolan standing alone on the rocky headland beside the chapel. And Bran told how, when he looked once more within, he could see no sign of the woman who had occupied the great chair, and that the light was gone from the altar.

After that the two brothers hastened back to the shore and sailed back across the strait, which was now peaceful and calm. Nor did they speak at all until they were safely home and sat together inside the bothy with the fire banked and platters of steaming food before them.

Then Bran looked across at his brother and asked the question he had most need to ask: 'Why did you follow her, brother?'

And Sgeolan looked back and wrinkled his brow and said, 'Because she was the Queen.' Whether he meant the woman in the litter or their passenger, Bran could never discover, for Sgeolan refused to talk of the event again. But it is told that after this the two men could not settle to their old way of life, but became wanderers through the land, until in time they came to the court of the Emperor Arthur and took service with him. There they learned of the days, not long past, when a terrible blight lay upon the land, when the king himself fell sick and the queen journeyed far from the court in search of a remedy for his malaise.

For long months she remained absent, then one day the people heard birds singing where they had been too long silent, and when they looked out of their houses they saw the first green of spring upon the trees and in the fields; and that day the queen returned, and it was soon known that the Emperor was well again, so that there was much rejoicing throughout the land.

And whether it is to be believed that the queen was indeed she whom Bran and Sgeolan saw lying sick unto death in the Island of Sorrow and Joy, or whether it was she whom they carried to the island, I will not say; but it is said that the brothers became great warriors in the service of the Emperor and were known by other names in the tales that are told of those times. But when first they came into the presence of the Lord and Lady of the Land, the queen leant forward and smiled at them and said, merely, 'Welcome.'

The Hermit

The visitor to Iona can sit in the circle of tumbled stones called the Hermit's Cell, on the isolated western side of the island. There is no historical proof that it was a hermit's cell, though the location seems a likely one. The hermit of this story is a typical Celtic individualist, seeking enlightenment in his own way but within the broad fold of the Celtic Church. This was by no means unusual, and eccentric hermits persisted until surprisingly late in Britain. In Malmesbury, for example, Christina, daughter of Henry of Somerford, was licensed in 1250 by King Henry III to remain shut up in the hermitage in perpetuity. It is interesting to find that by this time, within the Roman Church, hermits were made legal by royal licence, presumably for a price.

Today, the Catholic Church has strict rules regarding permissions for monastics to live as hermits — Thomas Merton being an outstanding and rare modern example. But our hermit bridges the pagan Druids and the evangelist Christians . . . indeed, he finds his own brotherhood too pagan to endure, and like many a grumpy Scots visionary before and since, retires to solitude. There he finds one of the most curious and enduring traditions of spiritual enlightenment and transformation, that of physical *vanishment*. For like Enoch in Jewish tradition, and like the shamans, Druids and magic workers of the chthonic traditions worldwide, Patrick the Hermit vanishes physically into the Otherworld. Perhaps he takes the form of a bird, or perhaps he is called home so powerfully that his very body is taken too. But like all hermits he spent many hours mortifying the flesh with fasting, so he may simply have blown away in the high winter gales. I leave it to you to decide what his fate was.

In summer, the sky and sea were open far to the west, and Patrick the Hermit would sit for long hours staring over to the horizon. He had only recently remembered that his name was Patrick, and found this annoying, as it was a sign that his human life had not entirely left him. Here he was, no property other than his weathered robe, no tokens of the world other than a stone-and-turf shelter covered now with summer flowers. And even this cell had been built long ago by another, and Patrick (honourable name but annoying) merely slept within it occasionally.

The long look to the west reached where sea and sky met, where the burning works from the Forge of God were cooled. The hermit knew that if he could abandon his humanity, he might fly to that Gate. So he fasted, and looked, and contemplated, and when he could remember the words, he prayed. Prayer was a problem for Patrick, for when he prayed he could somehow hear the brothers praying in their new-built church on the east of the island. They prayed often, and it was rumoured among the people of the isles that God heard their prayers.

There was also the problem of the goat, or as Patrick thought of it, The Goat. Whenever he prayed aloud, for it was fitting that the world should hear holy words for its purification and joy, the goat would clamber up on to the roof of his cell and start bleating. It was difficult to decide if the foolish creature was praising the Trinity or damning Patrick for his prayers. The great prince, Columba, had frequently declared that all living creatures praised God aloud – but in his company they would hardly have dared to do anything else. However, Patrick the Hermit set himself tolerance of the goat as a test, perhaps as a penance or a fee for his own entry into the animal world. For Patrick sought to transform himself into a bird.

This had not been an easy or reasoned decision, and had come long after his original seclusion. The role of hermit was an honoured one among both Picts and Scots, pagans and Christians, so there had been no problem in gaining permission from Segine, the Father of the community, to withdraw the short mile or so to the traditional cell built high upon the western hills. No conversation with fellow men was allowed, and a regimen of fasting, prayer and contemplation was demanded. Regrettably, people from the Island would come to visit the cell to request prophecies, reminding whoever dwelt there that such had been the purpose of the cell long before Colum had sailed from Ireland, and that purposes outlasted people.

But as time passed, and as Patrick forgot his name and most of his words, living on to an age that seemed miraculous to the monks of the community, the island people strangely began to leave him alone. An occasional gift of milk or bread would appear upon the well-known paths that he walked in all weathers, but no one came near, as if all the Picts and Scots of the Western Isles had agreed that he must pupate in peace. For they all knew that he was going to transform into something . . . though opinions varied as to what that something might be.

Two generations of brothers had mingled within the community, and thus Patrick was assumed to be at least one hundred years old. It was said that as a boy he had known Columba, and had accompanied the great preaching and miracle-working missions into the heart of Pictland. It was certain that as a young brother he had been given the honourable task of polishing the bell shrine, and that he had polished until the day of his withdrawal as hermit. It was said that a feather had floated down from the roof of the shrine every year upon the anniversary of this day – but that was nonsense.

On days of high wind, and there were many of those in spring and winter, the hermit would run into the gale flapping his arms up and down vigorously. He would leap from high rocks to land tumbling on the thin, peat soil. Sometimes he would strike stones and pebbles, but after so many years he knew all the soft spots well, and avoided the seams of rocks that jutted from the earth. A saying began to spread around the island to add to all the other weather lore: 'Patrick will be flying today'. But, of course, he was only leaping.

The brothers, far into the woven pattern of prayer, service and inspiration, were building a fortress of light that drove all shadows far away. But Patrick had chosen the harder path, for he was open to all the subtle forces that passed by, within, or through the island. At first it had seemed to him that the way of endurance would purge out the intimations, the visitors from other worlds, the visions . . . and at first it did so. But the keening of the fairy washers and murmur of the sea people were heard by all who lived in the isles, so their loss was of as little importance as their presence. No one-legged creatures hopped around Patrick's cell, no long, silver arms reached down the smoke hole at night to strangle him, and no tall, fair, shining people came up out of the earth to sing to him. Very well, he was indeed a prophet with his perceptions cleared of those everyday visitors ready for something so terrible and bright that people even sailed from Ireland to accost him. But that had been years ago, and most of those who had sought him out as a prophet were, of course, now dead.

The people of the island had realised that he would utter no truth concerning the Otherworld or the Queen of Heaven, but all agreed that he would turn into a creature of wonder, the like of which had never been seen before in that place or any other. But it would also be true to say that as the years passed, even they tended to forget about him, and that his fame in the Western Isles diminished considerably. Like the wind and the rain, and the movements of the fish through the year, Patrick was part of the land, ever present, never fully seen.

But he himself had accumulated a large collection of feathers, and spent many hours studying them minutely. He was familiar, from his younger days, with many of the Greek and Druidic doctrines of transformation and transmigration: he knew that if you concentrated, imagined, and visualised a thing, you would in time become that thing. And on long sunlit days, at dawn and at dusk, he had seen the glowing Gates in the far west, and knew that only a powerful and enduring bird might reach them before they vanished.

One such day, sitting upon the pinnacle of rock not far from the tiny spring of Eternal Youth (once an object of pagan worship), Patrick remembered his dispute with the father. This had occurred when he was no longer young, but at that strong age when men jostle for power within the Church. It had been about the doves, and no one had ever forgiven him for it, or so he thought. The truth was that most of the brothers concerned were now dead, and those few left had so utterly transformed the tale that it seemed to have occurred in another place and with other people.

Because of his boyhood association with prince Columba, Patrick had studied many curious books. Books were something of a touchy subject with the great evangelist, and he would often call them the curse of the world, but there was a library of scrolls, and many of the earliest brothers were trained bards with prodigious memories. It was from one of these bards, and from a little scroll of Greek script — still locked away in the church — that Patrick had drawn his argument against the doves, despite the strong tradition of Colum's own name, which meant Dove. But doves, argued Patrick, were the birds of the love-goddess, Astarte or Venus, and were not fitting to keep in a Christian church. They were upon the island from the days of the great Druid college, and were sacred to the Goddess, used in auguries and even in sacrifices. One had only to consider the great and terrible shrine of the goddess Brigit, now become a saint, in Ireland. The father (had it been Laisren or Ferna-Bret? So hard to remember) was not pleased, for the doctrine of the Holy Spirit as dove was well advanced, and he for one believed in it implicitly. The doves remained, and Patrick became a hermit. Somewhere the Goddess smiled gently.

So here was Patrick, listening to the goat and wishing to be a bird. Today when he muttered the *Litany of Angus*, the goat told him that a certain Oswald, who had once been a pupil upon the island, had now become king of Northumbria. This, said the goat, was to be of great importance for the Word of God, for Oswald would soon receive, from the seniors of the community, the brilliant evangelist, Aidan, who would found a new Fortress of Light upon the cold, sea-washed isle of Lindisfarne. Patrick flapped his ragged-sleeved arms at the goat, who stopped talking and began to chew the thin grass upon the hut roof. Not long after this news had been received from the goat, Patrick fell into a wasting fever.

The Hermit of Iona.

Winter came early that year, with hardly any autumn. Great grey walls of sea and cloud mounted up, and raging winds tore the plants from their shallow roots. Patrick was huddled in his cell, racked with burning and shivering, and when the great storm blew away part of the wattle-and-daub church and the brothers struggled to keep the holy relics safe, no one thought to look for him in the gale.

Within the tiny, stone cell, the raging of the storm was muffled. Patrick smiled to himself, for he was sure that the goat must have been blown away long since. He saw many strange things blow past the doorways; Colum looked in for a moment, his pastoral crook hooked onto the doorpost to keep him in place for a moment, and smiled at Patrick: 'You were always a good boy,' he said, 'remember to polish the bell for me' . . . and was gone. The saint seemed to herald a rush of people. Some Patrick knew well, others were of a strange breed, tall with long, fair or red hair, wielding bloody swords. A great king rose up and laughed a deep, booming laugh, and a hoard of foreigners staggered past carrying – great sacrilege – the holy Stone of Kingship in their unpurified hands. Patrick shivered violently, and when he opened his eyes again, he saw great ships of iron moving over the land as if it were water, and a city of stone so tall and vast that it seemed a blasphemy against the Creator, abusing the four elements and torturing the blessed land with its foul presence. Patrick heard many voices gabbling and shouting together, and the screams of the damned souls in torment. He tried to remember the Prayer of Grace, but the pain in his chest was so huge and hot that his brain became numb.

Determined to fight this terrible flow of vision, Patrick climbed slowly to his feet, clawing his way up the rough, stone wall for support. The moment he stood upright, utter silence fell. A silvery bell chimed three times, and there was the beating of wings. It seemed that a woman's voice, his mother from so long ago, spoke deep within him: 'Arise, my child, and come home . . .'. And beyond the door of his cell, the sky divided into a Gate of Light. For a moment he was astonished, and simply stood with his jaw hanging down and his arms at his sides. Even as he lingered, the Gate began to close, and suddenly remembering his purpose, Patrick leapt forward, flapping his arms vigorously up and down.

After some days had passed, one of the younger brethren walked out to the cell, to see how mad Patrick had weathered the storm, and to tell him the good news about Aidan. The cell was empty, and the poor goat moped around the door, as if pining for a friend. Patrick's worn, ragged robe lay upon the earthen floor, but of the hermit himself there was no sign. After days of praying to Oran and then Colum for guidance, a new hermit was appointed from among the brotherhood. But the goat ran away and would not have anything to do with him, and she made her new home in one of the tiny farmsteads near the coast, much to the delight of the Pictish farmer. On stormy nights the goat would come into the low, turf house, along with the other animals. 'Ah, here she is,' the wife would say, 'Patrick will be flying tonight . . .'

10·the orkneys: islands of the otherworld

THE ISLES OF THE DEAD

O MAP OF legendary Britain would be complete if it failed to include the Orkneys. These islands have been inhabited for as long as there have been settlers in the far north. Neolithic, Bronze Age, Celtic, Norse and Scottish dwellers have left their mark on the language and culture of the islands.

But there has always been something that is considered strange, even mysterious about the place. In common with most of the more remote islands around the coastline, they were long held to be the abodes of the dead – borderlands between this world and the next.

This stems in part from the fact that they were actual necropoli (burial grounds of the sacred dead), and it is a well-known fact among archaeologists that one cannot walk far in any direction in the Orkneys without falling over a tomb or tumuli, once (or in some cases still) the last dwelling-place of some famous chieftain or hero, perhaps ferried there from the mainland, their names long since forgotten.

Some, of heroic and legendary mould, have not been forgotten – at least not by students of the legendary history of Britain. Gawain, Gareth, Gaheries and Agravain are remembered among the most famous of Arthur's warriors; even their dark half-brother, Mordred, has not yet passed from the annals of the world, while their mother, sometimes called Morgause, sometimes Morgan le Fay – few fail to remember her!

The Orkney Clan, T. H. White dubbed them in his famous book, *The Once and Future King*. Lot, their father, was Lord of Lothian and Orkney, and also Arthur's bitterest opponent during the troubled early years of his reign; yet his sons were among the first to sit at the Round Table in Camelot. Perhaps in the sixth century they were political hostages to ensure there would be no further rising among the northern tribes. By the time of the great medieval romances, other and more subtle reasons lay behind their coming. Not only was Camelot the greatest centre of chivalry in that far-off legendary time, but there was also

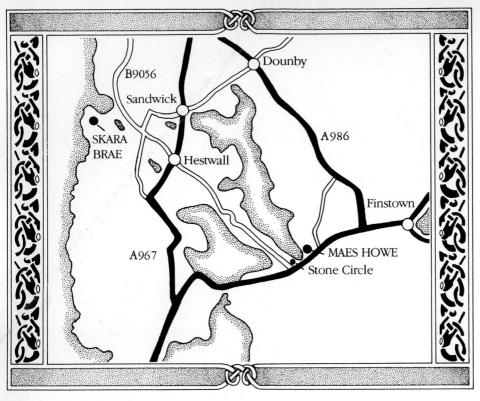

Mainland Orkney.

a complex web of relationships between Arthur and his Orcadian knights.

After the wars in which Lot fell, his widow came to the court of the new, young king, bringing her young sons with her. And, so the story goes, Arthur became enamoured of her, not knowing she was his half-sister, each sharing the same mother, Igraine of Cornwall. Thus Arthur begot the child who would be his own downfall – Mordred.

This seems to have been Morgause' revenge for the death of her father Gorlois at the hands of Arthur's father, Uther Pendragon. Certainly, though she is not represented as Arthur's implacable enemy, it seems likely that she knew of the forbidden consanguinity of their relationship. Incest was always a fearful thing, forbidden by the Church and abhorrent to God.

Yet, if we look at this story again, we see that Mordred had a very real claim to the throne of Britain. He is both nephew and sister-son, which by more ancient laws of the land would have marked him out for particular favour in the eyes of the people. None of the texts name Mordred hero, yet it is possible to see a context in which he would have found it easy to secure support for his claim to the throne.

It has often been assumed by Arthurian scholars that Morgause and Morgan were in fact one, rather than sisters as they appear in the major romances, and that as such they were once a primal character who had been, as so often occurs in the Arthurian matter, split into two. If this is so, then the most obvious contender for the original identity of the two women is the Celtic war-goddess known as the Morrigan. Certainly, this ancient and fearsome deity shares a number of points in common with Morgan/Morgause. Both have the

150

ability to change their shape, particularly into that of a crow; both are merciless, both are queens (Morrigan means 'Great Queen'), and both rule over isles of the dead.

We may recall that at the end of the Arthur cycle, the king is put into a barge with three queens aboard, one of whom is Morgan, and taken to the Otherworldy island of Avalon to be healed of his wounds. Again, in the *Vita Merlini* of Geoffrey of Monmouth, we find Morgan and her nine sisters ruling over an island to which, once again, Arthur is carried to be healed. And, Morgan/Morgause is Queen of the Orkneys, long identified with the Isles of the Dead.

It is interesting to note that Geoffrey of Monmouth — that indefatigable source of Arthurian material — also mentions the Orkneys several other times in his *History of the Kings of Britain.* He names one of their kings, Gwanuasuis rex Orcadum, a name derived from our old friend Gwynn ap Nudd, also King of the Dead (see pp. 86–90)! Perhaps Geoffrey was aware of the reputation held by the islands; perhaps he knew that they were also called the Orcades, a name deriving from the Greek *'orcus'*, death. Morgan herself is sometimes known as Morcades, a clear enough indication of the way her role was understood in those times.

It may well be, then, that we have vestiges of a tradition that makes the Orkneys more than symbolically islands of the Otherworld, and that Arthur himself may have come there to be healed of his wounds . . . their actual history is no less remarkable.

PREHISTORIC ORKNEY AND THE SETTLEMENT OF SKARA BRAE

NE OF THE most immediate reactions made by the visitor to Orkney is to marvel at the sheer number of ancient works. Standing-stones, settlements, tombs: it is not possible to move any distance on Orkney without coming upon the evidence of ancient culture. It has often been assumed that these remains, in general well preserved, are due to some special sacred quality of the islands — and to a certain extent this may be true. But we should remember that at one time mainland Britain held far more of the works of megalithic or neolithic culture than it does today: we need only look back a mere two centuries to find substantial differences between famous sites in Britain as they stand now and as they were before deliberate policies of destruction were undertaken. Excluding the obsessive destruction of neurotic materialists and puritans, there has been an enormous long-term toll upon ancient works through the daily action of farmers and builders. Preservation is, after all, a very modern concept indeed. Many of the early antiquarians and archaeologists, who started the modern trend for research and preservation in the eighteenth and nineteenth centuries, were little more than refined looters.

There are still sites virtually unknown in Britain, and certainly seldom visited. Many locations have vanished beneath the plough, into church or

Viking ships from a ninth-century coin.

house walls, and more recently under roadways and housing developments. Thus it is to the isolated places, such as the Orkney Islands, that we may turn for a pristine insight into early culture.

The settlement of Skara Brae, on the Bay of Skaill in Orkney, is some five thousand years old. For many centuries it lay covered in sand until a storm in 1850 revealed the remains. Stone was used extensively in the structure, and the low tunnel entrances and high chambers within are reminiscent of the chamber tombs also associated with the period. Within the single room of each house we find beds, dressers, and cupboards, all made of stone slabs. The first impression to the modern visitor is of a slightly comical, uncomfortable dwelling, the mock 'Stone Age' house – but this is far from the case.

The village of Skara Brae seems to have stood originally by a freshwater lake, though now it is close to the sea shore because of erosion and weather changes upon the coast. Seven buildings, one set apart from the rest, make a very close village, linked by low passages. The stone chambers were originally covered to a considerable depth with midden, a good old British word for domestic refuse and earth. This thick covering of decaying matter would have provided constant warmth for the occupants, deep within their chambers, roofed over with skins and timber. The modern visitor might think that this use of midden was due to insanitary ignorance, but this is not so, for the dwelling also featured separate toilets with drainage – the midden was a deliberate energy-conscious design feature. We might visualise a situation where in summer the roofs were open in fine weather, but in winter the dwellers kept warm and dry without consuming vast quantities of rare wood for fuel.

The stone furniture would have been suitably padded, covered and decorated. Evidence shows that the people kept animals, fished and grew

Skara Brae. Interior of the house with its characteristic stone furniture.

Plan of Skara Brae.

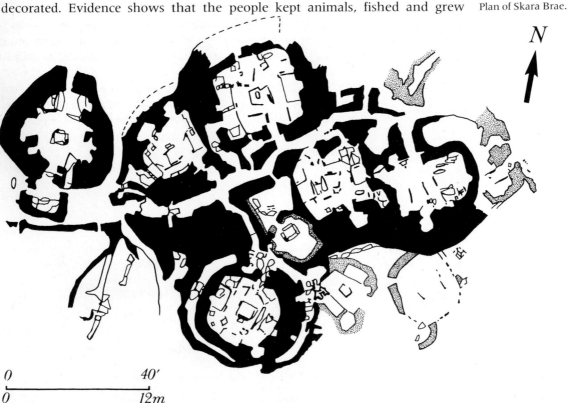

N

0   40'
0   12m

152

cereal crops. They made stone and bone tools, and the slightly isolated building in the village may have been a workshop, for it contained the remains of burnt and chipped stones. The people of Skara Brae also made strong pottery jars decorated with bosses, spirals and lines, known to archaeologists as Grooved Ware.

The inhabitants of this close-knit village of fifty or sixty people (apparently a fairly constant figure over the period of 600–1,000 years) would have been involved with the massive ritual structures such as Stenness, the Ring of Brodgar, and the fine chamber of Maes Howe nearby. This raises the immediate question as to the density of the population on Orkney, for the massive works seem to demand large numbers of people over long periods of time. Agriculture and weather have undoubtedly destroyed many other prehistoric Orkney settlements, and there are certainly others still undiscovered beneath sand or earth, or even under the sea. The superstitious reverence attached to the megalithic remains meant that they were relatively untouched, so it is the domestic structures that have vanished over the centuries. It is tempting to assume that Orkney had a large prehistoric culture; certainly the stone circles and mounds suggest this . . . and there are parallels with the great Wessex culture in the south of England that was certainly the result of an extensive population. It is also a strong possibility that the islands, only 11 km (7 miles) off the northern coast of Scotland, were visited at ceremonial occasions by people drawn from a wide area, and this is supported by the legendary associations of sacred islands handed down through tradition.

Two elderly women were found buried in the wall of one of the Skara Brae houses, and this burial has raised many questions for researchers. Clearly, the great tomb of Maes Howe was reserved for ceremonial burial, as were similar chambers the length and breadth of Britain – but why were two women interred in the walls of a humble house? We find echoes of a foundation ritual in the sacred island of Iona in the Hebrides, where Saint Columba is said to have buried one of his monks alive to found the church, so such practices were still circulated (at least as legends) as late as the sixth and seventh centuries, two thousand years or more after the building of Skara Brae. It is tempting to assume that these women were blessed ancestors, protecting the close-knit village, perhaps as household spirits consulted by those who lived in the settlement. Another theory, equally supported by folk tradition and ritual practice, is suggested in the story, *The Mystery of the Women* (see pp. 164–70).

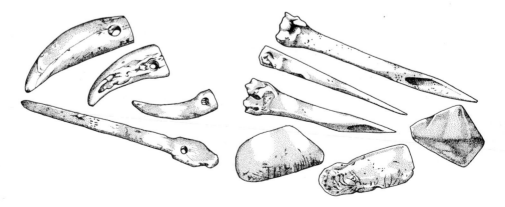

Prehistoric bone tools and ornaments, such as were used at Skara Brae.

Genealogy of the Earls of Orkney.

Eystein
- Rognvald of More
  - Turf-Einar
    - Arnkel
    - Erlend
    - Thorfinn Skull-Splitter
      - Arnfinn
      - Havard
      - Hlodvir
        - Sirurd the Stout (d. 1014)
          - Sumarlidi
          - Brusi
            - Rognvald (d. ?1045)
          - Einar Wry-Mouth (d. 1020)
          - Thorfinn (d. 1064)
            - Paul
              - Hakon
                - Paul (d. ?1137)
                - Harald
                  - Erlend (d. 1154)
                - Margaret
                  - Harald Maddadarson (d. 1206)
            - Erlend
              - St. Magnus (d. 1117)
              - Gunnhild
                - Rognvald Kali (d. 1158)
                  - Ingirid
                    - Harald the Young
      - Ljot
      - Skuli
  - Hallad
- Sigurd the Powerful
  - Guthorm

Valkyrie welcoming a slain Viking hero to Valhalla.

WOLVES OF THE SEA

HE VIKINGS FIRST reached Orkney in any numbers in *c.*AD800, more than two thousand years after the building of Skara Brae. These tough and expert seamen made light of the voyage across the stormy Northern seas. They recognised the vital position of the islands, which lay within easy reach of the riches to be pillaged from both Scotland and England, and above all, gold-rich Ireland.

Pictish warriors from Orkney.

Norse settlers from the west coast of Norway soon established a powerful earldom over the Northern Isles, changing the names of the islands and native settlements and imposing their own language, religion and culture on the inhabitants, most of whom were forced into thraldom.

But the Vikings were traders and farmers as well as ruthless plunderers; they brought a variety of rich goods from all across the world, and established thriving farms on the fertile volcanic soil of the islands. Thereafter men of the Orkneys fought in every corner of the globe: at Dublin with Sigurd, by London Bridge with King Olaf, in Paris with Rolf the Ganger, and in Constantinople with the Varangian Guard, and at Stamford Bridge with Harold Godwinsson.

The Northern Isles remained in the possession of the Earls until 1195, when the Shetlands became subject to Norway. Orkney continued Norse until 1231, when Magnus, Earl of Angus, became the first Scottish ruler, though still owing allegiance to Norway. Finally, both Orkney and Shetland became pledged to the Scottish crown as part of the marriage settlement of Margaret, daughter of Christian I of Denmark and Norway, to James III of Scotland.

The story of the Nords Earls' rule is told in a remarkable text known as the *Orkneyinga Saga*, written in thirteenth-century Iceland. It tells an extraordinary story of violence, adventure, death and betrayal.

Pictish symbols found in Orkney.

154

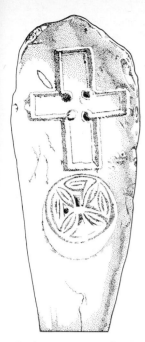

Ancient grave stone from Orkney.

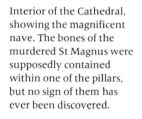

Interior of the Cathedral, showing the magnificent nave. The bones of the murdered St Magnus were supposedly contained within one of the pillars, but no sign of them has ever been discovered.

One of the most famous of the earls was Thorfinn the Mighty. He ruled both Northern and Western Isles, as well as a large part of Scotland and part of Ireland from the Brough of Birsay, a small tidal island where he also built a cathedral that seems to have reflected both Christian and Norse traditions in its design.

Tradition associates Thorfinn with the almost legendary figure of Macbeth, in some instances identifying them as a single figure; while another tale relates how the two men journeyed to Rome together to seek absolution for their bloody deeds. The latter sounds like a later pious interpretation, but there is sufficient evidence to support the identification of Thorfinn with Macbeth to make at least a possibility. When Thorfinn died, his widow, Ingbjorg, married

155

Bishop's Palace. The ruins of the once-splendid mediaeval building that bears testimony to the wealth and power of the Church in Orkney at this time.

Malcolm Canmore, who was responsible for the final defeat and death of Macbeth. Speculation reaches an interesting level when one considers that this makes Ingebjorg the Lady Macbeth of Shakespeare's tragedy, as well as the wife of his murderer!

Thorfinn's grandson, Magnus Erlendsson, is probably Orkney's greatest hero. A deeply peace-loving man, he shared the earldom with the savage Viking leader, Haakon Paulsson, with whom he quarrelled so often that both men's advisers finally suggested they meet on the tiny islet of Egilsay to discuss their differences and settle their disputes. Magnus readily agreed and went unarmed, only to meet his death at the hands of his treacherous enemy. This took place in 1117; within two decades of that date Magnus was canonised and followers of his cult were widespread throughout the islands and the mainland. His nephew, Earl Rognvald, founded the Cathedral of St Magnus in 1137. It is still one of the finest churches in the whole of Britain, having escaped battering at the hands of the Reformation.

Rognvald himself is perhaps the most attractive of the Norse earls. He was a poet and an accomplished musician as well as a soldier whose adventures read

Cathedral of St Magnus. Modern stained-glass window in the church, depicting the martyr in the robes of a bishop.

Standing-Stones of Stenness. Part of the complex formed by the Ring of Brodgar, containing some fascinating alignments to the seasons of the year and the movement of the stars in the heavens. It has a central burial site and has likely associations with the nearby massive Maes Howe chamber.

Ring of Brodgar. This vast stone circle, one of the largest in Britain, forms part of a complex of standing-stones, earth mounds, and ritual circles that spans the whole of the Orkneys. It shows the grand scale on which the prehistoric culture built and worshipped.

like a modern historical romance. At sea between Spain and the coast of Africa, he made this verse:

> Constantly north-curving
> the coast: a roaring
> sea makes sport
> of our sturdy timbers.
> My verse flows – vain
> you envy, villains –
> seaward from Spain
> slips my slim prow.

(trans. Paulsson and Edwards)

After his death, Rognvald, too, was canonised. As one writer puts it, 'There have been more devout saints, but never one more attractive.'

The history of Christianity in the Orkneys began in 995 when the Norwegian King, Olaf Tryggvason, enforced the adoption of the religion on all his subjects, including those in Orkney; but the work of conversion was begun earlier through followers of St Columba, whose own work was mainly concerned with Pictish Scotland, but who sent out monks to spread the faith in the Northern Isles. Thus Orkney came into contact with the thriving Celtic Church, whose adoption of native religious practices within the framework of the Christian teaching made it strong throughout the islands, though it later came into conflict with the Roman Church and was forced to conform.

These varied strata of culture, religion and adventure made Orkney what it is – a pattern of the past that can be read in the faces and language of the people to the present. It is a deeply magical and mysterious place, as anyone who visits the Ring of Brodgar or Maes Howe or the Brough of Birsay on one of the long, light evenings towards midwinter will discover for themselves. The islands truly deserve the title of Otherworldy, for here one is in a place where the veils between the worlds are thin.

The Hidden Runes

This tale is an attempt at a piece of historical guesswork. The runic inscriptions carved on the stones of Maes Howe really do exist – more or less as quoted here. They were put there by Viking invaders and colonisers of the Orkneys at various times during their association with the islands, but more than that we cannot say. Nor is it possible to visit the site without wondering by whom and why they were made. The true story will probably never be known, but sufficient references exist to throw some light on the mystery. *The Orkneyinga Saga*, already mentioned, tells how a party of warriors under the leadership of Earl Harald Maddadarson were forced to take shelter at the site during a storm. The text remarks, with typical laconic understatement, that next morning two of the men were stark mad 'which delayed them somewhat'. What happened to these two men we are not told, but a transcription of certain of the runic messages inside Maes Howe gives one pause for thought. They have been followed up in the accompanying story. Once again, the theme is of guardianship of the land. The Celtic practice of appointing the spirit of a long-dead ancestor to such a tomb is well known, and is discussed elsewhere (see R. J. Stewart, *Underworld Initiation*, Aquarian Press, Wellingborough, 1989).

There was a man named Ketil Bignose who lived on the main island of Orkney, and this is his story. Ketil was not one to go Viking. He had sailed across the wild sea from his home in Norway in search of good land for the ploughing, and having found it he settled down to a life of hardship and unending toil, though he did find time to marry and sire three healthy children.

The woman he married was called Ingebjorg and she was, as everyone said, a fine-looking girl. In fact, no one could quite understand why she had married Ketil, who was less than handsome, having no outstanding features of any kind except for the nose that gave him his name. But they seemed happy enough and, after a while, as their family grew, people forgot their puzzlement – though they continued to remark on Ingebjorg's beauty and her fine figure, which she seemed to keep despite birthing Ketil's three sons.

Everything seemed so settled and happy at Ketil's stead that no one gave any credence at first when rumours began to get about that Ingebjorg was seeing a lot of a certain Hermond Sigurdsson, who had a small, ill-run place adjacent to Ketil's. Hermond was not much liked in the islands, being a loud-mouthed fellow much given to boasting about his past exploits while a Viking with Hardrada. There were those who said that he had never fought in a raid at all, but had come by enough money to buy his farmstead through other means. There were even rumours of a price being put on his head, or of a feud with a family in Iceland; but there was no real proof of this, and so people left Hermond alone as much as they could.

Another reason he was disliked was because of his friendship with another unpleasant character named Gukr Inarsson who was known to have killed several men, supposedly all in fair fights and with the right price paid afterwards. He was a grim man to look at. He also had a great scar from the wound that lost him his right eye and some of his teeth, and a broken nose got in a fight with Herli Grondesson, soon after he came to the islands. Together these two were considered a thoroughly bad lot, which is why no one could believe that Ingebjorg could possibly want to have anything to do with them.

And they might have been right, but for one thing that no one really knew about Ingebjorg – that she very greatly wanted to better herself, to have a bigger farm, more thralls to man it, and have sufficient money to buy silk from Miklegard and a golden chain to hang about her neck. She had probably been in love with Ketil to begin with, and perhaps she still cared for him in her own way, but she was bent on making more of her life than their poor farm and a gaggle of shouting children. She thought Hermond and Gukr were the people to get it for her, and the means was this.

On part of the land farmed by Ketil stood a great mound. It was known as Orkhaugr, a name of ill-omen to the Norse people, while the natives called it Maeshowe. It was said to be the grave-place of one of the ancient kings of the Orkneys, but whoever he may have been was long since forgotten, even by the islanders themselves. To the Norse it was a place best avoided, and rumours of the Haug-Bùi, a strange, fearful spirit who exacted terrible punishment from any human being who came across him, kept all men well away from Orkhaugr.

All men, that is, except Hermond, who – returning drunk from the tavern in Kirkjuvalgr – paused there for a brief rest, fell asleep, and dreamt a dream in which he saw himself carrying armloads of treasure out of the mound while Ingebjorg looked on admiringly.

It was this dream that brought the two of them together, because Hermond wanted to get Ketil's permission to dig in Orkhaugr but couldn't think how to do it without letting on the reason for it. So instead, he sought for and found an opportunity to speak to Ingebjorg in private and to put to her a proposition – that if she helped him and Gukr find a way into the Howe, she would receive a share of the treasure.

At first Ingebjorg was distrustful and angry. She very nearly went to Ketil and told him everything, but then she began to think about all that a share of the 'treasure' might buy, so instead she held her tongue and set herself to find a way to get Ketil out of the way long enough to enable the entry of the Howe to take place.

In the end she didn't have to bother, because the following week, Ketil broke the blade of their only plough, which meant that he had to go into Kirkjuvalgr to get it repaired. As soon as she was certain when he would be gone, Ingebjorg sent word to Hermond and Gukr, who set about preparing to enter the mound.

They were both rather afraid at heart, though neither would admit to the other, and they drank a lot of beer to hearten themselves before they prepared to set out on their fateful deed.

What neither of them knew was that Ketil, who was no fool when it came to the ways of the world, was aware of what they were planning and had decided to teach the three of them a lesson as well as getting the treasure for himself. To this end he had pretended to break the plough in order to give the two men the opportunity to break into the tomb. In fact, he planned to get in there himself the night before and to make quite sure there was nothing left for the robbers when they, in turn, found their way inside.

So when he was quite sure that Ingebjorb and the children were sleeping deeply, Ketil got up and went to where he had left the tools he needed, and set forth. As always, the sky was still light, for it was near midsummer, and though the sun was only recently set, the hour was late and no one was about. Ketil, therefore, had no difficulty finding his way. Soon the great bulk of the mound lay before him, grimly forbidding in that grey light. But Ketil was a hard-headed, determined man with a certain shrewd humour, and if he felt any fear, he put it firmly behind him.

He had seen more than one such mound laid bare by wind and weather, and had a good idea of what he would find. He went to work with a will, digging downwards through the roof of the Howe until he met stone. Muttering a quick word to Freyr, he carefully prised out the capstone with his knife and lifted it out.

A gust of stale air escaped through the stone roof and Ketil jumped back. Then, gathering his determination, he carefully lifted out the surrounding stones and lowered a hastily kindled torch down into the hole. It was a deep, hollow chamber, about the height of three men, he judged. He hammered an ash stake, brought for the purpose, into the earth of the mound and secured the rope he had over his shoulder with a firm knot. Then he took up the slack and tested the firmness to his satisfaction. This Howe was no cliff daily passed by fishing boats; if he fell inside he would have to dig himself out, for no one knew where he had gone. Draping the rope over one arm and one foot, he let himself down in to the heart of the mound.

Once down, he looked about and found himself standing in a high, corbelled chamber, shaped something like a beehive. Massive stone held the roof up and dark openings led off on each of the four sides. One of these – the long one – must have led to the entrance, sealed with a stone as huge as the rest. It would take much labour on the part of Hermond and Gukr to shift that. Above him he could see the tiny hole he had made, with the stars shining clearly in the pale sky.

The Hidden Runes.

Ketil looked at the dark openings on each of the three other sides of the chamber and his heart jumped: within must lie the treasure, along with the bones of whatever great men were laid there. 'Never mind', he muttered to himself, 'they have been dead these long years – long enough not to be troubled by me.'

Then, as he was about to approach one of the side chambers, he caught sight of a number of markings scratched on the face of one of the upright stones. Holding his torch closer, he saw with a shock that they were runes. What was more, they were in a language he knew – his own. As he traced them with a finger, a smile began to dawn on his face. The runes said:

HAKON ALONE BORE THE TREASURE OUT OF THIS MOUND. IT IS CERTAIN AND TRUE AS I SAY, THAT THE TREASURE HAS BEEN MOVED FROM HERE. THE TREASURE WAS TAKEN AWAY THREE NIGHTS BEFORE THEY BROKE INTO HIS MOUND.

And a little lower, Ketil read:

THESE RUNES WERE CARVED BY THE MAN MOST SKILLED IN RUNES IN THE WESTERN OCEAN, WITH THE AXE THAT BELONGED TO GUKR TRANDILSSON IN THE SOUTH OF ICELAND.

So he was not the first. Ketil's smile grew broader, until he began to laugh out loud. The sound was strange and unearthly in that place, but even stranger was the sound that followed it. A low, grating voice said something in a language older than Norse or anything else Ketil had even heard.

For a second his heart stopped beating, then he swung round, reaching for the hilt of his sword. What he saw drained his limbs of all power to move.

A huge figure stood there in the entrance to one of the side chambers, naked but for a skin breech-clout and some shell arm-rings. His black hair was pulled back into a long tail and his beard was full and long. Black eyes reflected the light of Ketil's torch fiercely.

For several seconds the two men stared at each other, then Ketil fell to his knees and croaked out a plea: 'Mercy, whatever you are. I meant no harm!'

Surprisingly, the other answered in mild tones, and in good, if halting, Norse. 'I will not hurt you, little man. Get up!'

Ketil stood up shakily, then dared to ask, 'Who are you?'

'I am the Guardian,' he answered. 'You have disturbed my rest for the second time in a hundred years. What reason have you for entering here?'

Ketil poured out his tale, holding back nothing, all the time staring and staring at the creature before him, who must have been dead for more years than he could properly imagine but who yet seemed hale and hearty as any Viking warrior.

When Ketil was done, the Guardian looked at him impassively. 'I have watched the stars of the inner earth for a thousand cycles, yet it seems that greedy men still walk the earth. It seems to me that these others shall be taught a lesson. Perhaps then I may rest in peace until I am called for a better reason than this.'

His black eyes regarded Ketil impassively: 'Go away from this place, little man, and be sure not to trouble me again, for I shall not be so well disposed towards you again.'

Ketil turned away and grasped the rope that would carry him to safety. But he could not resist one last question: 'What happened to the treasure?'

In his low grating voice, the Guardian answered, 'Did you not read the marking? "The treasure was taken away three nights before they broke into his mound." It is safe now, until it is needed again.' And somehow there came unbidden into Ketil's mind the image of a great sword, shining with light, hidden in a dark crevice between two great stones — though whether they were part of the Howe or of some other place, he knew not.

Then, he swarmed up the rope, not looking back, and as swiftly as he might he laid back the stone he had taken from the roof and covered it once again with earth, until only close examination could have told of his night's work. Wearily, he made his way back to the farmstead and slept for what was left of the night, though he was troubled by strange dreams.

Next morning Ketil left for Kirkjuvalgr as soon as day dawned, and made sure that he did not return till late. He found Ingebjorg waiting for him with a pale, pinched look on her face and their children gathered closely around her. In a trembling voice she told him what had happened.

At around midday she had heard a terrible screaming and crying coming from the yard outside, and on going out to look, she found Hermond Sigurdsson and Gukr Inarsson grovelling in the mud, with their eyes nearly staring from their heads. They were totally bereft of speech, being able only to make gobbling noises, and like beasts they ran about on all fours. Hermond's hair, which had been the colour of fox's fur before, was now quite white, and Gukr's one good eye was nearly shut and twitched the whole time.

Word spread quickly and other of Ketil's neighbours were soon on the scene. They finally took away the two men and shut them in a barn until it could be decided what was to be done with them, for they were both, clearly, stark mad.

'What can have caused this thing?' asked Ketil, when he had listened to his wife's story in silence.

Ingebjorg had the grace to look guilty, but Ketil did not press her. Indeed, looking at her, all flushed and breathing quickly with fear, he saw exactly what it was people meant when they said she was the fairest woman for miles.

Hermond and Gukr remained mad, and the Thingmoot declared that they should be cared for and given such work as they were able to do. Neither lived long after that time, however, and they were buried side by side on the shore, looking towards their old homeland. Ingebjorg never spoke of the affair again, nor did Ketil seek to remind her. He went once to the great mound and found it seemingly untouched. He could only guess at what had occurred there, to deprive the two robbers of their minds.

As for the Guardian, he remained undisturbed for many years thereafter, until the time came for the sword to be wielded again. But that is another story . . . .

The Mystery of the Women

This short tale, set in the prehistoric village of Skara Brae, seems at first to contain some of the elements of the dark side of tradition, such as were preserved in folk-tales for centuries. There is no suggestion whatsoever that the actual Skara Brae is a haunted or frightening place. Indeed, on my visits to the village I found it to be a peaceful (if somewhat wind-blown) place, and felt that here were a truly civilised and harmonious people, living at one with their land.

As often happens when writing a tale, I began with a very simple idea – the mystery of the women buried in the wall, and the apparent lack of male burials in the village. From these two simple but puzzling items of information the rest of the story unfolded and told itself. To my own surprise what began as a sombre tale turned out to be much more, and just as Skara Brae itself is a miniature of human culture and development, so did the theme of individual vision in service of collective society suddenly appear at the heart of the story.

The house was very warm, filled with the friendly scents of home; of fish, curing skins, fermenting seeds, and the strong perfume of cat glands, worn by the priestess. Six women sat in a circle around the fire, each painted in different patterns of brilliant red and blue dots and spirals. The oldest woman, the priestess, with the luxury of heady scent upon her skin declaring her status, laid her hands palm-flat upon the wall. The youngest withdrew to sit patiently waiting to one side, while the remaining four set up a low droning chant, accompanied by rhythmic rasping of notched antlers, rubbed vigorously together. Each woman crossed her right arm over her left, and rubbed the antlers held out on either side by her partners. Their muscles glistened in the firelight, well rubbed with fat and accustomed to long hours of labour.

When the rhythm was established, the youngest girl, with only one spiral upon her forehead – her skull still rounded and not yet flattened by the long hours of carrying baskets supported by a headband – scattered a bundle of dried herbs upon the tiny driftwood fire. The house was filled with a choking, resinous smoke that seemed to linger and to refuse to leave through the open smoke-hole above. The rhythm changed subtly, accompanied by a lifting of the women's shoulders and a dipping of each of the four heads in sequence, like the dipping of birds into a fish pool. The girl waited for some time, carefully counting to herself, then reverently drew a few tiny fragments of dried fungus from a leather pouch, and laid them on the smouldering herbs.

The multiple rhythm of rasping antlers and droning chant began to accelerate. The thick smoke-filled air grew hot, but the women began to shiver and wail, keening the cry of the cold, the homeless, the lost. The priestess rubbed her dark, work-callused hands over the stones, and began a tearing high-pitched screech that penetrated through the skin roof out into the cold winter night.

Across the freshwater lake, on the shore opposite the settlement, men sat around an open fire. They were well wrapped in great, thick, elk-hide robes decorated with shells and feathers: they looked nervously at one another. The keening and screaming from across the water grew louder, and the men began to mutter a hunting song, slowly at first, then with greater enthusiasm. One picked up a dried fish, coloured rich red, and defiantly bit into it, smiling and laughing, spitting out bones and scraps of skin. Another opened a decorated pot of strong fermented milk, tearing off the thick goat-skin seal, hurriedly downing a mouthful before passing it to his companion. The pot went around the fire, the fish followed it, and the hunting song grew brave and defiant. Out in the dark they could hear the tame animals moving and worrying in their pen. The flock always knew when certain things were due, as did the birds, and the deer, and the bees that dwelt in the hollow rocks. The screeching from the women's place reached a shrill, wavering climax, suddenly underpinned by a low droning that seemed to come from the earth itself, manifesting out of the rasp of horns and voices, yet continuing beyond their cessation. The men fell silent and hardly dared to breath. The pot was empty, the fish was eaten, and it hung heavy in their churning stomachs. They pulled the hoods of their robes over their heads, and slowly their courage faltered and faded away. It would not be long now.

In the stone house, the priestess jerked and foamed at the mouth, her eyes blank, trembling whites, her skin pouring sweat. The four women sat in silence yet the droning endured, and the youngest girl stared in astonishment as two old, old women seemed to walk straight out of the wall towards the fire. These were the oldest women she had even seen, perhaps forty summers or more. They were not wavering or insubstantial like male spirits of the mounds, but solid brown flesh. Every part of their skin was covered in the most elaborate patterns of dots and whorls, faded to dim brown and black but standing out as if engraved into the flesh. They smiled, revealing jagged stumps of teeth, and stretched their withered hands to the tiny flames.

Upon the stone slab nearby stood a heap of boiled grain, red-coloured fish, dried meat, and a stew of shellfish in a thick decorated bowl. The old women leaned over and with a great slobbering and munching devoured the feast. One belched loudly while the other wiped the juice from her hairy chin. The seeress had become rigid, in a crouched foetal position, her head tucked into her knees and her arms over her head. She might have been dead but for an occasional twitch of ragged breath. The air grew cold, and a grey vapour condensed along the walls to drip down to the floor. The fire blackened and died, and the two crones began to sniff loudly like hunting animals and to look around the chamber, as if searching for something more to eat.

The youngest girl knew what to do, for she had learnt the secret verses of instruction all through that long, hot summer when the sun hardly set. She pulled a large, pink-and-brown shell from beneath a cushion woven of brightly coloured grasses. Not daring to look behind her, she darted for the tunnel, and stooped low to crawl down the passageway to the night beyond. As she emerged, she saw great wheels of stars turning above her, and the frosted air was welcome after the damp chill of the house – the house usually so warm and snug and kind. Behind her she heard a slithering sound, and she quickly clambered over the soft, steaming mound of refuse, up to the top of the thick stone wall.

Across the water the glow of a fire could be seen clearly, and beyond that other tiny fires, and beyond those the flaring of great beacons that lit the stones of power where the winter gathering would soon begin. She longed for the gathering, for it would be her first, her transition into womanhood. But before then, before the blood-kin from other islands and places far to the south over the roaring waters were welcomed and feasted, something must be done. She put the large spiral shell, carried by storms from a distant ocean, to her lips. The note was clear and mellow, and as it sounded she could see the silhouettes of a group of men – the first time in her life that she had ever set eyes upon a male – rise hastily and smother their fire.

A scrabbling sound as of claws came from behind her, then a rushing, flapping as of wings, and with a blast of icy air two dim shapes sped off across the water to the spot where an instant before the fire had shone. The girl heaved a sigh of relief, and waited for the high-pitched screams of a dying man to begin. Now she could relax.

In the morning the girl was allowed to sleep late. Usually she was up before the sunrise to assist the priestess in the gathering of wood for the sacred fire. Today she lay in her comfortable box bed, surrounded by the sweet smell of dried heather and strong herbs, a fringed canopy of hide tooled with many tiny pictures over her head. This was the mantle of story-telling that had been used for her instruction of seven winters. She knew it all now, but not all of its many implications. Although the house was dimly lit, for the roof had not been rolled back to admit the high winter sun, she could see each tiny picture clearly. They were patterns of dots, swirls, lines, bars, squares and very occasionally an image that looked like an animal or a person, though she had soon learnt that they were not intended as such.

Someone had left a bowl of dried berries and a tiny fragment of honeycomb, mixed with flakes of fish, by her bed. She refrained from eating. She knew that she had to assess the terrible dream of the previous night. The symbols on the story-mantle could be read in different directions, in lines up and down, or across. They could also be read in jumps and turns, each carefully learnt by the girl from the priestess. She knew that she had dreamt a story backwards or sideways, and as she had been trained, closed her eyes and reviewed the images that sprang before her perfect visual memory, ready to turn them again into their true order and meaning.

The house, first of all, the house, and the village, were the centre of priestess learning for the islands . . . here a close community of women had lived for several generations, passing on their mysterious knowledge by secret teaching, using magical aids such as the mantle (which to an outsider would seem to be merely a decorative cover), the rhythms of rasping deer antlers, and the crystal stones. Without the insight and the memory of the senior priestess, no king nor warrior could enter the Womb Chamber safely, and no new guardian nor ruler could be set between the worlds. This was the learning, the mystery, that the girl was about to enter. Her first seven winters of training had ended last night; now she could attend the great midwinter ceremony when the stars known as the Seven Women reached a certain position in the bowl of the sky. She must also choose a man to stay with her, comfort her with his body, make children.

Allowing the images from last night's dream to run through her mind, she knew that the terrible vision was connected to this major threshold of her life. The next seven winters would be concerned with raising children, making judgements for the other villages, learning and dispensing medicines and healing spells. Then, after another threshold that she knew nothing of, just as she had known nothing of this present initiation until it occurred, she would return to the Village of the Women, and become once again part of the secluded sisterhood and the mysteries.

Two images remained, crystallising out of the dream sequence: the two crones in the wall, and the terrible death of the young man. She reflected upon them, as she had been taught, in reverse order of importance. The man came first. She considered that she might be unwilling to take a partner, hence the dream of terrible death. Surely such an interpretation was too crude and simplistic. She looked upon the story-mantle above her head, and saw there the jagged mark, like a lightning flash, that represented sacrificial death. The sacred death was a matter of beauty, joy and great illumination. What she had dreamt was terror, hunger and degradation. There was no symbol upon the mantle for this type of death, so she paused to reflect upon its possible meaning to the victim. If you dream, the priestess had taught her, waste no wood-gathering time on what the dream means to *you* – you will gain more wisdom by considering what it means to the people in the dream. As soon as she moved her imagination thus, she released the meaning of that part of the dream: some poor young man was going to be married to a trainee priestess. His freedom to boast and shout and leap would be taken away, he would have to keep a stately and grave appearance at all times, even when he wanted to run and drink fermented milk with his brothers. He was singled out for great office for seven years. No wonder it seemed like death; the men were all in awe of the House of Women, and especially of the strange sources of knowledge and memory available to the priestesses. Very well, thought the girl, I shall make deep changes that no woman has ever made before: I shall begin by teaching my man, whoever he may be, some of the memory symbols. This thought shocked her for a moment, then she contemplated the *feel* of it – it felt right. The story-mantle, with its signs that could be read in different directions, would remain an inviolate secret, but certain arts of memory could be passed on to men now . . . the reasons were good, there was no terrible struggle to survive, and the great temples of stone were almost complete. Let the men and the women exchange some of the mysteries now, for a new age was about to dawn. For a brief moment the girl felt a staggering illumination blossoming within her head, then it slowly faded and she reflected upon the nature of the two crones in her dream.

Within the wall of the house were two blessed mothers, the women who had founded the House of Women in the time of the great winters, or so it was said. Yet the great winters – memory of which was preserved in the long story-tellings – had surely been before her people had come north to the islands, so the time of founding was not intended to be taken literally. One thing was certain: two elderly women had been buried right in the wall of the house as a mark of great honour and respect. They had founded the Village of the Women, and had certain insights that the houses were to be made to a high standard. The design had been kept for many generations, becoming increasingly formal and consistent as the centuries passed. The Mothers in the Wall were treated as household guardians, but were never regarded as sources of terror.

It was customary for the women to chatter to the mothers, as if they were still alive and sitting in the circle and colouring fish for the evening meal, or helping to scrape skins or sort seeds. Sometimes the mothers appeared to women in dreams, telling them of shoals of huge fish approaching the coast, or of the movements of the vast flocks of birds that followed the changing seasons. The mothers were very, very old, and they came from what the girl considered to be a simple world. They knew nothing of the great stone temples, or the

The Women of Skara Brae.

ancestor chamber, the Great Womb. They had, perhaps, worked towards these sophisticated structures, when they established the first, very simple house, but had never seen the great stones set up. In dreams they talked of small sacred stones and trees, and guided women to find underground water courses. It was as if the ancient spirit of the mothers inhabited the physical burial of two women, as if there was a line of mothers stretching back forever through the wheeling of the stars. The girl remembered that the mothers knew of weaving, but not of complex patterns, of fishing, but not of weighted lines or nets. Of planting they knew very little, for their woven cloth had been made of hair and not of fibres.

The mothers represented the deepest levels of hearth and home, peace, love and security. Yet in her dream they had become terrible crones rushing out to feed upon human life: she took this dream in two ways, realising that each was closely connected. What, she asked herself as she had been taught, did the dream mean to the mothers? It meant that they were unsatisfied, and that they sought to break the mould of tradition. The girl paused to consider this revolutionary, almost inconceivable conclusion. She could sense instantly that this was why they had appeared in such a shocking guise, why they left the house, which would otherwise be unthinkable. The wisdom of the women was to travel out, no matter what the cost. This was the meaning of her dream. She clambered from her bed, and began to eat.

There was a shuffling in the low corridor as the priestess entered, who looked questioningly at the girl. The girl paused to lick her fingers, and merely nodded at her teacher. Both knew that the threshold time had come, not only for the girl's life and her passing into womanhood, but also for the people themselves. This would surely be a great midwinter ceremony.

The girl set her bowl upon the stone-slab table, and ducked under the fringed shell curtain into the corridor, out into the tiny street and from there into the sunlight. The priestess ran her finger along the story symbols upon the mantle, and saw for the first time a pattern that had never occurred to her before. Wrapping the skin into a tight roll, she paused to rub her palms over the wall to bless the mothers, and felt their deep love and care come through the stones into her hands. Then she, too, went out into the light.

afterword

Having traversed most of the island of Britain from stem to stern, we found that certain themes, common to many of the sites visited, emerged as reference points throughout the journey. In particular, the relationship of the king to the land, sometimes requiring sacrifice, has made itself felt, as has the peculiar consistency of tradition, the many layers of which have gone in to the making of what used to be called the Island of the Mighty. Each successive age has added its own layer to what was already there: religions old and new have resolved their conflicts in the flow of time; heroes have come and gone, or like Arthur, await their recall.

It is perhaps fitting that we should end in Orkney, for the north is the realm of mystery, and the spirits of the ancestors in magical tradition. Nor should we be concerned that our last story begins with a disturbing theme; if we ignore the dark side of legend and folklore, we are only pretending, and not making a true journey at all. If our explorations of tradition, in terms of people, places and powers, are to be more than quaint exercises in obscurity, they must encompass many varied aspects of human experience. And this is exactly what is found in legend and tradition, for tradition is collective and carries within it, through the centuries, the wisdom, love, joy, fear and despair of everyone who has lived upon a land or within a region. Legendary Britain can provide many journeys that, like those of Bladud, the Druid king, contain both dark and light simultaneously.

Bibliography

Bamford, C., 1987, *Celtic Christianity*, Floris Books, Edinburgh.

Barber, C., 1982, *Mysterious Wales*, David & Charles, Newton Abbot.

Barber, R., 1980, *Living Legends*, BBC, London.

Boswell, J., 1941, *The Journal of a Tour to the Hebrides with Dr Johnson*, J. M. Dent, London.

Brennan, M., 1983, *The Stars and the Stones*, Thames & Hudson, London.

Briard, J., 1978, *The Bronze Age in Barbarian Europe*, RKP, London.

Brown, G. M., 1981, *Portrait of Orkney*, Hogarth Press, London.

Burl, A., 1976, *The Stone Circles of the British Isles*, Yale University Press, London and New Haven, Conn.

Campbell, J. G., 1902, *Witchcraft and the Second Sight in the Highlands and Islands of Scotland*, David Nutt, London.

Child, F. J., 1892–8, *The English and Scottish Popular Ballads*, Dover Books, New York, NY.

Clarke, B. (trans.), 1973, *The* Vita Merlini *of Geoffrey of Monmouth*, University of Wales, Cardiff.

Cumont, F., 1956, *Oriental Religions in Roman Paganism*, Dover Books, New York, NY.

Cunliffe, B., 1969, *Roman Bath*, Thames & Hudson, London.

Davidson, H. R. E., 1977, *Symbols of Power*, Brewer, Roman & Littlefield, Cambridge.

Evans, Sebastian (trans.), 1912, The History of the Kings of Britain *by Geoffrey of Monmouth*, Everyman's Library, London.

Evans-Wentz, W. Y., 1911, *Fairy Faith in Celtic Countries*, Oxford, University Press.

Fairbain, N., 1983, *A Traveller's Guide to the Kingdoms of Arthur*, Evans, London.

Gantz, J. (trans.), 1976, *The Mabinogion*, Penguin, Harmondsworth.

Giles, J. A. (trans.), 1896, The History of the Kings of Britain *by Geoffrey of Monmouth*, Oxford Baxter, London.

Gordon, E. O., 1907, *Saint George*, Swan Sonnenschein, London.

Graham-Campbell, J., 1980, *The Viking World*, Francis Lincoln, London.

Green, R. L., 1956, *The Adventures of Robin Hood*, Penguin, Harmondsworth.

Grimble, I., 1980, *Highland Man*, Highlands & Islands Development Board, Edinburgh.

Harris, P. V., 1954, *The Truth about Robin Hood*, (privately printed), London.

Hartland, E. S., 1894–6, *The Legend of Perseus* (3 vols.), D. Nutt, London.

Holt, J. C., 1983, *Robin Hood*, Thames & Hudson, London.

Joussaume, R., 1988, *Dolmens for the Dead*, Batsford, London.

Keen, M., 1977, *The Outlaws of Mediaeval Life*, RKP, London.

Kirk, Rev. R., 1691, *The Secret Commonwealth*, reprinted by the Folklore Society, Mistletoe Series, London.

Laing, L., 1974, *Orkney and Shetland*, David & Charles, Newton Abbot.

Laing, L., 1975, *Late Celtic Britain and Ireland*, Methuen, London.

Laing, L., and Laing J., 1979, *Anglo-Saxon England*, RKP, London.

Lang, A., *History of Scotland* (various editions) 3 vols.

Levis, J. H., 1919 (1973), *The British King who Tried to Fly*, West Country Editions, Bath.

Loomis, R. S., 1963, *The Grail from Celtic Myth to Christian Symbol*, University of Wales, Cardiff.

Luce, Sir R. H., 1979, *The History of the Abbey and Town of Malmesbury*, Friends of Malmesbury Abbey.

MacCana, P., 1975, *Celtic Mythology*, Hamlyn, London.

MacCulloch, J. A., 1911, *The Religion of the Ancient Celts*, T.& T. Clark, Edinburgh.

MacCulloch, J. A., 1948, *The Celtic and Scandinavian Religions*, Hutchinson, London.

Macleod, F. (William Sharp), 1982, *Iona*, Floris Books, Edinburgh.

MacMillan, A., 1898, *Iona, its History, Antiquities etc.*, John Menzies & Co. Edinburgh.

Magnusson, M. 1976, *Hammer of the North*, Orbis, London.

Martin, M., 1703 (reprinted 1934), *A Description of the Western Islands of Scotland*, (privately printed).

Marwick, E. W., 1973, *The Folklore of Orkney and Shetland*, Batsford, London.

Matthews, C., 1989, *Arthur and the Sovereignty of Britain*, Arkana, London.

Murray, J. A. H., 1875, *Thomas of Erceldoune*, Early English Texts Society, London.

Newstead, H., 1958, 'King Mark of Cornwall', in *Romance Philology*, Vol. XI, no. 3.

Ottaway, P., 1987, *A Traveller's Guide to Roman Britain*, RKP, London.

Parry, J. J. (trans.), 1925, *The* Vita Merlini *of Geoffrey of Monmouth*, University of Urbana, Ill.

Paulsson, H. and Edwards, P. (trans.), 1981, *Orkneyinga Saga*, Penguin, Harmondsworth.

Paxon, D., 1988, *The White Raven*, Hodder & Stoughton, Sevenoaks.

Piggot, S., 1974, *The Druids*, Pelican, Harmondsworth.

Porter, H. M., 1971, *The Celtic Church in Somerset*, Morgan Books, Bath.

Ratchiffe-Barnett, T., 1937, *Border By-Ways and Lothian Lore*, The Moray Press, Edinburgh.

Ritchie, A., 1985, *Orkney and Shetland*, HMSO, Edinburgh.

Ritson, J., 1823, *Robin Hood*, C. Stocking, London.

Ross, A., 1974, *Pagan Celtic Britain*, Cardinal, London.

Ross, A., 1976, *Folklore of the Scottish Highlands*, London.

Ross, A., 1986, *A Traveller's Guide to Celtic Britain*, RKP, London.

Skene, W. F., 1886, *Celtic Scotland* (3 vols.), David Douglas, Edinburgh.

Skene, W. F., 1987, *Arthur of the Britons in History and Ancient Poetry*, ed. D. Bryce, Llannerch Publishers, Wales.

Tatlock, J. S. P., 1950, *The Legendary History of Britain*, Berkeley University Press, Berkeley, Calif.

Thorpe, L., 1966 (trans.), The History of the Kings of Britain *of Geoffrey of Monmouth*, Penguin, Harmondsworth.

Thorpe, L. (trans.), 1978, The Journey through Wales *of Giraldus Cambrensis*, Penguin, Harmondsworth.

Tolstoy, N., 1985, *The Quest for Merlin*, Hamish Hamilton, London.

Toulson, S., 1985, *Celtic Journeys*, Hutchinson, London.

Toulson, S., 1987, *The Celtic Alternative*, Century, London.

Walker, J. W., 1973, *The True History of Robin Hood*, EP Publishing, Wakefield.

Westwood, J., 1985, *Albion*, Granada, London.

Whitlock, R., 1979, *In Search of Lost Gods*, Phaidon, London.

Wilcock, J., 1976, *A Guide to Occult Britain*, Sidgewick & Jackson, London.

Wimberley, L., 1959, *Folklore in the English and Scottish Ballads*, Frederick Ungar Publishing Co., New York, NY.

Books by the Authors

JOHN MATTHEWS

The Aquarian Guide to British and Irish Mythology (with Caitlín Matthews), Aquarian Press, Wellingborough, 1988.

The Arthurian Reader, Aquarian Press, Wellingborough, 1988.

At the Table of the Grail, Arkana, London, 1987.

Boadicea: Warrior Queen of the Celts, Firebird Books, Poole, 1988.

Celtic Battle Heroes (with R. J. Stewart), Firebird Books, Poole, 1988.

El Cid: Champion of Spain, Firebird Books, Poole, 1988.

Elements of Arthurian Tradition, Element Books, Shafesbury, 1989.

Fionn mac Cumhail: Champion of Ireland, Firebird Books, Poole, 1988.

Gawain, Knight of the Goddess, Aquarian Press, Wellingborough, 1989.

The Grail: Quest for the Eternal, Thames & Hudson, London, 1981.

The Grail Seeker's Companion (with Marian Green), Aquarian Press, Wellingborough, 1986.

'Merlin and Grisandole', in *Merlin and Woman* (ed. R. J. Stewart), Blandford Press, London, 1988.

Merlin in Caledon, Hunting Raven Press, Frome, 1981.

'Merlin in Modern Fiction' in *The First Book of Merlin* (ed. R. J. Stewart), Blandford Press, London, 1987.

Richard Lionheart: The Crusader King, Firebird Books, Poole, 1988.

'The Tenth Muse', in *Tarot Tales* (ed. Rachel Pollack and Caitlín Matthews), Century, 1989.

Warriors of Arthur (with R. J. Stewart), Blandford Press, London, 1987.

Warriors of Christendom (with R. J. Stewart), Firebird Books, Poole, 1988.

The Western Way: Vol. I: The Native Tradition (with Caitlín Matthews), Arkana, London, 1985.

The Western Way: Vol. II: The Hermetic Tradition (with Caitlín Matthews), Arkana, London, 1986.

BOB STEWART (R. J. STEWART)

Advanced Magical Arts, Element Books, Shafesbury, 1988.

'The Grail as bodily vessel' in *At the Table of the Grail* (ed. J. Matthews), RKP, London, 1983.

Barbarossa, Firebird Books, Poole, 1988.

The Book of Merlin (ed.), Blandford Press, London, 1987.

Charlemagne, Firebird Books, Poole, 1988.

Cuchullainn, Firebird Books, Poole, 1988.

The Giant Who Ate Porridge, Macmillan, London, 1980.

Living Magical Arts, Blandford Press, London, 1987.

Macbeth, Firebird Books, Poole, 1988.

The Merlin Tarot (2 vols.), Aquarian Press, Wellingborough, 1988.

Music and the Elemental Psyche, Aquarian Press, Wellingborough, and Inner Traditions, Vermont 1987.

The Mystic Life of Merlin, RKP, Arkana, London and Boston, Mass., 1986.

The Prophetic Vision of Merlin, RKP, Arkana, London and Boston, Mass., 1986.

The Second Book of Merlin: Merlin and Woman (ed.) Blandford Press, London, 1988.

The Underworld Initiation, Aquarian Press, Wellingborough, 1984 and 1989.

Warriors of Arthur (with J. Matthews), Blandford Press, London, 1987.

Waters of the Gap, Bath City Council, Bath, 1980.

Where is St George?, Moonraker Press and Blandford Press, London, 1987.

índex

Aaron 19
Abbey of St Gall 9
Abbot Blathmac 132
Adam of Domerham 30
Adamnan 129
Agravain 149
Aidan 146,148
Aidan, King of Scots 130
Alain, King of Norway 136
Alan-a-Dale 94, 105
Albion xiv
Amangons 15
Ambrose 35
Ambrosius Aurelianus xi, xii, 21–24,
    26, 27, 32, 37
Andret 10, 11
Anglesey 65, 66, 126
Annwn, Lord of 90–92
Apollo 39, 70
Apollo, Temple of 68, 70
Apuleius 35
Aquae Sulis xi, xii, xiii, 29, 49, 63–68
Argante, Queen of Faery 85
Arthur, King xi, xiii, xiv, 1–4, 10, 18,
    19, 21, 29, 30, 32, 33, 35, 37, 38,
    53, 71, 72, 83–86, 93, 96, 101, 103,
    111, 133, 137, 149, 150, 171
Arthur, Emperor 15, 91
Arthuret, Battle of 115
Arthur's Grave 30, 85
Arthur's Table 18
Artorius 27
Artos 27
Atlantis 6
Avalon 29, 30, 85, 151
Avebury viii, 47, 52
Avon Gorge 64
Avon River 73

Badbury Rings 2
Badon, Battle of 1, 2
Bailbrook 71

Barbarossa 53
Barnsdale 100
Barnsdale, Forest of 101, 103
Bath x, xi, xii, xiii, 1, 2, 34, 63, 64, 65,
    67, 70–73
    Pump Room 64
    Roman Baths 63, 64
    Romano-Celtic Temple x
Beckery Island 83
Bede, The Venerable xiii, xiv, 19
Bedwyr 18, 27
Bel 16, 51
Belin 16
Belinus 16
Beroul 8
Bevidere 2
Bishop's Palace 156
Bladud, King xi, 34, 50, 51, 68–74, 171
Blake, William xiv, 50
Blond, Bligh 83
Bodmin Moor 2
Boudicca xiv
Bran 137, 138, 140–143
Briggidda 67
Brigit 67, 83, 146
Bristol 64
Broceliande 12
Brough of Birsay 155, 157
Brutus 98

Cadbury Camp 1, 2, 4, 18
Caer Bladon 73
Caer Lleon 16
Caer Siddi 14, 15
Caer Usk 16
Caerleon xi, xii, 16–20
    Roman Amphitheatre 18, 26
Caliburn 29
Cam River 1
Camden, William 85
Camel River 1
Camelot 1, 18, 149

Camlan, Battle of 1
Canmore, Malcolm 133, 156
Carlisle, Earl of 103
Castle Dor 7, 8
Ceriddwen 96
Chapel Point, Mevagissey 7
Chalice Gardens 82
    Hill 82
    Well 82
Chertsey Abbey 9
Chester 17
Christina of Somerford 143
Clas Merddyn xiv
Clust 19
Colonsay, Island of 127
Cornwall, Arthurian 1
    Royal House of 10
Creiddelyadd 91, 92
Creiddylad 86
Creuddilad 96
Cruithnechan 128
Cuildremhue, Battle of 128
Culhwch, Prince 19

Dabutius 33
Daedalus 50
Day, Mabel Leake 98
Decius, Emperor 19
Dee, John 80
Demon of Socrates 35
Destiny Stone 130
Diana 68, 70
Dimetia, King of 34
Dinas Emrys xi, 28, 31, 32–37, 39, 40,
    42
Dinas Ffaraon Dandde 40
Dindraine 137
Donegal 21, 128
Dozmary Pool 2, 3
Dragon Hill 51
Drostan 9
Drumelzier 115

Drust, son of Talorc   9
Drustan   9, 10, 14, 137
Drustan's Ghost   10
Dublin, Trinity College   128
Dumnonia   12, 15
Dumnonia, King of   10
Durrow, Monastery of   128

Earlston   114
Edward I   111, 130
Edward II   99, 100, 101
Edward III   99, 100
Egilsay, Isle of   156
Eildon Hills   xi, xii, 38, 110, 112, 113
Eildon Tree   114
Eisner, Professor Sigmund   9
Elfland, Queen of   119
Elliott, Professor Ralph V.   98
Emrys Wledig   21
Epona   51
Erceldoune   123
Erlendsson, Magnus   156
Essyllt   9
Excalibur   2, 3, 29
Eyri Mountains   23, 40

Fairy Queen   xi, xii, xiii, 41, 111, 113,
    114, 120
Fell, Professor Barry   39
Fiend's House   98
Fionn mac Cumhail   86
Fisher King   xii
Flaming Head   72
Fliolle, Emperor   18
Flying Man   73
Fowey   8
    estuary   7
Franks Casket   50, 51
Frederick I, Emperor of Germany   53
Friar Tuck   94, 106

Gaheries   149
Galahad   137
Gareth   149
Gaveston, Piers   101
Gaul   22
Gawain   18, 97, 149
Geoffrey of Monmouth   xiii, 1, 16–19,
    21, 31, 33, 35–37, 40, 52, 68–70,
    136, 151
Gerald of Wales   17
Gereint   18
Gildas the Wise   21, 84
Giraldus Cambrensis   17, 19, 21, 30
Glaesting   85
Glaestinga-burgh   85
Glastonbury   xi, xii, 1, 29–31, 79, 80,
    83, 85, 86, 92, 112, 113, 130
    Abbey   83, 84
    Tor   79, 80, 82, 85, 86, 88, 92
Glewlwyd Mighty-Grasp   19
Gorlois   150
Grail, Fortress of the Holy   79
    Holy   10, 79, 83, 136
    Island of the   135

King   137
    Quest for   xii, 83
    Repository for Holy   1
Green Chapel   98
Green Gome   97, 104
Green Man   97, 99, 104
Greidyawl   91
Grondesson, Herli   159
Gruach   133
Guilmerius, (Monk)   73
Guinevere   9, 10, 31, 84, 137
Guy of Gisborne, Sir   94, 105
Gwanuasuis rex Orcadum   151
Gwri   24
Gwynhyvar   91
Gwynn ap Nudd   75, 85–88, 90–92, 96,
    112, 151
Gwyther ap Greidawl   86, 92
Gwytheryn   22, 23
Gwythyr   91

Hadrian's Wall   17
Harald Maddadarson, Earl   158
Haug-Bùi   159
Hawthorn Tree   113, 114
Hebrides   126
Henry III   143
Henry VIII   99
Hephaestus   50
Hereward   xiv
Hermit's Cell   134, 143
Hood, Adam   100
Hood, Robert   100, 101
Hood, Robin   xi, xii, xiv, 93–97, 99–101
    Grave   100, 101
    Well   103
Hotwells   64

Icarus   50, 68
Igraine of Cornwall   150
Inarsson, Gukr   159, 160, 163
Ingebjorg   155, 158, 159, 160, 163
Iona   1, 111, 125–131, 133–137, 143,
    153
    Abbey   129, 132
    Abbot of   132
    St Martin's Cross   134
    Well of Eternal Youth   134
Ireland   21, 128
    King of   136
Isca Silurum   17, 23, 24
Island of Glass   79, 85
Island of the Mighty   xiv, 137, 171
Isolt   4, 8, 9, 10, 14, 15, 112, 113

James VI of Scotland   115
Janet   41, 42, 44
Jesus   79, 113
John of Salisbury   83
John, Prince   94
Jones, David   xiv
Joseph of Arimathea   79, 80–82, 113,
    136
Julius   19

Kei   18, 19
Ketil Bignose   158, 159, 160, 162, 163
Kirk, Reverend Robert of Aberfoyle   xi,
    112
Kirkjuvalgr   159, 163
Kirklees Priory   100, 104, 108, 109
Kynvarch   9

Lancaster, Earl of   100, 101
Lancelot, Sir   6, 9, 10, 84
Land's End   7
Lantyan   7
Leinster   128
Liddington Castle   2
Lindisfarne   136, 146
Little John   94, 95, 105, 106, 109
Lizard Point   7
Llevelys   39
Llud Silverhand   91
Lludd   39
Llychlyn   136
Llyn Cerrig Bach   66
Logres   xiv, 137
London   ix, 68, 98
Loönis   9
Lot, Lord of Lothian and Orkney   149,
    150
Lothian   9
Ludgate Hill   98
Lud's Church   98
    Town   98
Luna, Goddess   65
Lyonesse   6, 9

Mabon   39
Macbeth   133, 155, 156
Macleod, Fiona   135
Maes Howe   153, 157, 159
Magnus, Earl of Angus   154
Maid Marian   94–96, 104, 106, 108,
    109
Maiden Castle   7
Major Oak   103
Malmesbury   73, 143
    Abbey   73
Maltwood, Katherine   80, 83
March ap Meirchiawn   9
March, Earl of   111
Marcus Cunomorus   9, 10
Marcus Flavius Cunomorus   10
Margaret, daughter of Christian I   154
Margaret, wife of King Malcolm
    Canmore   111, 132
Mark, King   7–10, 15
Matilda, wife of Robert Hood   100, 101
Matthews, Caitlin   137
Mecca   135
Melrose   110, 113
    Abbey   110, 111
Melwas   84
Melyagraunce   84
Mendip Hills   64
Merddyn   21, 22, 27
Merddyn Emrys   23
Merlin   xi, xiii, xiv, 1, 21, 28–35, 37–42,
    52, 53, 85, 111, 112, 114, 126

Merlin's Enclosure   xiv
  Grave   115
  Observatory   19
Merton, Thomas   143
Mevagissey   7
Michael, Archangel   51
Miklegard   159
Minerva   64, 67, 68, 70
Mithras, Romano-Oriental God   ix
Modron   39
Monro, Dean of the Isles   133
Mons Eris   35, 40
Moresk, Forest of   8
Mordred   1, 149, 150
Morgan le Fay   97, 104, 149, 150, 151
Morgen   126
Morholt   7
Morrighan   150
Morrois, Forest of   8
Mount Erir   33
Much the Miller's Son   94
Mull, Isle of   128

Nan Tor   98
Nemesis   17
Nennius, (Monk)   19, 21, 36, 39
Nimue   41
North, F. J.   6
Norway   136, 154

Oak-Head   55, 56, 58
Olaf Tryggvason, King of Norway   157
Olwen   19
Oran of Latteragh   127
  Land of   128
Orkhaugr   159
Orkney, Genealogy of Earls of   154
Orkneys   xi, xii, 126, 149, 151, 152,
  153, 154, 157, 159, 171
Oswald, King of Northumbria   146
Owein of Clun   105

Patrick, the Hermit   143–146, 148
Paulsson, Haakon   156
Paxson, Diana   9
Pennick, Nigel   6
Pierce, Robert   70
Port-a-Curach   129
Procopius   30
Prydein   xiv
Prysig Field   17
Puck   96

Relig Oran   133, 134, 148
Richard the Lionheart   93, 99
Ridgeway Road,   47, 48, 52
Ring of Brodgar   153, 157

Riothamus Uthyr   22
Riu Blas   94
Robert the Bruce   110
Robert of Huntingdon   100
Robin Goodfellow   96
Robin of Locksley   100
Roche Rock   8
Rognvald, Earl   156, 157
Rome   72

St Anne's Well   103
St Augustine   126
St Austell   8
St Bride   67
St Collen   85–88, 90–92
St Columba   111, 127, 128, 131–134,
  144, 145, 146, 153, 157
St Columba's Bay   127
  Shrine   131
  Tomb   131
St Dunstan   83
St George and Dragon   51
St Magnus Cathedral   156
St Mary Magdalene Hermitage   83
St Michael's Mount   7
St Michael's Tower   79, 81
St Patrick   127
St Sampson's Church   7
St Sampson's Isle   7
Samson Island   7
Sarras   137
Scarlet, Will   94, 105, 106
Scathach   126
Scilly Isles   6, 7
Scott, Walter   99
Segine   144
Segontium   52
Sgeolan   137, 138, 140–143
Sgilti   19
Sharp, William   135
Sheriff of Nottingham   94, 105
Sherwood Forest   xi, xii, 93, 103
Shetlands   154
Sigurdsson, Hermond   158, 159, 160,
  163
Silures Tribe   17, 22
Skara Brae   151, 152, 153, 155, 164,
  168
Skye, Isle of   126
Snowdon   35, 40
Sock-Head   55, 56, 58
Solsbury Hill   2, 71
Sone   136
Spiral Castle   14
Stenness Standing-Stones   153, 157
Stone of Kingship   27
Stonehenge   viii

Suetonius Paulinus   126
Sulis, Goddess   65, 67, 68, 70
  Temple of   64, 77
Swainswick   71
Swainswicke   70

Taliesin   12, 29, 30
Tell, William   94
Tennyson, Lord Alfred   2, 20, 41
Thingmoot   163
Thomas of Erlstoun   111, 112
Thomas the Rhymer   xi, 4, 37, 38, 41,
  52, 53, 110-115, 117, 119, 120
Thorfinn the Mighty   155, 156
Thorpe, Lewis   30
Thor's Hole   98
Thurshole   98
Till Eulenspiegel   94
Tintagel   xi, 3
  Castle   1
Tir na nog   14
Titus, Emperor   24
Tolstoy, Nikolai   39
Trinovantum   68
Tristan   xi, xii, 4–10, 15, 112
  Ghost of   12
Tristan's Leap   7, 8
  Stone   8, 9
Tuck, Friar   94, 106

Uffington Castle   48, 51, 52
Uther Pendragon   32, 150

Vale of Neath   86
Valkyrie   154
Vanburgh, Sir John   103
Vikings   154
Virgin Mary   95
Volund   49–52
Von Strassberg, Gottfried   4
Vortigern, King   xi, 21, 33–36, 38–40
Vortigern's Tower   21, 32, 35, 37, 38

Wagner   6
Wakefield, Manor of   100, 101
Warenne, Earl of   100, 101
Wayland Smith   xii, 48, 50, 52, 56, 96
Wayland's Smithy   xi, 47–49, 51–53
Wearyall Hill   81, 82
Weland   48
Wetton Mill   98, 99
White Horse   47, 48, 51, 52
  Vale of   47
White, T. H.   149
William of Malmesbury   30, 73

Ynys Avallach   30
York   17